Julius Rupp

Reason and religion

Julius Rupp

Reason and religion

ISBN/EAN: 9783337131944

Printed in Europe, USA, Canada, Australia, Japan

Cover: Foto ©Lupo / pixelio.de

More available books at **www.hansebooks.com**

REASON AND RELIGION.

BY

DR. JULIUS RUPP.

TRANSLATED FROM THE GERMAN.

With a Biographical Sketch of the Author

BY

MME. A. C. RASCHE.

London:
SAMUEL TINSLEY & CO.,
31, SOUTHAMPTON STREET, STRAND.
1881.
[All Rights Reserved.]

THIS TRANSLATION

IS

Dedicated to

MY FRIENDS AND PUPILS

IN ENGLAND,

AS A TOKEN OF MY AFFECTION FOR THEM.

CONTENTS.

CHAPTER	PAGE
TO THE READER	vii
BIOGRAPHICAL SKETCH OF DR. JULIUS RUPP	xi
I. ON PRAYER	1
II. VIEW OF LIFE WITH WHICH PRAYER IS INCOMPATIBLE	15
III. THE LIFE OF HIM WHO REJECTS PRAYER	31
IV. ON PRAYER AS A MEANS OF SELF-EDUCATION	49
V. PRAYER AS TAUGHT BY THE CHURCH	68
VI. LORD, TEACH US HOW TO PRAY	83
VII. HOW ARE WE TO RESUME THE WORK OF SELF-EDUCATION BY PRAYER?	98
VIII.—A. OUR FATHER WHICH ART IN HEAVEN	115
VIII.—B. OUR FATHER WHICH ART IN HEAVEN	131
IX.—A. HALLOWED BE THY NAME	146
IX.—B. HALLOWED BE THY NAME	166
X. THY KINGDOM COME	184
XI. THY WILL BE DONE ON EARTH AS IT IS IN HEAVEN	202
XII. GIVE US TO-DAY OUR DAILY BREAD	219
XIII.—A. FORGIVE US OUR TRESPASSES	237
XIII.—B. FATHER, FORGIVE US OUR TRESPASSES, AS WE FORGIVE THEM THAT TRESPASS AGAINST US	253
XIV.—A. LEAD US NOT INTO TEMPTATION	269
XIV.—B. LEAD US NOT INTO TEMPTATION	283
XV. DELIVER US FROM EVIL, OR FROM WICKEDNESS	299

TO THE READER.

The Reader will find, in the following Discourses, a few expressions that are not in common use. Philosophers frequently introduce new words to express new ideas, or take old words and restore them to the original meaning from which they have been diverted, and use them in a more extensive or more closely defined sense. The word JUSTICE, for instance, is used by Dr. Rupp in the same wide sense as by Plato, never in the narrow sense of its common application. The word COGNITION is, perhaps, not flattering to the ear, but it is the only one which the translator could find to render with some force the German term—*Erkenntnisz*.

Should the dissertations in the foot-notes appear superfluous to those who are familiar with philosophy, they may remember that this book is addressed to the general public; that, in order to understand one another accurately, it is always safer to determine the exact value of words, even when they are not quite unusual; and especially when ideas detach themselves from old notions and diverge from them, is it necessary to warn the Reader; as a sign-post directs the traveller when the road divides before him.

It is no less necessary to draw the attention of the Reader to another difficulty which might not strike him at first, and would unavoidably prevent him understanding the author. Dr. Rupp considers the doctrine of Jesus as having been misunderstood on some essential points, even by His earliest disciples, and he invites us to go back to this teaching in its pristine purity. It is therefore absolutely necessary, in reading this work, to keep all pre-conceived notions in abeyance, and notwithstanding the well-known subject, to read as if it were new. This is the only way of dealing fairly with a treatise in which old views are presented under an entirely new light. This keeping in abeyance applies equally to orthodox and rationalistic or other scientific views. Men of science, who find in religion a stumbling-block, generally argue against it from a point from which nothing of it is visible but the errors imported into it. May we be permitted to remind them that Religion may be presented to them from a standpoint from which they have never looked at it, if they only will betake themselves to it with an unprejudiced mind and the same devotion to truth which they bring into scientific researches?

The data given in the Biographical Sketch of the author are derived from the same source as those of the article on Dr. Rupp, in Brockhaus's "Conversations-Lexicon" (Leipzig), and we owe a large tribute of thanks to a German friend, L. Ulrich, of Koenigsberg, who, having followed closely the author's public career from its beginning, has been able to give us authentic information concerning it.

We gladly avail ourselves of this opportunity to address our thanks to the friendly committee of gentlemen who read the translation in manuscript and favoured us with their frank advice, as well as to other friends who helped us in the revision of it, and in the verification of some quotations, and generally showed their interest in the work.

We are fully aware that the style leaves much to be desired, it being far below that of the original; but if the Reader is not discouraged, and finds, in the imperfections of the English rendering, a cause to go to the source itself—the German text—it will be a solace for us not to have altogether missed our object, which is to put into due prominence a work of great value.

THE TRANSLATOR.

FALLOWFIELD, CHISLEHURST,
November, 1880.

BIOGRAPHICAL SKETCH

OF

DR. JULIUS RUPP.

Dr. Julius Rupp is one of the thinkers who have devoted their lives to the solution of the philosophical and religious question, and have made *volition* the fundamental principle of their view of life and of the world. His earnest and scientific mode of thought, joined to a deeply religious and moral spirit, has fitted him to be the leader of a reform party which, small as it is, has persevered through great trials in its efforts for reform in Church matters. Dr. Rupp's loving reverence for the character of Jesus, shows itself in the supreme importance which he attaches to his teaching.

Possessed from his early youth by the conviction that there are many individuals, as there no doubt have been in all ages, scattered on earth, devoted to truth and faithfully attached to the thought of eternal justice, whose isolated efforts only need to be combined to carry out a work hitherto unknown in history, he has devoted his life to form this association of "free men" who would, with steadfast steps, follow the path on which humanity is destined to reach her goal.

He was born on the 13th of August, 1809, in Koenigsberg, East Prussia, where his father held the office of accountant in one of the Government offices. As a boy, he frequented the Gymnasium of the Altstadt, until the year 1827. He then passed on to the University of his native town, and studied theology and philosophy (under Prof. Herbart). As proposed by the College of Theologians, he went to Wittenberg as a member of the seminary for preachers, a privilege granted only to students distinguished by a decided talent and an irreproachable conduct. In 1832, Rupp took his degree in the faculty of philosophy at Koenigsberg. After having been a private tutor for a few months, he exercised the functions of a master in the Royal and City Schools for boys, from the year 1832 to 1835, and gave lectures at the university as "Privat docent" on literature, history, and philosophy; and was one of the masters (*Oberlehrer*) at the Gymnasium of the Altstadt. During these years, he had on Rothe's* suggestion written the "Bishop of Nissa, his Life and his Opinions" (Leipzig, 1834), a theological work of great value and of a scientific character. After that, he published a summary of universal history, for the higher classes of gymnasia, with genealogical tables and maps (Koenigsberg, Bornträger, 1837), a work distinguished from others of the same kind by the systematic

---

* Rothe, a professor of theology at Wittenberg, and later on at Berlin, who died a few years ago, the "Saint of the Protestanten-verein."

arrangement from the Christian-Germanic point of view. Then he published a collection of extracts from classical authors, for the higher classes of gymnasia and higher middle-class schools.

In his preface to this last-named work, and in two treatises on "Pedagogy," Dr. Rupp (Koenigsberg, 1842) shows that the weakness of our age in matters of moral organisation and the indifference concerning religious affairs, the absence of, at least, all connected efforts in this respect, could be remedied only, in view of a religious education, by promoting the establishment of religious communities among the people.

In the year 1842, Dr. Rupp was appointed "Divisions Prediger," *i.e.* chaplain for the Garrison of Koenigsberg, a high position in a country where the army ranks as high as it does in Prussia. At this time, owing to his high character and the uncommon power of his eloquence, he had a large circle of fervent adherents. The Church of the Castle (the old and venerable church in which all the Kings of Prussia have been crowned, and which was built by the German knights) could scarcely hold the number of his hearers, some of whom were men of science who had hitherto appeared entirely devoid of religious feeling. Through all Dr. Rupp's sermons of that period, as well as in the subsequent series, runs the idea that Christianity, such at least as Jesus had really conceived it, was the belief in humanity. If we may explain the idea in our own words, we should qualify it thus : humanity called to prove its divine origin by a life divine. He held that the words "son of man," and "son of God," not only designated the same person, but also that the meaning of the two expressions is identical.

Soon after his promotion to this office, Dr. Rupp found himself involved in a double disciplinary trial by the clerical authorities. This was caused by two speeches which he had delivered in the "Deutsche Gesellschaft," a scientific society in his native town. The subject was —"The Christian Commonwealth, and Theodor von Hippel and his Doctrine of it" (to be found in Prutz's Literarisches Taschenbuch, Hanover, 1845). Although these speeches did not attack orthodoxy, to hear them from the lips of a member of the Clergy was enough to cause anxiety to the ecclesiastical court, whose object it is to uphold the State; for the orator placed a new ideal of the State in opposition to the old one hitherto maintained by the State on which these ecclesiastical authorities themselves lean. But this was not all; it happened just at that time that the first sitting of the Prussian Synod was to be held. During the preparations for this new institution, Dr. Rupp publicly declared that such a synod could not be considered as a legitimate representation of the Church if the laity did not send representatives freely chosen by the parishes. The Royal Consistory addressed to Dr. Rupp a serious admonition, accompanied by the threat that persistency in such views was incompatible with the office entrusted to him by the Church.

In the course of the same year the town of Koenigsberg elected Dr. Rupp as the head-master of the Gymnasium of the Kneiphof. (Koenigsberg consists of three towns of ancient date, now merged into one: Altstadt, Kneiphof, and Löbenicht.) The Government refused to confirm this election, being probably irritated by Dr. Rupp's speeches, and still more by a pamphlet of his, entitled "The Compulsion of Creeds and the Protestant Liberty of Conscience and Liberty of Teaching," (Koenisberg, 1843); also by essays concerning the liberty of theological teaching, as well as by his contributions to the *Christliche Volksblatt*— Popular Christian Magazine.

Determined to bring the necessity of a new reform in the Church to a crisis, Dr. Rupp preached a sermon condemning the anathemas of the Athanasian creed against people of different persuasions. This took place on the last Sunday of the year 1844. He wrote to the ecclesiastical authorities requesting them to take the subject he had treated into consideration, and to seek the advice of the Church on the matter. The answer was that the Consistory had ejected him from his office, on the ground of his repeated gross offences against it, and his obstinate refusal to recognise as such the faults of which he was accused, and to promise to avoid them in the future. (See the "Proceedings of the Koenigsberg Consistory against the chaplain of the garrison, Dr. Julius Rupp, with explanatory notes and remarks from Dr. Julius Rupp," Wolfenbüttel, 1846.)

All the petitions addressed to the clerical authorities against this decision, signed by a large number of the clergy and laity, remained without result. Therefore Dr. Rupp's adherents met together on the 19th of January, 1846, to form a free religious community, the first of this kind in Protestant Germany, and elected him as their pastor.

Dr. Rupp made his acceptance dependent on a few points, first that the free Church, while declaring herself independent of creeds and clerical government, would at the same time maintain both her membership of the Evangelical Church and retain her characteristics; secondly, that she should keep her members together through the strength of religious life only, without the compulsion of a creed, and that in order to prevent all possibility of encroachment from the pastor in office on the rights of the congregation, a statute should be passed prohibiting any participation on his part in the business management of the Presbytery.

A last condition showed the purity of Dr. Rupp's intentions, as well as his wisdom and his knowledge of men: politics occupied men's minds at that time more generally than religion, and though a sincere patriot himself, he felt the want of a religious distinction which would free his community from associating with those who might use religion as a means or a pretext of political opposition. He therefore proposed to his adherents to introduce among themselves the use of the word "thou," as typical of brotherly love. At once the political departed from him and returned to the National Church, while those who really had the reform of the Church at heart remained faithful, although the use of the word "thou" was not attractive to them. When this sifting was effected, Dr. Rupp desisted from this last condition, which his friends represented to him as inexpedient, and which, having but the importance of a form, was used optionally only. He has ever since been the pastor of the Free Evangelical Community.

The persecutions he and his adherents have had to bear in the years of political reaction would alone form an interesting chapter in the history of his noble life; but Dr. Rupp carries the practice of Christian principles so far that the wrongs done to him, which would have embittered a character less strong and less disinterested, have dwindled down in his eyes to an almost invisible speck in the past, and he does not consider these judicial persecutions as worth mentioning. "The persecutions," he once wrote to a friend who cannot forget, "only took place during the confusion of the years that followed the Revolutions of '48."

At the time of his trial, the German Reformed Church—a branch of the Established State Church—in Koenigsberg had elected Dr. Rupp as its minister. The Government persistently refused to confirm this election, even years after, when this religious body addressed a direct request to the King, Frederick William IV., to confirm their choice.

Dr. Rupp wrote at the same time a circular letter to the Evangelical Church in Germany, in which he, referring to the question mooted by the Protestant Friends in Saxony—also called the Friends of Light—"the Letter or the Spirit," (*Ob Schrift, ob Geist*), put the question: "Creeds, or God's Word?" He also presented an open letter to the Consistory of Koenigsberg, and, conjointly with other liberal-minded men, published a periodical under the name of the "Free Evangelical Church"—*Die Freie Evangelische Kirche*. To this period belongs also a collection of his sermons on the same fundamental principles of Christianity which runs through all his works.

In the year 1844 a branch of the Gustavus Adolphus Association* had been opened at Koenigsberg, and Dr. Rupp was chosen as its representative at the general meeting of this society, then sitting at Berlin. The assembly at Berlin declined to receive him, on the ground that he no longer belonged to the Evangelical Church. Against this resolution, which transformed the Gustavus Adolphus Association into a fanatical court of creeds, petitions poured in from all sides. A war of newspapers and pamphlets kept all its members in a feverish state, until after the lapse of a year Rupp's voluntary withdrawal from the Koenigsberg Gustavus Adolphus Association prevented the threatened schism. He expressed his opinion on this affair in a public letter to Archdeacon Wolf, of Kiel, published by the *Hartungsche Zeitung* (Koenigsberg, 1846, No. 255), and at a greater length in a paper entitled, "Koenigsberg der Gust. Ad. Verein und die Evangelische Kirche, von Julius Rupp, zur Zeit vorsitzende des Haupt Vereins, in der Provinz Preussen," (Altenburg, 1847) — Koenigsberg, the Gustavus Adolphus Association and the Evangelical Church, by Julius Rupp, at the time President of the Central Association in the Province of Prussia.

The revolutionary year '48 stopped for a time the many accusations and punishments which hung over Dr. Rupp on the ground of unauthorised ministrations.

* The object of this association is to give encouragement and help to Protestant communities scattered among the Roman Catholics in Germany.

At the beginning of the year 1849 Rupp published the *Ost Preussische Volksboten—Popular Prussian Messenger*—a political and religious weekly paper which aimed at placing politics on a basis of justice, "because the growing power of a *party of justice* alone can be a guarantee that the efforts made to obtain liberty will lead to a satisfactory result."

The same year Rupp, being elected one of the members for Koenigsberg in the second Prussian Chamber, addressed through his own organ to his constituents a series of letters in which he expressed himself fully on the resolutions and debates of the Chamber; these were followed by a series called "Democratic Letters." The *Popular Messenger* was suppressed by the authorities in the year 1851, after Rupp had been condemned to an incarceration of several months for press offences.

The impressions made on Dr. Rupp's mind and religious life during these trials are well expressed in the sermons preached during these years—"Christliche Predigten," 1849—(Christian Sermons). Having not only hearers of his own congregation, but also outsiders, he could reach the public ear, and he protested against the idea of having his religious community considered as a kind of monastic society looking contemptuously upon public life, its experiences, and their results; or as one of those popular assemblies whose convictions and resolutions change according as the victory remains with those who erect the barricades or with those who attack them.

The harsh measures taken by the authorities and the persecutions that lasted through the years of political reaction after 1848 made it necessary for Dr. Rupp, if his community was to enjoy the legal right of meeting for religious purposes, to declare that *he left the National Evangelical Church of Prussia according to the regulations of the Patent of* 1847. But he lost no opportunity to declare that this formal act, to which he had been *compelled* by outward circumstances, *had in nothing altered his feeling of attachment to the Protestant Church.* Notwithstanding the acceptance of this "patent" by the Free Evangelical Community, the accusations, money-penalties and incarcerations by the authorities and dissolution of the meetings by the police were continued.

In July, 1851, the Prussian ministry withdrew Dr. Rupp's patent as an academical lecturer without even consulting the competent authorities of the University. In the month of August in the same year the Free Evangelical Community was dissolved under the false accusation that it was a political club. In October, 1853, it reconstituted itself under a new name. Only through indefatigable activity could Dr. Rupp make it possible to maintain his family through public lectures in the Town-hall, private teaching, and writings which became a new cause of judicial penal sentences. He, at the same time, had to overcome innumerable difficulties to keep in existence the community of which he is the pastor.

From 1856 to 1862 he was the editor of the Koenigsberger *Sonntags Post*, the Koenigsberger *Sunday Post,* for religion, public life, science and art, the aim of which was the promotion of humanitarian culture, or education in self-government. That object was to be pursued in the sphere of national life by the advocacy of the inherent dignity of the individual as a preparation for the government of the people by themselves. Secondly, this object was to be pursued in the domain of Natural Sciences by the acknowledgment of the principle that, on one hand, Natural Sciences are to abstain from all judgment in the concerns of Justice,* and on the other hand by the acknowledgment that all attempts to set limits to the inquiry of Natural Sciences, far from arising from reverence for the Spirit (*der Geist*), on the contrary, proceed in every instance from the fear of it. Thirdly, in the domain of general culture this object was to be pursued by combating the false notion that, as far as the cognition of truth is concerned, the generality of people are divided into two classes; the minors or ignorants, who must, owing to their supposed incapacity, be guarded and guided by the learned, and the so-called cultivated, capable of finding out for themselves moral and religious truth concerning the essence and aim of human life. Lastly, this object was to be pursued in the domain of the Church through the testimony of the Gospel against the prevalent so-called Christianity.

The other works of Dr. Rupp are "Von der Freiheit ein Zeugnisz für das Evangelium"—Of Liberty a Testimony for the Gospel (Leipzig, 1856), one portion of which now appears for the first time in an English dress in the present volume. These discourses draw a sharp line of distinction between what Christianity is

* Justice is considered here in the same large view which Plato took of it.

and what the Gospel demands of men; the Christianity being but a combination of Judaism and Hellenism, whilst the Gospel stands in relation to it as *thought and action united in a living principle,* in reference to which all speculative systems and all programmes of political and social parties are but instruments and means of practice, or, to express it in the words of Kant, *results* of regulating principles. In 1857, from Rupp's most industrious pen came "Immanuel Kant, the Character of his Philosophy and its Relation to the Present."

In this work Dr. Rupp presents to us the fundamental thought of Kant's theocratic philosophy, as a thought by which Kant has placed himself in absolute opposition with the whole development of philosophy such as it now stands. Rupp goes on proving that Kant's fundamental ideas in the practical domain of philosophy are no others than those which Jesus has introduced into history.

The appendices which follow this work contain important remarks on the data from which philosophy necessarily must start, and they rectify most important points in the opinions expressed by Schopenhauer on Kant's æsthetics, and clear Kant's character of the accusations of Schopenhauer. (See also Kant's " Stellung zur Reform des Christenthums : Religiöse Reform, 1873; *i.e.* Kant's Attitude towards the Reform of Christianity).

In 1862 and 1863, Rupp again represented Kœnigsberg in the Second Prussian Chamber. On this occasion, as had been the case once before, in 1849, one speech of his was enough to make him known as one of the first orators. The first time (twenty-sixth sitting of the Lower House, 1849) he spoke on the importance of the right of printing and publishing of printed matter. On the second occasion (thirty-eighth sitting of the Prussian Chamber), when he spoke on the appointment of Jews as teachers in public schools, he produced the same deep impression on his hearers.

In 1863 he undertook the editorship of a political paper, appearing twice a week, and called *The Friend of the Constitution*. From 1867 to 1876, at one time he was editor, and afterwards contributor, of the *Religiöse Reform*, the object of which was to be of service to readers of all denominations, by examining afresh all fundamental questions of moral and religious life, and by presenting to them scenes from real life from the Middle Ages down to modern times, as exemplified in the lives of Thomas More, Zwingli, Sebastian Frank, John Knox, Fénelon, Lamennais, W. Penn, Lessing, Schleiermacher, Parker, etc. Also new events in the domain of literature, and news of important facts in the Church, were treated of in the pages of the *Religiöse Reform*.

Dr. Rupp, being afflicted with cataract in both eyes, was completely blind during some time—1869 and 1870—when an operation gave him back the sight of one eye, but very much impaired. Notwithstanding this infirmity, Dr. Rupp never relinquished his almost youthful activity as the pastor of his congregation, and is as enthusiastically devoted as ever to the cause which he has created and kept alive.

No one has ever heard a complaint pass his lips, and, in the worst times of persecution, he prevented all ex-

pressions of condolence on the part of others, with the
most serene benevolence towards all. His silvery and
refined laughter cheered all who came to him with
feelings of despondency, and many went away comforted by him whom they came to condole, who never
admitted any ground of complaint or dissatisfaction.
A friend who was accustomed to see him in prison,
and always found him everywhere in the same gentle
and cheerful disposition, once wanting advice from
him, went there, and, completely forgetting the character of the place, asked whether Dr. Rupp was at
home? "This calm attitude of mind, always above
attacks and injuries, may best be understood on reading an article of his in the fifteenth number of the
Reform Blätter, of which he is a frequent contributor.
The subject is Delff's way of dealing with the sentences passed on Socrates and Jesus, in his 'Beiträge
zûr Religion's Geschichte' (Contributions to the History of Religion). Dr. Rupp, though in no way
bringing forward his own case, directly or indirectly,
shows in his article the view he takes of the relation
between the secular power and men who, in virtue of
their convictions, bring the inner authority of the
individual into conflict with the outward authority of
society at large, without even a wish to put themselves in opposition with the law of the land, and notwithstanding their respect for it, find themselves in
this opposition in consequence of their allegiance to
the inner law of duty towards society, conceived as a
moral and collective being from which they cannot
sever themselves.

No one who comes in contact with this truly great

and holy man remains uninfluenced by him. The ennobling feeling of his presence in his large family-circle is rendered still more attractive by his simple bearing and the striking modesty with which he listens to others; and, when drawn out by them, imparts information on the most varied topics out of the extraordinary store of his knowledge of politics, art, and literature, of all ages and countries.

The Reader may justly ask how Dr. Rupp found time for all that he has done; to which we answer: He works hard early in the day; three or four o'clock finds him in his study. If you want an interview with him, he will appoint any time for it before eight o'clock a.m., the rest of the morning being mostly taken up by business engagements. Dr. Rupp knows the necessity of relaxation in the interest of health and good work, and knows how to respect and obey the laws of nature. Asceticism and abuse are, in his eyes, equally dangerous to the practice of goodness. He goes early to rest, and, as long as his health allowed, took regular walks, and never failed to go to a *café*, where he read the news and saw as much of his fellow-citizens as his spare time would allow. It is proper here to say that no one can possess, in a higher degree, the art of withdrawing from conversation the moment it ceases to be what it ought to be. The least personal criticism causes him to retire, but so quietly, that the offender may go on for a time speaking, and suddenly find him gone. Then he knows how to use the willing minds, hands, and eyes about him. We must not raise the carefully-drawn veil of his private life, tempting as it is to do so for the benefit of those who have not had the privilege of visiting, in this admirably regulated house, the picture of frugality, order, neatness, peace, and activity; but we may say, that, unlike Milton, he has been fortunate and wise enough to raise in his house and in his congregation a generation of men and women who all deem it an honour and a happiness to be employed by him in the interests of a sacred cause. The veneration for the head of the family is as striking in this house as the cause of it is real; and this feeling is extended to the grand-parents, who have been dead for many years. On the writing-desk of Dr. Rupp stands a portrait of his father, evidently held in great honour by the family at large, for it is generally decorated with a garland of flowers, frequently renewed by gentle and artistic hands. His mother is the object of a profound gratitude on his part, and some hymns of Paul Gerhardt, which she taught her boy to repeat daily before sleep closed his eyelids, are said to have been to him a source of comfort and strength through a life of trials.

The Reader will be pleased to hear that Rupp, great as he is as a preacher, as a philosopher, as the expounder of Jesus, whose plan he lays before our eyes with such depth and originality of thought, *is equally great in the practice of his principles;* with him, the thought and its embodying action *are one.* No one who knows him ever denies this fact; the writer of these lines has repeatedly heard it confirmed privately by the Nicodemus of his native land, as well as by those who keep away from him because they do not share his views, or because they belong to that class, unfortunately growing in number, who hold ideas and principles in contempt, and smile at those simple-minded people for whom ideas and principles are the one reality of life. Even these realistic people—to whom God has, in spite of themselves, preserved the perception of what is good—will tell you that they respect Dr. Rupp for his thorough consistency of principles and action. In all relations of life he is an ideal man; as a husband, a father, and a relative, as a friend and as a leader of men. His acts of benevolence and charity are never known but when brought to light by those who are the objects of them. A direct advice, as far as I know, he never gives, considering it as tending to weaken the judgment and the will of him who has to act; but he helps by general hints, throwing light on the question, and, if needed, by most effectual help when the person concerned has determined upon the course to follow.

Such a eulogium may appear fulsome to those who do not know how true is every word here advanced. We venture, for the sake of truth, to express this eulogium, to declare before the public that there is such a man; but that is done in direct disobedience to him who is the object of it, *in defiance of his positive prohibition of all praise of him*. He has too long prevented his disciples from thus doing him justice, and the writer of these lines—which will never meet the eye of Dr. Rupp before they are printed—has but one regret, one *most painful regret*, and that is the certainty of incurring his displeasure. This, however, being done for the sake of truth and justice, as well as to satisfy the most natural and justifiable curiosity of the Reader, the consequences must be borne.

As a preacher, Dr. Rupp has recourse to no artificial means of success. The truth and the indwelling force of his argument is sufficient for him; the depth of his thought and feeling is nobly expressed in a language always simple in the choice of his words, but the fulness of his ideas, their abundance, show themselves in a complexity of construction which requires great attention on the part of the reader or hearer; the imagery soberly employed is always fitting and beautiful; his immovable attitude the very picture of concentration; his spare figure standing in full view of his audience; his hands folded before him, apparently growing more tightly clasped as his thought and feeling grow more intense, and his firm, sonorous voice alone give the measure of the subdued emotions of a soul vibrating under the effects of thoughts, each betokening an act of his powerful will and spirit.

Such are the means through which Dr. Rupp keeps his audience spell-bound during the whole length of his sermons. Difficult as the uninitiated find it to follow him, he commands their unwavering attention, and no one goes empty away, not even those who are unable to grasp the whole thought of a discourse.

There is a whole education in listening to him, and an education it is, in the fullest sense of the word, the belonging to his congregation. The Sunday services are but part of the many means of edification he gives to those under his spiritual care. His aim being to form independent thinkers and active labourers for life in all directions, he is the rallying centre of many meetings during the week, the object of one of them being to discuss the sermon of the previous Sunday.* At other times, written questions are put by various members, without signature, in a box under the care of the chairman, and are discussed with much animation. Dr. Rupp, generally seated in some remote part of the room, carefully avoids, if he can, the giving an opinion until all who desire to speak have done so. These discussions are of a highly philosophical character, though always brought back to their application in daily life. The members of the congregation belonging to various ranks of society with more or less culture, it sometimes occurs that a speaker is not understood, and excites some hilarity or a keen opposition. Nothing is more surprising than the lucidity with which Dr. Rupp exposes the real meaning of even the most awkward speeches, throws the brightest light upon it, and the laughers are, without any unkind words, brought back to their proper level and the just appreciation of the contribution to the debate so lightly received at first.

When the Free Community sprang up, Dr. Rupp founded a school with the help of three young clergymen, and later on with that of some young men who had left the university and devoted themselves to the same cause. Two educational establishments were also opened under his direction and the care of some eminent members; but the Government's rough treatment, when after the year '48 the reaction set in, soon obliged these institutions to be closed. There has

---

* In the days of his full physical strength Dr. Rupp had the discussions immediately after the sermon, as will be seen in a note further on.

since been no possibility of re-opening them. Under the present reign, however, Dr. Rupp has, to the great satisfaction of his community, resumed the religious teaching of children above eight years of age. This teaching he continues until their confirmation, when his addresses to the candidates are particularly impressive and uncommonly well adapted to the needs of young people entering society as active and responsible beings.

A literary committee of the congregation has been in existence for many years, and sitting every week (with an exception during the absence from town of most people in the heat of the summer), has produced a most valuable collection of religious and philosophic extracts from authors of all times and countries within their reach, in which the Free Community recognises her own aspirations, the German element naturally preponderating considerably. Some of the writers represented in this collection, called "Die Stimmen der Freiheit" (Voices of Freedom)—Ernestine Castell, Countess Schwerin, Karl Schmidt, for instance—have poetically expressed the feelings and partly the views of their community with much felicity. E. Baltzer, member of a Saxon Free Community and an excellent poet, has given to this collection most valuable contributions; the Commission has also published for the use of free Christians an abridged edition of the Gospels.

These are but a few hints as to the life of this interesting society, which has been gradually thinned by the many cases of forced emigration during the years in which the Prussian Government of Friedrich

Wilhelm IV., misunderstanding the noble aims, the peaceful, though active, tendencies of this community, dealt to it the most unjust and arbitrary blows. Under the present ruler, an honest and brave soldier and a benevolent sovereign, the persecutions against the free churches have ceased, and the Free Evangelical Community of Koenigsberg, like others in the empire —widely different from each other in their tendencies —enjoys the peace and liberty granted to subjects who, for the sake of their consciences having left the National Church, are tolerated, but otherwise not favoured, and even the most eminent talents among them are left unemployed by the country.

Nevertheless the activity described in these pages shows that the vitality of a good cause does not depend on a numerous membership, and that a religion founded upon living principles will maintain a vigorous life through good and evil report, through persecutions and in spite of the indifference of the surrounding world.

Though now sorely tried by infirmity, Dr. Rupp is a living proof of the power of the spirit in the fulfilment of duty amid trials of all kinds, a living proof of the efficacy of the will in those whose strength is in God and whose rest is secure.

ANNA C. RASCHE.

REASON AND RELIGION.

I.

ON PRAYER.

NOTHING can be more encouraging in our first steps in the search after spiritual truth than to find others whose views agree with ours. When we, with tottering steps, first venture on this search, not having acquired yet the firm assurance which truth gained by independent thought alone can give, we consider the great number of those who think with us, as a proof of the soundness of our views. When we no longer require to be confirmed in our opinions and strengthened against our own doubts, the growing number of those who accept what we consider to be truth, becomes in our eyes a guarantee of a progress in the right direction, a hold gained on public opinion by the right principles, which we hope will soon tell upon the tendencies of society, and bring about a marked change in the manners, customs, and institutions of the country. It is certainly encouraging to find ourselves carried onward by a large community bent on the application of our own principles to real life.

The sympathy of others spurs us on in our efforts in the search in which we are engaged, and gives a real impetus to our aspirations. The share which we take in such concerted action will always be the best touchstone of our moral and religious faith and tendencies. Indeed, if we wish to test the soundness of our moral and religious principles, and of our aspirations, that cannot be done better than by examining them in their application to daily life. It is in the laws and institutions, and in the general features of society at large, that its principles will show themselves as they really are. And no attempt to verify the worth of our principles can be fairly made except by a community, the members of which are bound together by the same moral and religious aim, a community in which all classes, all ages, all professions, trades, arts, and all modes of life, are largely represented.

Nevertheless, the advantage and satisfaction derived from conformity in our profession of faith are not all in all. The most important question is this: Does this conformity imply unity, or is it a conformity of words only? If it should be no better than a conformity of words, the illusion would be fatal. We all know, not only from the testimony of others, but by our own experience, how frequently it happens that we use the same words—the same symbols—not only in a different, but even in a contradictory sense; and even terms applied to the fundamental laws of human nature are exposed to this misuse.

We often use among ourselves words referring to

general principles, such as Self-Government, Free-will, Justice, and Charity, in order to ascertain accurately what are our notions of God, of Christ, and of the operation of the Divine Spirit in collective humanity. Now, our first and most important duty is to ask whether we do not delude ourselves when we take the frequent recurrence of these words as a proof of the harmony of our respective convictions. Subjects for which we are accustomed to use certain words in a special sense, peculiar to our own community, might from this very fact be misleading in an inquiry concerning the positive meaning of our religious language and our respective tendencies. There are some subjects to which we have adapted no expressions peculiar to our community; they may afford us a better test for finding out whether we really agree when we use the same words for our leading principles, or whether, notwithstanding this uniformity of language, we may not be gradually drifting into divergent paths. Any of these subjects belonging to our system of thought, which we have left aside in the course of our Sunday discourses, will answer this purpose. They form quite as important a part of our moral and religious life as those with which our attention has been engaged more recently. Now, the best qualified of them for such a test is Prayer. I think we shall be able to look back without regret upon the Sunday mornings devoted to the inquiry as to what Prayer really is, and we may hope that the discussions following upon these sermons will afford us the satisfaction of ascertaining what are our respective positions towards each other. This we can but consider as a decided gain.

1—2

Those of my hearers who regularly meet in this place of worship will have noticed that my mode of reasoning does not consist in bringing forward an array of arguments of all kinds, in order to compare them and weigh their several issues against each other. I am convinced that with such a method it is only the inclination of the hearers and the ability of the speaker, not the intrinsic value of his cause, which make the scale sink on this or that side, and that very little advance towards truth can be made in this way. I accept the wise maxim of the Brahmin, who says:

> "If any matter seem to have
> More roots than one, dig down
> Yet deeper, and thou'lt surely find
> There's left thee only one."

I shall, not, therefore, be able to speak with the misleading glibness usual to those who have not found the one root, the one ground of their argument, or who pretend not to have found it. All that I can offer is the frank testimony of what I consider to be the truth. I cannot believe that life can be sound without prayer, and at the same time I can no longer pray as the Church taught me to pray. The fundamental thought which has led me to this twofold conviction will form the basis of all my discourses on this subject.

We shall not, however, be able to treat of the matter itself to-day. We must limit ourselves to stating the fact which is to be made the starting-point for the series of discourses upon which we now enter. This important fact is—that prayer tends more and more to disappear from the Christian world, and more especially from among the members of our Protestant

Church. There certainly is no lack of complaint on the part of the Roman Catholic clergy of the neglect of prayers prescribed by the Church, but this neglect is generally very different from the lukewarmness which Protestants have shown of late towards prayer. Our clergy have noted this symptom long ago, and this phenomenon is as old as the Church herself. It shows her incapacity to influence man in all phases of his life equally, or to influence society at large. This phenomenon we find among the adherents of all religions. Youth in the thrall of passions; men enslaved by the hardships and cares of business; the rich seduced by the charms of pleasure, and held in its bondage, have always and everywhere forgotten the fealty and reverence demanded by their respective Churches. In short, this carelessness as to prayer, which now afflicts the Roman Catholic Church as much as it did the Protestant Church of former days, shows that part of mankind neglect, or appear to neglect, more than others, *that* which they admit to be right and necessary for their moral welfare. The general repentance which seized those who had carried this neglect to its extreme limits, and the confession of it on the part of many at the hour of death, sufficiently proved that the outcry of the clergy was founded upon this ever-recurring fact.

But this old experience has nothing in common with the fact now in question. The change which is taking place in the Protestant Church at the present moment does not consist in omitting prayer from levity, but in the conviction that prayer *ought* to be dismissed altogether.

The decline of prayer among Protestants at the present time does not consist in a casual neglect of it. From the beginning of the movement, the omission of prayer never has been considered as an offence that ought to be followed by regrets proportionate to the frequency of its occurrence. On the contrary, it is the result of a new conviction, a change in the mode of viewing life and the world in general. Far from being disturbed in mind and conscience, people who entertain these opinions are proud of having arrived at them; proud of rejecting a useless, unmeaning, and artificial duty; proud of having recognised in it a superstition which the sooner it is dismissed the better.

Such, at least, is the state of mind of those who originated this new point of view. Different is the feeling of the numerous class of people who have been seized by this change, and are carried along this new channel of thought, but on whom the recollection of the old faith has, nevertheless, retained a certain hold. They follow the new current, but not without repining. Whilst the originators of these new views do not pray because they *will not*, the others seem to wish to pray and not to be able to do so. Some of them bewail their incapacity to pray any longer. They look back to the happy time when they could turn to the Eternal Father and pour out their feelings to Him in ardent prayer; they look back to that time as to a lost Paradise.

But they now make resignation to the depressing incapacity a duty, because the sweet days of youth are over, and they are told that this childlike faith of a soul that can pray is but one of the many blossoms on the tree of life which must needs pass away when the spring is over, in order that the fruits of knowledge may obtain their full maturity. But there are many others to whom such resignation is impossible, for what they feel is more than a regret: it is a self-reproach to have lost a faith which they find is beyond their power to regain. They still hear the warning voice in their hearts, reminding them that the tree of knowledge, nourished by the sap of eternal life, and not being subjected to these changes of the seasons, produces at the same time, with equal abundance, luxuriant fruits and fragrant blossoms. But alas! as often as this warning voice strikes their inward ear, the feeling of loneliness and desolation which closes their lips to prayer comes upon them and refuses to leave them, notwithstanding all their self-accusations. And none of those who would still pray, if they could, can, even with the greatest efforts, distinctly remember the time when, and the exact circumstances under which they entered this gloomy phase of their existence in which they now must follow their course half-hearted and with a divided mind. They all join in the confession of the noble poet, who says:

> "How first I entered it I scarce can say,
> Such sleepy dulness, in that instant, weighed
> My senses down, when the true path I left."

But by far the largest number of people among those who never pray, consists of the indifferent, who neither brought about the change nor suffer from the contradictions which so painfully perplex earnest minds concerned in it; they did not help the movement in its origin, nor are they conscious of it; they blindly follow the impulse given elsewhere, without even knowing it, and without troubling themselves to inquire if their state of mind is similar to that of others or not.

When we say that prayer is on the decline, that it is falling rapidly into disuse, and that this is one of the characteristics of our time, we are prepared to be flatly contradicted by a certain party. It will be argued that the fact was true twenty years ago, but that since that time a decided change for the better has taken place. We cannot agree with this opinion. We readily admit that, for some little time past,* there have been more prayer-meetings in the churches and elsewhere, and that in many parts of the country unusual efforts are being made to revive old customs which had almost entirely died out. A superficial observer, judging by these appearances only, may consider these efforts as the token of a real change. But if we wish to judge of the spiritual development of society by a true standard, very little importance must be attached to changes brought about by special orders, which, according to our own experience, only hasten the ruin of the very customs and institutions the decadence of which they were intended to prevent. To judge soundly of the religious spirit of an age, it is not in the province of law and reigning authorities that we must gather our information; the private character and the habits of family life, the inclinations, the notions thus kept up in the minds of men, will show themselves with less restraint; and in them we find the true symptoms of the spirit of the time. No one will deny that, at the

* These discourses were delivered in the year 1853.

present time, that love of private prayer and family worship which gives the nation its true moral tone is at its lowest ebb. Is the number of families who meet for common worship not decreasing from day to day? Do many mothers consider it their duty, as in days of old, to hear their little children say their morning prayers and their evening thanksgiving when they rise from their beds or go to their nightly rest? I know that many of you will agree with me that this custom was not by any means always the expression of a truly religious spirit in education; and it would be jumping to a hasty conclusion if I were to say that the life of a family is absolutely devoid of piety because this custom is not kept up in it. Our object is not to weigh the worth and efficacy of the ways of the present against those of former days, but to show that prayer, which man was formerly taught to offer to Heaven almost from the cradle, is now disappearing, in the towns at least; when the country people, who so readily accept innovations from the towns, follow their example in this matter, and give up the family-worship still kept up among them, outwardly at least, in some places, then the last link between the spiritual life of the nation and this ancient religious custom will be broken.

In order to make ourselves thoroughly acquainted with the character of this change, which ere long we shall be obliged to regard as an accomplished fact, we must trace back its course to its very beginning. Doubts were raised as to the rationality of customary prayers, simultaneously with the first attacks ventured upon, in our fatherland, against the fundamental principles of the old creeds a century and a half ago. For a long time, few people outside the circle of the learned had become acquainted with these new opinions which had only been gained by laborious inquiry. At last they found their way among the general public. The poets were then among the first to take up the theme and to popularise this systematised opposition to the old tenets, and to clothe it in a language intelligible to all. This spirit of opposition is best illustrated in the following lines of the poet, who, on his first appearance in the field, was heralded as the hero of a new age, and who marked, for all those whose hearts had turned from the old religion, the new track which they were henceforth to follow. It was customary at that time to make historical persons, gods and demi-gods, express the opinions of the author. He therefore puts his cry of indignation into the mouth of Prometheus,* whom mythology represents as the creator of the human race, and says:

> " When I was yet a child,
> And knew not where to turn,
> I raised my erring eyes
>   To thee, O sun ;
> As though beyond thee were
> An ear to hear my cries,
> As though he had a heart like mine,
> To feel the griefs that made me pine.
>
> " But didst thou help me ?
> No ! not thou ! A benefactor do I know
> My heart in thee—with heavenly fire glowing,
> Youth's lofty impulses bestowing,
> While to a God, in vain, I poured my heart.
> Grateful for good in which he had no part.

---

* Goethe.

On Prayer.

" Why should I honour thee ?
When didst thou ever solace pain ?
Or hear the oppressed one's cry ?
To thee fear-boding man
    May weep in vain :
To mankind have I moulded been,
By masters, who are thine,
    I ween,
Strong time, eternal fate !"

We set aside for the present all criticism on the thoughts here expressed. My task for to-day is merely to determine the extent and importance of their bearings. Man may turn away from the prayers which he used to address to the heavenly powers, because his heart has turned away from the objects of his desires. He may no longer pray, because he no longer cares for the things which he demanded, and is ashamed of his heart's dictates. Of this feeling there is no trace in the words; the reason for renouncing prayer is altogether of a different nature. These lines tell us plainly that the entreaty for the fulfilment of the desires expressed was entirely justified, as it expresses the seeking of what is supposed to be best in human life, the ardent craving of the heart, in the youth and bloom of life. There is, perhaps, also a feeling of humiliation in the words of the poet whom we have quoted; but this humiliation is not regret for having asked what he did, but for having been mistaken in the choice of the means he used. He is not ashamed to have fixed his will on a wrong object; he is ashamed of having misdirected his wishes and hopes; he blushes for having expected anything from the one whom he addressed, for having expected help where no help was to be had. The words are a cry of indignation, uttered by a man who at last opens his eyes and becomes conscious of his error.

We pray and entreat, and our prayers and entreaties are vain. This is, condensed in a few words, the sum-total of the experiences which lead people to reject the old belief. On that is based the new way of viewing the life of man and the government of the world. But was this experience a new one? Do not all nations, known to us, go through this experience in every century? Is not the complaint that the prayers which mortals send up to Heaven remain unheard and unfulfilled, as old as the world? It is undeniable: this experience has often repeated itself; and nevertheless we may say with truth, that at the time it was new in this sense, that the impression, then made, was a different one from the impression it had created in all preceding centuries of the Christian era. The successive changes of the seasons and the changes of the weather also repeat themselves in a similar way, and still the effects they produce on us, when in health, are totally different from the series of impressions they cause in times of illness. The sounds that delight us in days of health 'and happiness, give us, in times of sorrow and illness, the most painful sensations. That very few prayers are fulfilled, has been proved by the experience of all generations: but it never before had reached this climax, and shaken the spiritual organisation of man to its very depth, as it did at the time we speak of. Just then it could not be otherwise; never before had sentiments and longings made themselves the masters of society as they did then. In truth all human faculties were reduced to feelings.* Never before had the demands of life, with its realities and duties, been so entirely swallowed up and forgotten in the enjoyment of sympathy, the delights of friendship and love; the craving for the rapture of these feelings had never reached such a height of passion, and brought hopes and expectations to such a climax. Hence the maddening resentment and wrath at every disappointed expectation.

Carried away by the violence of these new impressions, created by the renewed experience of unanswered prayers upon the morbid spirit of that time, a large majority of people took up the words of the poet which so forcibly stigmatised the old belief on which prayer is founded, as an error of childhood, as a superstition of former ages, to be set aside as soon as the age of reason and maturity begins. Weary of the enervating excess of longings and feelings, men have entered on new paths of thought and action, but the impression made by the experience of unanswered prayer on that period of dreamy, lazy longings, has remained behind. Our prayers are vain! This idea is now inherited from father to son, and, the more ground it gains, the larger, of course, is the number of those who will not, or cannot, pray.

And the stronger the conviction grows, the more it penetrates the inner life of the nation in its various channels, the freer it is in its actions; moulding, as we shall show later on, human thoughts and aspirations according to its own shallow character, its own hazy, comfortless spirit.

But, say those decided scorners of prayer to us,

* The time when Goethe wrote " Werther's Leiden."

who, conscious of the reasons for retaining prayer, are determined to do so, can you deny the general experience that prayer remains unanswered? will you close your eyes to facts clear to everybody else? We entirely disclaim this reproach. We, least of all, even think 'of denying this experience, as we clearly see why that which has been called prayer never can be granted. We only wish that those who rest on this experience would not stop there, half-way to the goal. But whilst acknowledging the experience itself, we never shall agree to the untenable conclusion which you hastily draw from it. Our prayers, you say, remain unanswered, therefore there are only two alternatives; either there is no one to hear our prayers, or there is one who hears them, but cannot fulfil them, because he also is subject to the inflexible law of fate, and the two alternatives are equal in their results. Certainly they are, but you forget that besides these two alternatives, there is a third, namely, that there is a God who hears our prayers, who is hindered in His power by no law of fate, but that *He will not* fulfil them, that He ever rejected and ever will reject them. This third alternative is the only admissible one for any man who has come triumphant out of the chaos of conflicting opinions in which a man is ever the fool of his own imagination and desires, for anyone who has worked himself up to the power of recognising the holy, Almighty Spirit who manifests Himself in the unchanging order of things, and remains ever the same in the overflowing abundance of creation, the fulness of which human sight cannot encompass. Because Thou art love, Eternal Father, Thou rejectest the foolish prayers of Thy children! Open Thou our eyes, and let us see that Thou hast rejected our prayers even then when they seemed to have been granted. Open Thou our understandings, that we may see how often our prayers have been rejected, even when we thought we came to Thee with pure desires. Help us to see clearly that Thy very love most frequently *must* reject those very prayers dictated to us by our affection and care for those nearest and dearest to us. Let this thought, sharp as a spur, sink deeper and deeper into our souls, that it may drive out our imaginary griefs, that we may feel with double acuteness that our souls still crave and mourn for that which those never miss who walk in Thy sight. Compel Thou us to recognise that every time Thou rejectest our prayers, the burden which we have ourselves put upon our shoulders, the chains which we have entangled around us are taken from us! We thank Thee, Eternal Father, for every one of Thy denials! only when this Thy love that brings the denial has quickened us to love, then only can we obtain the necessary vigour to throw off the burden of imaginary benefits, and to break the chains of vanity. Then only we walk in ease and safety on the tossing waves of time and fate.

II.

VIEW OF LIFE WITH WHICH PRAYER IS INCOMPATIBLE.

The rejection of prayer in these later days is founded on the belief that there is no one to hear and answer it. The rise of such a conception is one of the changes which constitute the real history of the human race and its development. The majority of the so-called educated people are, so far as such changes are concerned, in a state of perfect ignorance; for their attention is chiefly directed towards events like war, disturbances, and civil reforms, the discoveries of new gold mines, technical inventions which tickle curiosity, and are more or less intimately connected with political economy, its gains and losses; things that never bring any essential progress, and only indicate, like the hands of a clock, some mechanism at work in the background. Events apparently so important form the whole staple of knowledge of these so-called educated people; and therefore the sole object of their interests. No wonder that when conversation turns upon any religious or philosophical questions, they have no more to say than the inhabitants of the earth about the bodies in the firmament most distant from us. The infinite, the spiritual world of liberty, known under the name of moral and religious questions, appears to them like a speck in which they can distinguish nothing. So with prayer; they can say nothing about it, except that, in their eyes, it is a superstition from which they expect society to be freed by the growth of education, for, according to them, it is based only on a deceiving appearance of truth. But where is truth itself to be found, instead of its deceiving appearances by which they say that people allowed themselves to be misled? and how can we protect society from a relapse into this superstition? these are questions concerning which they never have thought seriously. In short, what the majority of the so-called educated people have to say concerning religious and moral development is an empty phraseology, lying entirely outside the pale of the true cognition of truth. Where they end, there for us begins our labour, if we will devote ourselves to the holy work of the cognition of truth.*

We feel above all the craving, the necessity of gaining a correct view of the change that is going on. That prayer formerly penetrated the whole life of man, and that now the wise of the day will set it aside as a superstition, *that* is the contrast which strikes us at once. But what were the transitions that led us from the old belief to the new one? Just as the poisonous

* The word *cognition*, although not commonly used and pedantic at first sight, must be used here to render the meaning of the original in its full force. There are many ways of obtaining knowledge : you may acquire it by means of books, or by the teaching of fellow-men. Knowledge of spiritual truth so acquired is of absolutely no value, unless it is made our own by the spontaneous effort of a special faculty of man, an insight of the conscience, the intellectual power of the moral faculties, if I may be allowed this expression, a second deeper intellect, which every man, even without any special education, is endowed with for purely moral purposes ; that is, the cognising" power. In this sense it is, I say, that this faculty is peculiar to man, for no other creature is endowed with moral power ; and again, it is either dormant or paralysed in those who cultivate their intellect alone. Philosophers, Kant in particular, have made use of the words " cognising " and "cognition "—*erkennen, Erkentniss;* and if I am to illustrate it, I shall refer the reader to St. Paul. He refers, though in a concrete form, to this power of grasping moral truth, or " cognising " it by one's own insight, which is developed in those of whom he says that their wisdom is foolishness to others who have not developed this power of appropriating it by their own cognition, being blinded by their own worldliness, their over-mastering inclinations, and having become unfit for the work of " cognition."

and the healing plants have needed a long time, the first to bring their deadly power, and the latter their life-renewing virtue, from their first germs through their roots, their stalks, leaves and blossoms to their matured fruits, so also what we call error and truth have their first causes in scarcely perceptible germs of thought, and must pass through manifold transformations before they reach their last development and become tenets of public opinion, and in this shape exert their fatal or salutary influence over whole nations during succeeding generations. And as the agriculturist who would destroy the injurious weeds in his field obtains the desired result, not by the destruction of the fruit thereof, but by digging up and destroying their very roots, so the man who would till the ground of the cognition of truth considers the training of public opinion and customs back to their very origin as all-important. If we wish therefore to gain a clear understanding of the present contempt of prayer, we must examine what is the root of it, what is the ground whence it arose, and from what it derived its nutriment. This contempt, which may be considered in itself as a phenomenon, derives its origin from the same view of life as the general opinions and aspirations predominating in the civilised world of the present moment. What, then, is this modern view of life? We cannot presume to give in a few words an exhaustive expression to a complex system of thought. We must content ourselves, for the present, with hinting at the leading thought of this modern view of the world and of life, and so we can only touch upon the collateral ideas, *i.e.*, consider one side of this leading principle connected with the rejection of prayer. This principle, this leading thought taken in this connection, appears to us to be the *want of respect for the individual human being.**

When I speak of a human being, I here understand the one principle of life, the one organism which we presuppose in any being to whom the name of man or woman can be applied—I mean the one principle of life, the one organism common to all whom we comprise in the human race, setting aside all differences produced by climate, the age of the world, and the degree of civilisation; in short, I apply this name to all who bear the uniform characteristics forming the common basis of all individual human beings. The importance of man, the degree of dignity attributable to him, depends on the position assigned to him in the universe, according to the various systems the aim of which has been to account for this enigmatic phenomenon of human life. These systems form two dis-

---

* The individual human being here meant is not the concrete individual whose rights are so much respected in this country, and are more and more thoroughly vindicated with every stage of civilisation. The author, as will be seen in the course of this sermon, points to the current conception of the human being in the abstract. No one will deny that the view taken for some time of the unimportance of our planet and its inhabitants has tended to reduce the high opinion men had of themselves, and that it was and is with a certain pride that people exhibit their progress in the knowledge of the universe and their conviction of the very small place we occupy in it. The idea of the unimportance of the earth and that of its inhabitants as an infinitesimal fraction of the boundless universe was extended to the nature of men. The author contends that nothing can justify the contempt for *man's moral nature*, whatever may be the rank of our planet in the universe considered as a body among other bodies.

tinct groups opposed to each other: on one side are those that place man as far as possible from a divine origin, from the first cause of all things that exist. On the opposite side, we find converging together all the opinions placing the human being as near as possible to the eternal origin of all life and being. According to the first of these two groups of opinions, the human being is but one of the innumerable leaves on the tree of life which we call creation ; nothing but one of the innumerable leaves belonging collectively to the different forms of growth of this tree, but every one of which can fall off or be destroyed without injuring or diminishing in any way the vigour or fertility of this tree. According to the second group of systems the opinion is, that the individual human being is an integral part of the organic functions of the tree of creation ; so much so, that the individual power and action constituting the essence of every human being is present and in action, from the root to the fruit, in all stages of the growth of that tree.

No one has more emphatically proclaimed this latter opinion than Jesus of Nazareth. Anyone having, through independent thinking, freed himself from the prejudice which places Jesus beyond the limits of human nature, and makes Him an idol, must acknowledge that the *absolute importance* attributed by Him to every human being, without distinction or exception, is one of the fundamental principles which most sharply distinguish His doctrine from that of all other systems of religion and philosophy, either before or after Him. If we thoroughly enter into the view He entertained of the individual human being, as such, we might say there was not alone one Adam, the only primitive man of creation, whose descendants we are, but rather that in every one of us, without exception, is the Adamitic primitive force renewed; every human being of to-day still is, in the same way that Adam was, according to time, the one begotten of the Eternal Father. Every one of us is now as *he* was then, and in the same way, the object of the individual solicitude of the Eternal, as Adam at the beginning of the history of our race, when he was materially not only the first, but the only one. Jesus applies to every man, without exception, the words that all hairs on his head are counted. In order to leave no doubt of the fact that the importance He attaches to the individual human being is quite independent of the degree of development he may reach on earth, at any time, He adds, in the figurative language of His nation, speaking of children: "Their angels do always behold the face of our Father in heaven!" If we once acknowledge that Jesus always calls Himself the Son of man, and represents Himself simply as an individual human being, we must, to be consistent, also apply to all human beings that which concerns His nature, but not what concerns His work. We shall then find that what He says of Himself is applicable to every one, without exception: "Before Abraham was, I am;" that is to say, the real essence of every human being goes further back than all history: every one of us is anterior to that which we call the world. In short, every individual human being is, consciously or unconsciously, as the Apostle says, in the spirit of his Master, an associate and co-operator in the holy work of the Eternal.

Taken all together, these views will justify us when we say that no founder of any religious system has conceived man as being so intimately connected with the originator of all being, no one has attributed to man a work so absolute, a nature eternal in its essence, as did Jesus of Nazareth.

This doctrine, proclaimed by Jesus, never has been generally acknowledged, even within the pale of Christianity. And never have Christians been further from it than at the present time; their whole way of viewing life being chiefly characterised by the very small place the individual human being holds in the estimation of the general public. The contempt of the individual is intentional, and we can trace its origin back to the war waged against the enemies of light, at a time when the belief in miracles, on one side warping the minds of believers by an irrational enthusiasm, and on the other side craftily used to deceive the simple, was found to be an insurmountable obstacle to the progress of national education. As an argument against this mischievous belief, creation was then represented as a superior mechanism, betraying high art in its construction, the motive-springs of which were perfect, and maintained so uniform and infallible a regularity, that no interference or repair was ever required on the part of its Maker. This regularity of motion became the standard of criticism; and hence a habit of mind was contracted according to which everything and every phenomenon became classified according to the relative position it occupied in the world, establishing in the latter a system of endless gradation. Nearest to perfection were those motions which could be proved to occur in the most regular rotation. But imperfection was found to exist in some details of creation, subject to a limited regularity, and therefore to exceptions and contradictions; and these were disappointing to the notion of perfection. Individual life was one of these details in which exceptions and contradictions were most conspicuous and numerous. From the new point of view, individual man, like all other details of individual life, was then considered to be placed in creation furthest from the seat of the infinite life of the Creator; and from conclusion to conclusion, seeing in this individual life nothing beyond the limits of the senses, it was considered to be the seat of all imperfections and wickedness. It had become a current idea that the world assigned to the human race, the characteristics of which could manifest themselves only in the form of individual narrowness, must now needs be considered as a sort of exile to which the ever-creating Almighty was banishing man out of His presence. Individual life was supposed to be a dungeon in which the free spirit was bound in degrading fetters. It became a proof of high-mindedness and noble aspirations to wish to leave this prison, and a proof of manliness to burst open the gates of this gaol. Death was the only portal through which the spirit could reach a better life and enter into the contemplation of the infinite. The relation of the individual human being to Deity was supposed to be in no way different from that of the slave of antiquity to his master. The first was of such low extraction that it would have been incompatible with the dignity of his master to be in direct intercourse with him. His approach alone would have offended his lord. How far less could he have asked him anything! The master could do no more than give general instructions concerning the discipline and employment of his slaves; he did not care for the weal or woe of the individuals. In the same way, the solicitude and care of individual men appeared too trivial an occupation for the infinite perfection of the Eternal Spirit, who would not condescend to do any more than trace the general plan of the universe, and establish a general organisation for the economy of creation, the actual working of which in the inferior stages of existence was left to the powers of nature, whose functions were fixed in manifold gradation.

Their immediate influence could be visible only in the guidance of superior men and of whole nations. How the individual fared, driven round in his narrow circle by the instinct of self-preservation, was, as far as the realisation of the principle presiding over the universe was concerned, utterly indifferent.

The poets and the sages, in whose memory the fundamental thought of the Gospel was not quite extinct and the Church, which was, outwardly at least, still maintaining her dominion, all joined to express in their teaching their disapprobation of the contempt into which the individual had fallen; but this disapprobation lost its power over the public more and more as time went on, owing to the convergence of two changes just then taking place, both of which fostered this tendency to self-contempt. The first of these changes was *a false view, very generally spread, of the nature surrounding man.* For centuries together, nature had been the subject of poets' dreams and songs, without being in the least known scientifically. When at last a beginning was made, and all phenomena of natural life were studiously observed and critically compared; when the human eye, aided, sharpened, and strengthened by improved instruments, reached unheard-of distances in the firmament, and penetrated the secrets of the most minute organic forms, beyond the limits so far attained by the scrutinising powers of man, down to the most rudimentary manifestations of life, the new paths to knowledge, so long neglected, so recently opened, naturally engrossed the attention of inquiring minds; and with the astounding discoveries made in the novel field of the natural sciences, rose the fallacious idea that there was but the one side in nature now revealed by these sciences. Like to a child who, in sight of the new world to which the telescope has introduced him, would think, in his simple faith, that by further improvements in the glasses, thoughts also would become visible to the eye, people became a prey to the illusion that there was nothing in creation which could not be reached, counted, measured, weighed, and computed by observation and criticism; that time and fate, law and power, were nothing but numbers and proportions. In the hope of explaining and scrutinising all things in this way, the moral cognising powers of man were drawn into this experiment. The life of the human being was also now supposed to be but a sum-total of proportions. Under the influence of such views, the contempt for the human individual could but increase, for conscience will not be robbed of the conviction that all that can be seen, measured, computed, is superficial and shallow. Besides all this, the earth was, according to these new opinions, not considered as the temporary habitation of man, but as the mother of the human race. Now, in the new order assigned to the heavenly bodies, the earth must henceforward cede to the sun the honour of occupying the centre of our planetary system; how could her child now escape the humiliation of his mother? The more it became the fashion to make size and greatness the standard of power, significance, and worth, the lower must man, the inhabitant of this petty planet, sink in his own estimation.

Nothing was now wanting to bring this contempt of the human individual to the highest pitch but the *false view of what society is*, which then began to permeate public opinion. The Church had once formed a community whose influence was founded upon spiritual merits, and had from that high position made herself, by her moral and religious character, the guide of nations. But when she presumed to govern them she lost her influence. At the time of the Reformation, attempts were made to replace her by a community which would represent the power of thought. These attempts failed, and the world began to think that a society governed, not by moral and religious authority, but by the outward, compulsory force of civil power, was the most perfect work of human culture. But from the moment man is represented as being of such a nature that something exterior, some compulsory force, is required to subject him to the dominion of order and right, our conscience and reason will enter their protest, and refuse their esteem to such a creature of imagination. Men may wander ever so far away from the path of nature, but the voice of conscience cannot be silenced, and its verdict is that no being created for self-government who takes his refuge in compulsion can escape contempt.

These new opinions concerning God, nature, and society have not been laid before you in order to explain the cause *of this contempt of the individual*, for no error giving birth to a false appreciation of man has any other origin than his own egotism. As long as he does not free himself from self-love, he will, as often as he overcomes one error, fall into another exactly opposed to it. For centuries together man had been governed by the conceit and the stubbornness of his pride, which despises nature, and flatters itself that the universe is there for his sake alone. When this fallacy gave way to knowledge, while the self-love nevertheless remained, man must needs fall into the contrary error of that despairing feeling which loses its self-confidence, and then considers itself as a purposeless tool of the powers of nature. I repeat, it is not with the intention of showing the origin of the modern contempt for the human individual that we have reminded you of the new view taken of God, nature, and human society. We have done so in order to prove that this contempt reappears on all sides, though under a new form, and that it constitutes one of the fundamental principles of modern philosophy.

The love of *prayer* now dying away, the first doubts of its efficacy, the in-creeping indifference to it, are all of them special forms and symptoms of this fundamental principle. A heartfelt, confident prayer to God is incompatible with contempt for the human individual. Every request presupposes, for me at least, two conditions: first, that He to whom the request is addressed is able to grant it; secondly, that in order to have it granted, I must *ask* Him to do it. If it were not so, the request would be vain in the first case, and superfluous in the second. If owing to our conception of the relative position of man to God, we consider the perfection of the infinite as impossible in individual life by reason of the limits set to the latter, if we consider wrong and wickedness as inherent in the nature of limited beings, then the craving of the human heart that has set itself upon the deliverance from it and all the harm accompanying it, never can hope to be satisfied. Man, then, never can know whether the misery in which he entreats Heaven for help is not one of the inevitable imperfections of life against which there is no help—whether the prayer, the object of which is to remove these evils, is not useless. And he who begins praying with doubts, will certainly, sooner or later, cease to pray altogether.

Besides, the notion of God arising from the contempt of the individual, necessarily causes prayer to appear superfluous, for this reason: the person who is convinced that God and the individual man are the two extremes of perfection and imperfection, will by force of logic be obliged, whenever he attempts to realise God as a being, carefully to avoid any of the features peculiar to man, to any personality, since these features are imperfection itself. He will then find himself condemned never to let his thoughts dwell on any conception that he could grasp with his mind's eye by means of an image. Then, as it is natural to a human being to be moved by entreaty, he will at once regard it as a monstrous error to imagine that God can allow Himself to be entreated. It appears to him diametrically opposed to the majesty and goodness of his God, to wait to be entreated before He dispenses His gifts to His creatures. Nothing appears more certain to him than that God gives to man whatever He can, and will give it to him, whether he prays for it or not. Nothing can be more certain than that the man who, from habit, prays under this supposition, will sooner or later give up praying altogether, for his reason will not submit for ever to occupy itself with things that he himself considers as superfluous.

These few hints may suffice to justify the assertion that the contempt of the human individual, and the cooling zeal for prayer, are only different manifestations of the same fundamental principle. All experiences of our spiritual life from which we may derive light on this subject will confirm this connection of mental phenomena. We shall find that the longing for prayer dwindles away more rapidly as the contempt for the human being increases, and that people never have passed so rapidly through all transitions of a change of spirit as now, when this contempt for the individual governs public opinion almost without exception. There certainly will be many who will call this reproach to our time unfounded, and argue that it is just the boast of our day that the rights and well-being of individuals, as such, are made the principal object of public solicitude and care. Who could refuse to acknowledge these efforts and their merits? If only this tendency itself did not manifest also this same contempt for the individual of which we complain! For upon what basis is founded the claim of every individual to have his rights acknowledged, and to have his share of the enjoyments of this world? For those who may be considered as the wisest among the representatives of the reigning principles of the day, this claim, as is well known, is founded upon the idea that man can only fulfil his destiny on earth when he is not molested in his rights on any side, and is protected against need by existing institutions. What, then, is the destiny of man on earth? Has man ever any other destiny on earth than to fulfil the law of his conscience, and to carry out in word and deed the principles of justice? And you will affirm that man has not been, nor ever will be, able to fulfil this one duty before certain measures are taken! Can virtue be represented as the produce of laws and civil institutions? Can man ever be robbed of moral liberty and self-government? And is it possible to suppose, even for a moment, that those most sacred rights, which the Eternal Father has given him as the most essential principle of his own, of his innermost life, most essential principles of all true worth and dignity—can it be supposed for an instant that these sacred gifts can ever be replaced by a lifeless machinery of earthly power? You will help the living by putting him under the government of what is dead in itself? Never have the contempt and ignorance of the creative power manifested in the human individual come to light in a more barefaced manner, exhibited themselves more unblushingly than in the doctrines upon which are based the present efforts for the right and the well-being of the individual. Such a callousness towards the self-depreciation of man, such callousness under the ill-treatment which man practises against his own nature, has never yet manifested itself in public opinion as now, in our own time.

But we, who willingly renounce the self-approbation of the day; we, who will not take upon us the burden of ignominy which can be no man's share except by his own choice; we, who are resolved to keep free from this new-fashioned humility, consisting in condemning one's own nature in order to shine more conspicuously in one's own doings; we, who retain hold of the unity and indissoluble communion of the human individual with the Eternal God, we will not forget that it is in company with contempt for the human individual that we find indifference towards prayer. Tell me in whose company you are, and I will tell you who you are. This is true in this case as in others. Let the rejection of prayer ever so cleverly assume the sacred names of Liberty and Truth, we find no attraction in it, after having discovered in what company it is to be found.

III.

THE LIFE OF HIM WHO REJECTS PRAYER.

IN our last discourse we considered the views entertained by those who lead public opinion, and we came to the conclusion that, according to them, men could only free themselves from the errors in their prayers by rejecting prayer altogether. In order to judge fairly of their opinion, it is not only necessary to trace them back to their origin as we have done, but also to carry on the investigation from the premises of the argument down to its conclusions. Then we shall know its full significance in all its bearings.

The object of to-day's discourse is to investigate this second aspect of the question. We have seen on what ground arose the opposition to prayer. We will now see what are its results. We intend to set aside outward and isolated facts, for, whatever men undertake or carry out, their actions lie too much on the surface of life to enable any observer to be sure that he can see the motives that have prompted them, and their connection with the main tendencies in the life of a man. The names by which such single acts are called may be great and imposing, but they do not always convey a correct idea of their real character, and might be misleading in such an inquiry. It is therefore better to avoid them altogether. The association which we have called into life, the Community of Evangelical Christians, implies by its name that we have undertaken moral and religious reforms; nevertheless, we all know that similar as may appear the participation of most members in this common work of ours, the reasons that prompt the one to join in it, may be very different from those that prompt another to do the same. Although certain thoughts require the embodiment of action to show their real character, they nevertheless often happen to be ambiguous in their manifestations, and are of no use in our analysis of the results to which certain human tendencies infallibly lead, under any circumstances.

And so it is with the effects produced in real life by the rejection of prayer; they are so multifarious and so complex, that they will give us no distinct clue to the most important feature in the life of a man, his self-government. And of all his deeds, self-government is the one which he may consider as essentially his own. Whatever the judgment we may pass on the rejection of prayer, we never could consider the fact that man is good or bad as the result of this rejection. The rejection of prayer is a doctrine as well as the view opposed to it, which will have prayer to be a necessity; and though it is certain that a pure mind and a selfish one will not find the same satisfaction in the same doctrines, it is nevertheless impossible that doctrines and opinions should have the power of making pure or impure the feelings of those who entertain them. It is therefore an undeniable fact for us, that one may advocate and use prayer with the most heartfelt zeal, and nevertheless neglect his duty; and another, who most decidedly rejects prayer as an outgrowth of superstition, may nevertheless fulfil such duties as he acknowledges most faithfully.

If we wish to see clearly what are the fruits produced by the rejection of prayer, we must examine attentively all the stages of spiritual life that lie between the deed of self-government * on one side,

---

* The word "*Selbst-bestimmung*" we shall translate by self-government when taken in a general sense, and self-determination when it concerns the individual determination in special cases.

and the decisions that concern an outward existence. There are three different kinds of motives always acting together in the determinations of men. First, the choice between good and evil, *i.e.* self-determination, which alone determines the worth of the action in question; secondly, the way of viewing life, which determines our tendencies, *i.e.* the drift of our whole existence; and lastly, the consideration given to circumstances, and on which always depends the form and garb of the action. But again, the view we take of life has in every one of us its special development, and that is a complex one, with many ramifications, almost defying analysis. The germ of such an individual view of life lies hidden so deep in us, that language and consciousness alone never are sufficient means to reach it. In our last conference* we had an instance of the insufficiency of these means to follow such views of life in all the intricacies of their development, when we attempted to trace to its origin the contempt for the human individual. It is out of these germs, so deeply rooted in the obscure recesses of our consciousness, that our views of life and of the world around us grow and develop themselves into a multiplicity of thoughts of which we unavoidably become conscious more and more frequently. They at last attain the stability of general and leading principles,

---

* Dr. Rupp's audience are in the habit of discussing with him the subject-matter of these sermons immediately after they have heard it. These discussions are not only interesting but useful; they give the author the opportunity of explaining his meaning more fully, and moreover to make himself acquainted with the spiritual difficulties of his hearers, with their arguments, and the tendencies of his audience at large.

and become set points of view with which we grow so familiar, that they are always at our disposal whenever we want a basis for our determinations and a justification for our actions. Such is the ultimate result of the view of life which we form for ourselves, whether educated or not, and which leads us to these settled habits of mind that we just now recognised as our general and leading principles, or established points of view, to which we always return in all our dealings. These points of view and leading principles are the food of the life we lead as members of *society*. They give to all societies their real form, their organisation and constitution, independently of resolutions passed; nay, very often in direct opposition to the decisions of their majorities. Public opinion, that loosest but widest aggregation of human tendencies, is nothing else than the sum-total of these individual habits of mind, these points of view from which we start when we decide on anything, and which we, consciously or unconsciously, take as the standard of our judgments and the basis of our actions. Such general principles and leading points of view prove to be the "*natural powers*," superior to all established powers and authorities, and entirely beyond their reach. These "*natural powers*" alone bring about the progress or the ruin of national life, and of every community of any kind, according to the right or wrong objects they pursue. We can therefore find no better means of ascertaining which aspect the life of a man who rejects prayer will assume, than by making ourselves acquainted with the general principles and leading points of view which form the summary expression of the contempt for the human individual, and which, having their origin in the dislike for prayer, give the public opinion of the present day a background for the rejection of any form of prayer.

In order to keep present before our minds the effects which the inward rejection of prayer must have on the life of thought, let us ask what takes the place of God for him who does not care to pray, or cannot do it? or what remains of God to him, and if, for some reason or other, he continues using that name, what he means by it? We will express it in the words which have served us as a text for our considerations on the subject of prayer. In these lines prayer is rejected as a delusion of childhood, because He, to whom the child directed himself, neither can nor will help him; then he says: " I honour Him!" What for? Hast Thou assuaged the pains, etc.? Have not Time, the all-powerful, and Fate, moulded me to a man, my masters and Thine, I ween? Then Time and Fate it is that have taken the place of Him whom the man who prays calls his God.

What mean here Time and Fate? For the meaning these words have in the eyes of the man who prays, they cannot have in the eyes of him who rejects prayer. Even Time and Fate are a *part* of the manifestation of Deity in the eyes of the man who prays; they do not exhaust this manifestation; but here Time and Fate are the one and all. Besides these two elements, there is nothing that would share with them the dominion over the universe, far less any power the ministers of which they would be supposed to be. In this new sense, Time and Fate are synonymous with what we call the universe, the order and law of the universe, with one thing abstracted from it, namely, *justice*.* I do not mean that those whose God consists in Time and Fate will not have some meaning for the word "justice." There are things nowhere to be seen or heard, the symbols of which can nevertheless never be destroyed. Such a word is 'justice.' What would not the despots of all times have given if they had been able to wipe it out of the language of men! But there is, with the ground of their eternal fear, also the limit of their power. They can falsify the word, annihilate it they cannot. So those who do not pray, because their double God is Time and Fate, have applied the word "justice" to something indifferent or injurious in their description of the world. But what we mean by justice, this justice in the manifestation of which Time and Fate are simply instrumental, has no place in the endless order of their world. That justice which shows itself inseparable from the creative power of self-government and free-will, is necessarily excluded from the characteristics of a world whose fundamental law is limited to the narrow circle of visible and invisible causes and effects. If in this way you abstract justice from your conception of creation, what you will have left, instead of the eternal order and government of the world, instead of the omnipotent will of God, is mere power. If the guiding principle of education is power, man will learn to love, to admire power, and to aim at it as being the highest

---

* The word "justice" is used here in the general, comprehensive and higher sense attributed to it by Plato and Kant. See the note in the discourse on the text, "Thy kingdom come."

object of his aspirations. He who places his faith in power, sees in creation an endless gradation, in which, according to this system, a certain place is assigned to every being, by the fact that it overcomes others, and that it is in its turn overwhelmed by superior force. No being has any other vocation than to crush, or to be crushed. The eternal order consists in subjecting everybody to the double state of victory and destruction. Faith in power is the faith in eternal discord and eternal struggle; peace is nothing but illusion. The phenomena in the history of the world, nations, states, religions, present in their turn the same spectacle as the lives of individuals. Everyone of them has its time, and then it is irresistible; for everyone in its turn comes the downfall, and nothing can prevent this. When Christianity gained the victory over all other religions, in the eyes of these philosophers, the cause of this was that it was the newest. We are not allowed to say Christianity may perhaps pass away, and, if so, it will be because Christians misconceived its object; but we are to say Christianity *must* pass away, for it cannot escape the general fate, to grow old because it has been new, and to pass away because it has once come into life. What is just, or what is unjust, you are not to ask; this question has no sense for him who believes in mere power. He admits only of one question, What is just at the *present moment?* for just, to him, is only what is proper, *i.e.* expedient for the time being; and what is expedient for the time being is what has, so far, the power to maintain itself against all resistance. So far your power, so far your rights. As long as the Church had the power to burn heretics, she did right to burn them; as long as Europeans are more powerful than the inhabitants of Africa, slavery, and all that is done to maintain it, is just.

In this way mere force, mere power, takes the place of the omnipotent Will of God, in the eyes of him who does not pray, who does not see in the life of the universe a manifestation of justice, and enjoyment alone, enjoyment *for its own sake*, takes the place of the soul-inspiring surrender unto the Divine Will. The justice which one who does pray reveres, is eternal and unchangeable; that justice never required a beginning and never will pass away, and all that is connected with it and shares in its nature is by this very fact clothed with immortality. For him who prays, besides the enjoyment which years bring and take away, there is a blessedness in his feeling which, as the reflex and glory of justice, is eternal as justice itself. But for him who believes in Time and Fate, not seeing that this justice is the life of the world, nothing is left but the enjoyment that must fade away like the blossoms in the spring. For him who thinks he has found the true essence of things in the continual change of birth and death, in the eternal unrest, rising into being and sinking back again into rest, there can be no joy that does not bear in its bosom the germ of corruption and decay; thus for him there can be no love but that over which the fate of destruction hovers. Even friendship, of which he boasts that it outlives the transitory love of youth, is bound to the rolling wheel of time. The enjoyment of such a friendship owes its origin to the sympathy of kindred souls that find and draw each other; but that wherein they meet and attract each other is eternal only in this, that it changes and transforms itself. The never-ceasing unrest of Time and Fate forbids the confidence with which he who absorbs himself in prayer takes leave of the parting ones, and says: "We shall meet again." This friendship, this love of reciprocal attractions, not only goes to meet its doom, it always bears the sting of death in itself. It exists only on the condition that those natures which have most affinity with each other penetrate each other exclusively, rejecting all that attracted them previously, constantly fearing and keeping aloof everything and everyone that might, even from a distance, threaten to become more attractive, and that must, sooner or later, deprive one friend of the other. This jealousy, inherent in the errors of youthful passions, belongs also necessarily to the friendship of those in whom the belief in Time and Fate has supplanted prayer. This jealousy is the consciousness of guilt, inherent in mere enjoyment, the unavoidable verdict upon every existence that deprives itself of the pity of eternal justice. But, however grievously distorted this enjoyment may be by these blots of envy and jealousy, those who suffer in this way have at least not quite forgotten that happiness, if it is to satisfy human beings, must have its source in our very soul; whilst the vulgar crowd entangles itself more and more in the illusion that outward possessions are required to make us happy.

And as to those who have given up prayer, mere power takes the place of the omnipotent Will of God, and mere enjoyment that of soul-quickening love. So also, mere knowledge takes the place of eternal wisdom. He who says in his heart, "There is no justice," follows the old advice of the serpent, who said, "Eat of the forbidden fruit and you shall be like unto God, knowing good and evil." The knowledge of him who prays is the likeness of order, in which the eye of the conscience sees outwardly what lives in him whose eye it is; and in truth there is no other knowledge. No greater contradiction, therefore, than to be determined to know, to trust to the promise of an independent cognition, and all the time to deny the real, living source of knowledge and cognising power, and to declare obedience to the holy law of freedom to be a childish error. There is a deep meaning in these words of Schiller: "Woe to him who gets at truth by guilt"—that is to say—if the tree is cut off its roots, its fruit will never ripen. This root from which alone the fruit we are in search of—namely truth—can, according to the eternal order of things, grow fresh and healthy, is human conscientiousness. One who prefers to receive this fruit from the hand of him who scorns the law of conscience, will taste in it the full bitterness of death. For him even what is most salutary in itself becomes pernicious. Nothing is more favourable to progress on the true path of cognition than the consciousness of not knowing. But for him who does not make a distinction between the knowledge obtained by his conscience (the real cognition of truth) and the knowledge of the intellect,* the unceasing impelling instinct

---

* Dr. Rupp finely contrasts these two very telling words of the German language, "wissen" and "gewissen." Wissen, knowledge ; gewissen, conscience, literally *what is certain.*

in his consciousness of not knowing transforms itself into the bewildering illusion that it is *impossible* for us to know anything. The mere knowledge inseparable from the rejection of prayer proves to be, instead of a light to give light, a dazzling glare, when man gives himself up to this illusion, saying: " Let the sun shine from behind; we have light from its rose-coloured reflection." What he wishes really happens; his eye no longer perceives the eternal citadel of truth, and the thoughts he calls his knowledge are merely accidental opinions, casual ideas, suppositions no more closely connected than the glowing drops of the waterfall, which but for a short time mirror to our eye, in the glittering play of the rainbow, an imaginary unity. Mere knowledge is everywhere but a contradiction. The deeper the humiliation of this illusion of not knowing seems to be, the higher rises its conceit. He who prays because he knows this justice that brings order into the chaos of Time and Fate, and establishes in their very midst God's kingdom of liberty and peace, knows that in the whole horizon of his cognition nothing remains concealed that cannot and must not become visible to the eye of everyone who wishes to see. But he who does homage to mere knowledge, and turns his back on the light of truth because it hurts his diseased sight, always reaches the point where he proudly proclaims as the highest glory of knowledge that knowledge which must for ever remain an inaccessible secret to the majority of men.

Mere power, mere enjoyment, mere knowledge—these form the modern trinity; these are the three gods which, according to the belief of him who does not pray, govern the world. Obedience and its claims, that obedience that can be denied, the obedience of a free agent, does not exist in presence of these potentates of the world; for those who consider them as the only rulers of the Universe, cannot consistently acknowledge any other obedience than the compliance to which man is forced by nature, and which, therefore, no one can refuse. Such obedience is a mere link in the chain of causes and effects; and such effects being the result of necessity, can in no way be hastened or delayed by our will. Indeed, how could man presume to have any influence on the attainment of the end towards which Power, Time and Fate lead the world? What could goodness mean in such a world of inflexible necessity? What is there in common between them and the consciousness of what is good, *i.e.*, conscience itself? The belief that the world is governed exclusively by blind forces, sets man in antagonism with himself; it estranges him from his true self, from his conscience. For what other means has man to test truth than his conscience? What else can serve him as a spiritual eye with which to regard the whole economy of creation; as an eye with which to encompass its height and depth, its length and breadth; an eye for the visual angle of which nothing is too far and nothing too near; an eye for which every point of the universe is at once centre and circumference? If the forms or images this eye seeks to recognise are only dreams, then man is surrounded by an impenetrable night, be he for ever so wide awake. If we are driven hither and thither by Time and Fate alone, our steps must be tottering like those of a man who is blindfolded, so that he never knows whether he is not on the verge of a yawning abyss. Even his disposition, the only thing which to him appears to connect past and future, takes more and more the character of the unknowable. So man lacks every condition of a conscious participation in the work of Time and Fate. And if he notices how, in spite of this fact, in spite of himself, he retains the notion that in the course of the world something depends on his decisions; if he notices how this notion is at the root of his questioning and seeking, his cogitations and choice, his preferences and rejections, error appears to him as the thread which keeps together the whole tissue of his existence, and life becomes so unbearable a contradiction to him, that if he could pray, no wish would be nearer his heart than to beg that the burden of this existence should be taken from him as soon as possible, and that he might pass into the order of those beings which to him appear to be like plants and brutes, free from this evil fancy of self-government.

This is the bitter fruit borne by the life of thinking men after they have rejected prayer, under the influence of the new faith in Time and Fate. But are the effects of this new belief less fatal for the large majority of those who are unacquainted with the pain and labour of thinking? If Time and Fate are not ministers of eternal justice, if they are themselves the supreme lords of the universe, evil naturally loses its old meaning. Evil and good step into the order of those contrasts which, like day and night, frost and heat, dryness and damp, littleness and greatness, birth and death, are inseparable from life and the development of all beings. According to this new belief, St. Paul's saying, "that godliness is profitable to all things," appears to be an error. He who rejects prayer must consider it a duty to be on his guard against such one-sided moralists as Jesus and all the prophets, in order that he may never forget that the arbitrariness, selfishness, and everything against which these prophets and saints direct their attacks, are also necessary for the maintenance of creation. The man who prays knows that he has not to fear these enemies of goodness, for they are doomed to eternal weakness by a holy will; but according to the belief of him who rejects prayer, arbitrariness and self-love pertain to this force that always wills the evil and 'brings about the good.'* Thus arbitrariness and self-love also pertain to the perfection of the universe. Oh, how rich in deceiving consolation becomes life with the rejection of prayer to the mind that will not give up its guilt! "Do not torment thyself," says such a man to himself, "do not torment thyself with this hard duty of loving thine enemy and forgiving the wicked; do not torment thyself with the consideration whether thou dost not attribute imaginary vices to thine enemy, in order to justify thy hatred against him. Be that which moves thee ever so wrong, wrong must also be treated kindly; wrong also belongs to the great building of creation, as shade belongs to light."

With this terrible consolation in his heart, what wrong could a man, who rejects prayer, have to reproach himself with against his neighbour? True, he

* These words are a quotation from Goethe.

cannot conceal from himself that in such a throng of fighters as that into which society has been transformed by the greediness for wealth, for power, distinctions, and enjoyment, the individual can only rise by overthrowing his neighbours on the right and on the left. He must see that the greater the crowd and the pressure grow, the smaller must be the number of the few who reach the goal, whilst the battle-field strewn with the victims extends in proportion. He cannot overlook this fact, but it does not disquiet him. For him it is only the reflection of the broad law of creation, that must destroy in order to create new life. According to his opinion, it is that law that says to man, "One of these two alternatives is necessary;" thou must be anvil or hammer, there is no third possibility. Time and Fate, they say, cannot have moulded him aright who would grieve that his enjoyment, his distinctions, should be impossible, without the spoliation or humiliation of his fellow-man; that his happiness should make the misery of another.

And now consider the present time, and say whether men are not teachable. They listen to every word that shows the world under this light; they drink this sweet poison in long draughts; in their intoxication, they deem they have only just begun to live; such is the zeal and comfort with which they work at that self-education which is to lead them to arbitrariness and wrong, the result obtained in the forge of Time and Fate. Do not let us dwell any longer upon this painful picture. We felt obliged to mention at least the encouragement given by the belief that rejects prayer to the lowest propensities and passions to which man is prone. But far more important, it appears to me, to observe how paralysing is the action of the belief in Time and Fate on the vigour of better men, and how it becomes a hindrance to the results of their efforts. I mean those who in their aim agree with the Gospel, who wish to free society from various conflicting rights, the origin of which is as doubtful as their effects are injurious, and to subject public life in all its channels to an order always harmonious, founded on the nature of man; and, with this intention, try to prove that the causes of endless struggles of selfish interests are not to be sought in the laws of nature, but in the misapprehension of these natural laws, and that the true law of our nature points to the indwelling intention of giving to the common welfare a sure basis by a reciprocal advancement and help among men. Do these men not mostly proclaim the new belief in eternal Time and omnipotent Fate, the inevitable result of which is the rejection of prayer? And they do so even without being conscious that in this belief is the principal cause of their weakness, and of the barrenness of their efforts. They attempt to establish justice on earth. But man can help effectively that cause only in the victory of which he can believe. All the obstacles which tower upon each other against him, all the defeats he experiences, may even renew his courage and increase his strength, if there be this conviction in him, that the often hidden but irresistible power of eternal order is for him and against his adversaries. Be his thoughts and all his doings ever so sincere, be his devotion ever so admirable, without this faith he is himself the greatest hindrance to the final success of his undertaking—if he conquers—by hatred and exaggeration—if he is vanquished—by doubts in the possibility of success, of which he is not conscious, but to which he gives himself up without the resistance of will, whenever these doubts clothe themselves in the notion that the present circumstances are unfavourable, that nothing can be done for the time.

It is just this faith in the omnipotence of the principle which we wish to represent, that those of whom we now speak are lacking. They fight for what is right, but Time and Fate do not support them; for that Time and Fate in which they believe are the eternal change of birth and death. Time and Fate, this eternal power, are not on the side of right; on the contrary, they maintain the struggle between right and wrong, giving predominance now to one, now to the other. The victory for which they fight is itself in strife with the omnipotence in which they believe; all their efforts are directed towards a work which, according to their conviction, is impossible. In short, wherever we turn our eyes, the life of individual men, and that of society at large, who reject prayer, appears all round equally gloomy and empty. The records of the past tell us what were the effects of excommunication, that weapon so dreaded in all Christendom, when it was wielded by Popedom. In the country over which hovered the punishment of excommunication, the gates of the temples were closed, the bells that were wont to call for prayer were mute, and the priests silent; all were denied the means of salvation, through which, according to the faith of that time, the Church held hell at bay, and opened Heaven. No baptism, no marriage, no forgiving of sins, no rest in consecrated ground. It was as if God denied to such a people His blissful presence, and abandoned it to the powers of darkness. What, then, was mere imagination, becomes reality in the life of the nation which rejects prayer, because it will not believe that to justice belongs the reign, the power, and the glory from eternity to eternity. With the faith in justice which it rejects, it also loses the confidence and fidelity, self-assurance and self-respect. It praises as progress that which can produce nothing but error and spiritual impotence.

But, unavoidable as are these effects, they do not reach those depths of human nature in which for centuries a new life has been stirring, a new life of self-government, a devotion of self to earnest work, free inquiry, and active love. If the present age holds fast this freshness of life, the delusion which underlies the rejection of prayer, and which, through it, has grown more firmly rooted, will not prove to be the messenger of evil which precedes the in-storming destruction, but the last enemy who still delays the ultimate decisive defeat of evil. And so will this new life appear to us as a friend if we faithfully and conscientiously devote ourselves to the earnest work of our time. When this illusion is conquered the ground for the edifice of a true human community is clear. When the son of man has found again his Eternal Father, and looks up to Him with confidence, the old discord of man with himself is at an end; the long interrupted work destined to our race will begin again, and the eternal purpose of the Architect of the worlds will be realised on earth in the kingdom of God, of justice, and peace. Amen!

IV.

ON PRAYER AS A MEANS OF SELF-EDUCATION.

The word "prayer," as it is used in the Scriptures, has two distinct meanings. When the Apostle tells us to pray without ceasing, he means to exhort us to lead a faithful and conscientious life; to omit nothing, neither small nor great, and to keep in view every duty with unflinching watchfulness, so that we may be ready to give an account of every moment of it. On the other hand, when we are told that Jesus retired into the wilderness in order to pray, and elsewhere that He taught His disciples how to pray, the meaning is not that implied in the words of the Apostle, who evidently directs our attention to that ever-uniform and continual duty which we term self-government. The expressions: "Go into the wilderness in order to pray;" "Teach the disciples how to pray;" and other similar ones, designate a different kind of activity, *i.e.*, the one spiritual act recommended for special cases, and which it is necessary to keep distinct from other acts akin to it.

In the series of discourses on which we enter, we intend to deal with prayer in the latter and more restricted sense exclusively. We shall take into consideration the one side of spiritual life distinct from all others which can be entered upon and left again at certain times. Nevertheless, we keep to the old symbols of speech consecrated by the Church, and exclude from our consideration no form which prayer can assume in this sense. When we speak of prayer, we include in it all that presents itself as a feeling of devotion as well as all practices of religion. One person feels the nearness of God far from men, in solitude; another requires the presence of a congregation with whom he can celebrate the remembrance of our Lord in the repast ordained by him, and is thus enabled to gain a deeper and more vigorous conception of life. The one as well as the other is in a state of prayer. Here one stands on his mother's grave absorbed in earnest remembrance and blissful hope; there a woman, in the consciousness of her guilt, crouches on the steps of the altar and raises to the image of the pure Virgin a look of hope struggling with fear. And once in the time of heathenism, the priestesses trod with earnest looks and gestures in solemn dances, celebrating the feasts of their gods. All these are praying. Prayer may assume widely different aspects. Whether a man grapples with a thought in his aspirations to the cognition of divine truth, and strives to inscribe it with indelible features in his memory, and cannot be satisfied that it is his own until he can pour forth in words his spiritual gain; or whether in the whole repertory of his language he can find no expression for this new view obtained by so laborious an inner struggle and so anxious an inquiry, and is at last condemned to silence; or whether the feeling of delight break out in his countenance, in the expression of his eyes—all this is prayer. If, in the meetings of the first Christians in those times of persecutions in which the worship of the one God was punished with death, they did not allow themselves to be interrupted even by the sudden appearing of an informer in the midst of them, prayer became an act of saintly courage, for also in prayer, words may be deeds. Whatever forms the religious practices and life of the Church may assume according to the circumstances of the moment, the character of the nation and the manners and customs of the age, every one of these forms is a manifestation of the same spiritual activity which we call prayer, and which is indispensable to every human life if it is to develop healthily. Our notions of the value of prayer are intimately bound up with the notions of self-education. It is by analysing and realising vividly what self-education is that we can assign to prayer its proper place in life.

Self-education has nothing to do with the distinction and the choice between good and evil. The will which decides what is good or evil is, like eternal justice of which it is the image, one indivisible unit, and does not therefore admit of being taken in parts. In the *will* there is no beginning that could be linked to the past, and no end on which futurity should necessarily depend. Let us remember the words of Him who, hanging on the Cross, addressed His neighbour, saying: "Even to-day shalt thou be with Me in Paradise"—*i.e.*, "Thou hast paid due homage to truth, and hence guilt has no power over thee." In these words, and in a few other similar ones which He spoke on other occasions, is indicated the real nature of the will, which shares in the independence of the original being that rests in itself. But self-education is a work which proves to be subject to time, and to the law of progressive development, and must needs proceed out of a well-considered plan, and undergo the changes required by circumstances. Without foresight, and without a retrospective consideration of former experiences, it would have no happy results; it becomes a new task, now in this part, now in that. But the education we give ourselves is in itself no more able to make us good or bad than the education we receive from others. What it is our *will* to make ourselves will determine the worth and character of our self-education, for both the will that conceives and the realisation of this conception must be of one quality. The object of self-education is to appropriate to our use all the gifts of nature and the acquirements attainable in life, so as to make them subservient to us, to endow our will with power over outward things. It can succeed only if the *will* that conceives the plan, the aim of it, and also carries it out, is good. Self-education embraces the whole task of life: it requires the combined activity of all the means through which a gradual transformation of language can be brought about; and not that alone, but also the transformation of all that enters into the composition of the language, namely, our conceptions of the relations of things to each other. Self-education embraces the choice and use of all the means by which our intercourse with our fellow-men, our share in the manners and customs, laws, and social institutions, can be transformed in such a way and such a degree that the laws governing the development of nature and that of human life, finding all obstructions removed, can be brought to bear upon our whole action in all directions. Self-education thus consciously, intelligently, brought under the government of the fundamental laws of life, must enable us better to know, better to appreciate, and more wisely to administer the gifts of nature and of life. It must enable us to stop the effects of evil, to banish them from among us. And in the end it must enable us, by the help of the Good Spirit, to establish and extend further and deeper in the world the reign of the Good Spirit. The conception of self-education is expressed exhaustively in the words—prayer and work. These are two means which, taken together, form the whole extent of self-education. They complete each other like breathing in and breathing out in the life of the body. In work the mind expands and spreads itself in all directions, and enters into connection with all sides of life: in prayer it goes into and collects itself. Work finds in all incidents of outward life a call for bringing into action all the dispositions, all the powers of the soul, whilst prayer alternating with work re-establishes the balance and unity of inward life. Prayer is the sum-total of means through the use of which the soul recognises in the relations of all things to each other its own relation to itself; and however considerable may be the share it takes in the affairs of life, the mind gradually becomes more distinctly and more continuously conscious and sure of itself.

I fear that just those who value prayer will find it hard to reconcile themselves to the idea that prayer is only one of the two means which constitute self-education. They will say that prayer, considered as a means to an end, will thus be stripped of its sacred character. But it is this very view underlying this fear which runs counter to the cognition of truth. This view is no other than the old illusion which Jesus combated, that special articles of food, special times and places, special talents and occupations, were purer, more sacred and dignified than others. This fear is the consecration of feast-days and Sabbaths of the old dispensation, one of the innumerable garbs of that error which practises idolatry with what is elevated; and it is this very fear, this ancient error, which has opened the way to these confusing distinctions of what is small or great. Oh, might we never forget these words which came as a harbinger of our Saviour's work among us: "The valleys and depths shall be filled, and the mountains and hills shall be made low." May we never forget that other picture which represents Him as overthrowing the mighty from their seats, and raising the lowly! Also the conceptions which men form of God and of the superiority of certain gifts in the human mind, of the exclusive excellency of certain functions in society, are a manifestation of the pride against which Jesus directs His attacks. Does it never strike us that, when in order to do homage to prayer, we set it up as something higher, more dignified and majestic than work, we drag down the latter, deprive it of its own dignity, and debase it in our own eyes as the vulgar part of life?

Although work is undeniably connected with the various materials that we have to procure and to handle, has not God also introduced it into the economy of the world as well as prayer? It would be a salutary lesson to him who thinks prayer degraded, when put on a level with work, to hear the voice of the angel that exhorted Peter "not to make common that which God has cleansed." Every kind of work to which God calls us is as holy as prayer, and the notion that the latter would bring us nearer to God than work is an error springing up in the hearts of those who everywhere find a place from which they can look down upon others. By pointing to prayer as one of the two means, the use of which constitutes self-education, far from degrading it, we elevate it to be part of the holy law according to which all things are equal before God. For in all that pertains to the domain of what is useful, the Eternal no less reveals His presence than in nature and conscience. Whilst work is that means of self-education through which, by the right management of every task incumbent upon us, we gradually attain to an ever purer worship of God and knowledge of ourselves, prayer is the other means through which this worship of God and cognition of self is gained, by uniting and knitting more closely together the various sides of life in the human mind.

But how shall we practically apply this one means of self-education, which God has granted us in giving us the faculty of prayer? Like every other means. We must seize it, and through a continual practice make it our own, until we have attained in the use of it, a power and skill which has its life in itself, independently of the impetus given to it by special determinations. It is by making a beginning of this practice of the worship of God and self-cognition as best we can, that we seize and grasp this means of self-education, just within our reach, in our indwelling faculty of prayer. The only condition we have to fulfil in this compact evidently consists in doing our part in it of our own accord, *i.e.*, that we must not be brought to prayer by coercion, by any respect of persons, by any art of persuasion, by any fear of loss, or greediness of gain, lest we should be like a mechanism put into motion ; but on the contrary, that we pray by our own wish, and from a conviction that prayer is a necessity. In short, we must undertake it spontaneously. But many put off this beginning, having been told that it required a special inclination or mood for it, and they wait for this mood. They will wait in vain. They do not consider that if there is such a devotional mood to collect our thoughts, it has become quite a stranger to those who have long ceased to pray. They have allowed it to be scared away by the affairs of life, by its noises and distractions, so that they have ultimately become incapable of it. After these occupations and amusements, there certainly will be times of unwelcome lassitude, depression, weariness, and dulness ; but this devotional mood that invites us to collect our thoughts, is not one of the things that come without being sought. The warning voice of conscience, the appeals of which are wanting in the life of no human being, will perhaps also echo in their hearts as a feeling of longing for that which is eternal, but in the soul of him who does not pray, the remembrance of what has been lost and is now missing is the contrary of this devotional mood inviting to prayer, in which the fulness and affluence of spiritual life manifests itself. No, the important point is not to wait for this feeling of devotion, but to *make time for prayer*. This demand will appear to many as material and insipid. It is indeed incompatible with the tendency of those people who consider prayer not as something that, like their vineyard, their flower-bed, or their loom, will bring profits proportionate to the efforts they have bestowed upon it; but as disconnected from the sphere of our labours and the general activity which we consciously exercise. They see in it something like the effulgence of the stars; they shed their light, but we need not see that it be done. Is prayer really a concentration of the mind and soul, a special task of our lives, running side by side with work, then it is undeniably an absolute duty to find time for it. The only function of life which requires no special time, because it is always present and equally active in us, is the distinction between good and evil in which the undivided existence of free will, of reason, and conscience manifests itself. Any moment of our life may be dedicated to work or relaxation; the choice between fear and liberty, between selfishness and love, not only *can*, but *must* ever be made. But abstraction being made of the characteristics of self-government, everything else, like day and night, summer and winter, must have its special time. Is prayer to find place in my life? the time for it must be taken either from work or from relaxation. It is the case with the devotion for which we assemble here on Sundays, and that always is the case when we pray. If, included in the word prayer, we understand this special kind of self-activity which we contrast with work as a concentration of thought and feeling, as going into oneself and excluding from it all outward things, and we at the same time imagine that we can pray without appointing a special time for it, we deceive ourselves. This requisite is so evident that, with the exception of those who have been initiated into the dangerous art of finding arguments for and against every idea ever expressed, all who neglect prayer without rejecting it from principle, when they are reminded of it, say, We have no time for it. They would certainly not give this answer if they did not consider prayer as superfluous. The most certain proof that a man considers a thing as necessary is that he always finds time for it. But this answer seems to indicate also that there is the vague feeling that if we determine really to apply the means of self-education which God has placed within our reach in giving us prayer, the thing is not done in the few moments we consecrate to it on Sundays and holydays. And indeed prayer can only attain its object if we consecrate so much time to the use of it, that this means grows to be a power in us which manifests itself independently of momentary resolutions. It would certainly be a deplorable mistake if, like certain orders of monks, we came to consider life the more perfect in proportion to the time given to prayer, to the detriment of work. On the other hand, it would be equally misapprehending the true order of life, if we were to admit that the opportunities of worship offered by the Church were sufficient to give us the complete unity of life which we require. These occasional opportunities will sooner or later appear superfluous to anyone who has not, by his own experience, learned that this priesthood of the Gospel, this continuous worship of God, this close scrutiny of oneself is the best safeguard of a healthy growth and expansion of life. Work engrosses our attention now here, now there, accustoms our eye to the chequered and ever-changing scenes of life, and demands of us that we should grasp one side of existence and bestow upon it our undivided interest and thoughts. It is therefore necessary, in order to re-establish the consciousness of that unity which brings together all the aspects of life, and to help the soul to find itself again under all circumstances, that we should collect and consecrate our thoughts again every day. Without the daily prayer, daily work must make us strangers to ourselves. If we will keep the balance between our outward and our inward life, we must pray—pray daily; that is the reason why I cannot conceive a true human life without prayer, yea, without *daily* prayer.

The objections raised now amongst us, Protestants, against daily prayer, are well known. It is said that in this way prayer becomes a verbiage, that it again brings into use books of prayer and devotion and becomes a mere habit. It seems to me that these scruples do not arise from the cognition of truth, but from a sentimental, indolent, and supercilious character which religion has assumed for long, under the influence of the spirit of the time. It is thought that prayer can only be genuine when it comes of itself, when it rises without our intention from the depth of our hearts and pours forth of itself with irresistible power, when it overwhelms us like the sublime and the beautiful. It means this: Religion and prayer must be an enjoyment. When they require an effort and a self-denial they are dismissed as inconvenient and intruding guests. The apostle describes the state of his inner life by the words: "The good that I would, I do not; but the evil which I would not, that I do." Everyone must judge for himself whether he is so far advanced on the path of liberty that this description of the apostle is no longer applicable to himself. But for him who will not place himself above the apostle, there is no other course open, if he intends to advance in this religious and moral training, than to compel himself to bring to fruition this good in him that is so tardy in becoming active. It is so with prayer, and it is so with every good work. It certainly was an error when, in former days, people thought that nothing could be good that had not caused a struggle; but the contrary error, that everything must be evil which we impose on ourselves, must be far more suspicious to those who follow after Jesus. The gods certainly do not find pleasure in the torment of man, nevertheless they never cease to demand the fulfilment of a duty because man, through his own fault, has fallen into a state in which the earnest fulfilment of almost any duty causes him a grievous self-denial. Jesus tells us that His yoke is easy, and His burden light; but would this assurance have been required if He had not had to deal with people who first found it hard and overwhelming? No; my friends, never let us refuse to accept prayer as a duty when we are reminded of it, whether the warning come from within or from without, be it ever so inconvenient and intrusive.

This advice to keep ourselves to the habit of praying in spite of the calls to business and the attractions of pleasure, will meet with the opposition of many for this reason, that when we resolve to pray without feeling disposed to it, this resolution can hardly be carried out without the help of a book of prayer. And few things meet with so much disdain on the part of the so-called enlightened people as the use of books of prayer, not only of the bad ones, but of all such books without distinction, including also the best writings that might be read for this purpose. This disdain dates from the time when people set their highest pride on deriving everything from themselves, on never walking on a path trodden by others, and in striving to be (what was then called) original. At the same time the supercilious tone which aimed at distinction also crept into the feeling of religious circles, and only such prayers appeared to have any worth, the thought and expression of which had originated in one's own mind. It cannot be denied that to have thoughts and words at one's command, to express what lives in us, is no small privilege, and one especially enjoyed by people of culture; but in the kingdom of truth, not only are there no rich or poor, no man or woman, no free or slaves, but there are no distinctions between cultivated and uncultivated people. In one respect, prayer certainly must be my own work, and this condition is within the reach of the learned and the unlearned. Every prayer that is to contribute to my advancement must be my own, so far that it must spring from my own free-will, from a want perceived by my own reason, from the demand of my own conscience, from the conviction of its inner necessity, from my love for God, or can be traced to it. Is this the case—does the flow of prayer spring up from the source of free-will and self-government, then there is in it an indwelling force which has nothing to fear from the poverty of thought and awkwardness of expression, a force which will lose nothing from the fact that my mind is not practised enough to bring quickly all experiences of life to a living picture, and to give to each the most fitting expression. Accepting the help of a more skilled mind and using it to my advantage will in no degree weaken the force or efficacy of this spontaneous prayer. The thoughts thus found in a book of prayer are then no strangers, no unintelligible symbols; they are a common property which I enjoy in making use of them; they express my own wants, my own temptations, my own means, my own poverty, and my own riches. I only wanted the sharpness of sight to see what is in me, the lips to sound it in my ear.

And should I hesitate to realise what lives in me by using the words of a Jesus, of a St. Paul, of a Thomas-à-Kempis, of a Luther, and a Fénélon? No! if it was the love of God that made me wish to pray, even less glorious gifts than these will be for my good.

But of all prejudices against prayer, the most widely spread is the one based on the notion that the feelings which accompany prayer are stripped of their liberty and their beauty, and become a deadening habit when they are clad in the garb of language; that they lose their high character, and must therefore become common and trivial. No doubt, words as well as affected feelings can be dead and artificial; and it is equally certain that a servile habit is incompatible with the real character of prayer, or anything really useful and salutary. But one of the most dangerous symptoms of our age is that such a view could have gained ground. A coincidence of old and new errors has given rise to this prejudice. I can only consider it as a judgment of God that the fear of speech should have been engendered in the Protestant Church. It was through the power of speech that the Reformers obtained the most glorious victories—of speech as the bearer of the love of God—as bearer of the cognition of truth and liberty. They had a right to be proud of the use which they had made and taught men to make of this weapon of the Spirit. Had their Church persevered in this path, and not misused this weapon of the Spirit, and degraded it by making it a tool of scholastic subtleties and miserable contentions, the present fear of speech, even when applied to prayer, never would have arisen. In the last century a new error complicated this old guilt and brought prayer into disrepute — at least brought it into disrepute as regards the one form under which alone it can influence life deeply and everlastingly. An increasing love of pleasure arose in the hearts of the people, unguarded as they were against the temptations of their growing prosperity, and in the circles of the educated classes this phenomenon reached its highest point, and turned into sentimentality and a revelling in feeling which led them to satiety, loathing and torpidity; and this apathy has only in a few cases yielded to a restoration of spiritual health. Feeling then was raised on the throne from which justice was overthrown, and the intoxication of a feeling which does not speak, or at the utmost murmurs, was sought with idolatry. Speech firm and distinct, born out of an honest inquiry and sound research, was more and more treated as an unjustifiable stranger intruding into the sanctuary of Religion, and was ultimately driven out of it. "Feeling is everything," it was then said; "names are but sound and smoke, bringing darkness around the glow of heaven." Prayer could then only be conceived as the sweet enjoyment of solitude, and reminiscences after the fatigues and excitement of passions and pleasures; but this enjoyment had no greater enemy to dread than prayer: the quiet retiring into self would have made manifest the frightful emptiness of the mind. The weakness of judgment into which people then sank in the course they pursued, caused them arbitrarily to declare that feeling constituted the whole worth of human life, and quite as arbitrarily to declare speech to be nothing but a vain shadow. Then the worth of these imaginary things was, in good earnest, weighed against that of the other, and it was considered as beyond all doubt that feeling was as much better than speech, as the whole body of a living animal was to be considered better than the skin of a dead one. At the time when our forefathers respected the words of prayer, without servility to the letter, they knew that words alone and feeling alone were nothing, but that both being, what they are in reality, instrument, bearer, symbol and expression of the life founded upon liberty, were to be honoured equally, and were to be used with equal conscientiousness. We certainly have to take care, in our just dislike to the morbidness of sentimentality and dreamy enthusiasm, not to be unjust to the misused gifts of the Creator. For in the sacred order of the world, in the service of Eternal Justice, feeling is of no less importance than the power of considering and planning, nothing less than activity and law, institutions and customs. But feeling steps out of the place assigned to it by the Eternal, in the sacred order of the world, as soon as it looks down with contempt upon what stands at its side with equal dignity: the word which is the body of thought, and manners and customs which are the manifestations of perseverance and faithfulness. Truly there have been men whose feelings of prayer were so pure that they vainly sought for words in the distorted language of their time that would have expressed them; but we must not forget that speechlessness may also indicate poverty of thought. Thanks to the Eternal who has endowed us with feelings for prayer as for other objects, feelings which refresh us like the cool of the evening. But again, is there nothing but air in creation? Is there not also the shadow-giving and fruit-bearing tree, and the rock that even under the raging waters remains immovable? Should not the fluctuating feelings of prayer be allowed to consolidate and to organise themselves into words? Everything that presents a fundamental tendency of life, must, in order to attain its aim, present itself under all these forms at once, feeling, thinking, and doing.

And now, let us take our standing-point for this our inquiry outside the pale of prejudices which have hastened the decline of prayer, and we shall find that they are all connected with the indolent, supercilious, and sentimental character which for a long time has been distorting piety. They mostly can be traced back to the ascendency of privileges, to the prerogatives of so-called culture; they point to this aristocracy of the mind, so powerful among us and incompatible with the kingdom of Heaven, such as the Gospel describes it to us. These prejudices have their root in this fundamental error which will not be satisfied with goodness, with justice in its simplicity and unassuming character, and deems nothing worth our efforts that is not extraordinary, rare, great, and imposing. Do not let us forget that Jesus has come to exalt the valleys, and make low the hills and mountains. Let us learn humility, the humility of the free man, to which justice combined with the cognition of the law of equality will lead us; and we shall again find it easy to pray. Amen.

TRANSLATOR'S NOTE.—Sentimentality is perhaps not so much the cause of the decline of prayer in England as it has been in Germany, but singular as the comparison may appear, here also this crisis, in the religious development of the country, is caused in a great measure by a similar disparagement of one side of man's nature and the exaggerated importance given to another. What has been done in Germany by sentimentality and the disparagement of outspoken prayer is done in England by arguments of greater gravity. I mean an exaggerated importance attributed to mere intellect considered as the culminating point of evolution. Men of science doubt the spiritual element in man as distinct from his body. It seems so satisfactory to say: We shall soon be able to see the thoughts of man, to analyse his mind as we do his body, for mind must be the produce of matter! What was expressed as a doubt and an hypothesis by the learned, the thoughtless crowd of the ignorant proclaim as a fact based upon science: hence the contempt for prayer on this side of the German Ocean.

V.

PRAYER AS TAUGHT BY THE CHURCH.

ONE of the most valuable gifts which a kindly fate can bestow upon childhood and youth, is the possession of a home in which a man gradually and unconsciously enters into that spiritual communion that we call prayer, until it becomes a part of himself, before he is thrown into the throng of life. Once having learned to collect our thoughts, and to concentrate our attention by this long practice of prayer, we are able, whenever we enter into a sphere of action, to turn away from the many and bewildering impressions which threaten to estrange us from our better self, and too often chain us down to earth. We then find that the habit of retiring into ourselves at frequently recurring intervals has become an intimate want, as well as a power in us, always within our reach; that we can keep our eyes steadily fixed above the distracting scenes of the outer world, and come ever and again to the Eternal with our questioning minds, our wants, our longings, and our entreaties. Such spontaneous movements of the heart are for us the guarding and saving powers which poetry presents to us as the Guardian Angels under whose protection the traveller, shielded against the dangers that threaten him, follows his path undismayed and secure. The seeds sown in his infantine soul now bear their fruits: at the hour when others totter and fall, he stands upright; for at the decisive moment, under the overpowering impressions of which he might succumb, a voice that he knows and loves, loudly speaks from the depths of his soul, and says: "How could I do this wrong thing and grieve our Father in Heaven?" But the greater the power that such emotions exercise over those who have become familiar with prayer in early life, the more important it is that this power should possess no less purity than force, that the ideas inspired by the longing for what is eternal should be born of liberty :* that the feelings which at such moments turn into prayer should not, whilst they save us from the evil we perceive, conceal from us the evil we have not yet recognised.

For if so, the safety secured so far is inseparable from new temptations. And this is the danger to which all are exposed whose prayer, having been from their earliest days associated with their wants, their memories, and habits, is essentially, in its tenour, a mixture of error and truth. And this danger exists for every one of us, as long as we have not conscientiously examined that kind of prayer in which we have long participated in religious assemblies. Most of my hearers will probably agree with me, when I say that those who are advancing in the path of religious cognition and self-conquest find it from step to step more difficult to derive any satisfaction from prayer as

* It is perhaps not superfluous to explain the meaning attached by the author to the word "liberty," this expression having given rise to errors of a coarse character among several sects of Christianity, some of whom have thought that men once freed from their past sins, being purified by the blood of Christ, could henceforth do the same things without sin, provided they held fast to their faith in Christ. There is no trace of this gross superstition in the conception of liberty here mentioned. Liberty as here understood is inseparable from the cognition of good and evil, and plainly means the perfect independence given to man to choose the one or the other.

taught by the Church. But will this agreement still exist between us, when we ask what it is that we dislike in the Church prayers, when we examine the reason why, from the present standpoint of our inner-life, we no longer can pray as we are taught by the Church? I fear that just those points in prayer, such as the Church teaches, which render it dear and precious to me, are repugnant to many of our friends; that many reject in that prayer, as a superstition, just that which appears to me a pure and noble expression of truth.

Firstly.—Many people suppose that the address to God is an essential part of prayer, and make it a ground of objection to prayer; asserting that it is incompatible with the majesty of His omnipotence and His infinite nature to make Him like one of us, a sort of perceptible object. But the Church never made the address to God an essential characteristic of prayer. She has only blamed those people who avoid addressing Him for the reason we just mentioned; and to my mind the Church is right in this. He who does not wish to banish God from his language altogether, has no other alternative than to speak either of Him or to Him. When I speak to Him, I conceive Him to be present; when I speak of Him, I conceive Him to be absent. Unfortunately there are vast numbers of people who know Him only as absent and far away, and are unable therefore to describe Him otherwise without difficulty.

Nothing appears to me to be more devoid of foundation than the assurance that our conception of God approaches His greatness and infiniteness more nearly when we are speaking of Him than when we speak to Him. Whatever we may do, we cannot help with our finite faculties picturing Him to ourselves as finite and limited. And why should we avoid this? The cognition of truth, far from gaining, could evidently only lose by the vagueness of our conception of what is infinite. Is it not a peculiar feature in the essence of God to manifest Himself in what is finite without losing, for all that, the character of His infiniteness and inexhaustible fulness? Is it not a characteristic feature in God to manifest Himself in the most limited space, in the most scanty form, in a grain of sand, in a drop of rain, in the airy atom; and there to show Himself in the plenitude of beauty, perfection, glory and power? It is indeed a striking feature in His perfection, that the boundless Universe is no more before Him than the grains of dust that move about in a sunbeam, for His divine perfection is in everything, and everything dwells in it. He who is afraid of offending God by addressing Him like a limited human personality, seems to forget this altogether. Also in the finite human personality dwells the whole affluence of divinity. The entire value of our prayer consists in realising in the act of prayer that this is so; in feeling that God's eternal reason manifests itself in our finiteness; in short, our prayer is perfect only when it embodies this truth, when it is its living reality.

The old and beautiful custom, according to which man addresses the Eternal as his God and his equal, reminds me with more simplicity, naturalness, genuineness, and persistency than anything else, that also when I pray it is my first and last duty to acknowledge the eternal power and wisdom as being present in every pulsation, in every thought of human life, and to see the eternal order and love as realised in every decree of fate. He who imagines that he honours Him more when he worships Him under the form of the forces of nature, under the form of phenomena, which at first sight do not remind him of the semblance of man, will soon come to this, that he gradually understands less and less the way in which God speaks to his conscience, until it becomes quite unintelligible to him. But he who seeks and finds God in the manifestations of his own conscience, thus enters into the meaning of the whole creation; he reads clearly in his own being as in a mirror the manifestations of God in nature; he sees there the same creative power of liberty which is at work in his own will, creating that which is good, and itself destroying the evil it had chosen before. The time has not come again yet in which the sacred poet records that the earth was the garden of God, in which He walked with His children, the children of men; and where all served Him in peace and joy. But until this time has returned, I deem nothing comparable to this enviable picture of that lost reality, I conceive no more gracious memory of those days, no more sacred inheritance of the past, no more elevating promise of a glorious future, than the expression of childlike candour and confidence with which man even in this our time addresses God, as if He still walked in the cool shades of the garden—and I thank the Church from the inmost depth of my soul that she has kept up for us this beautiful, pure, and pious custom of praying to God.

Secondly.—Another fundamental notion in the prayer of the Church, even more objectionable to some people than the first, is that God should require to be entreated, that He should not give men those things which they require, and which are destined for them, until they ask for them. But in what consists this supposed error? It is said, even an earthly father, who loves his child, does not withhold a good gift he has prepared for him until the child petitions him in words, and no man in whose soul there is any mercy keeps back his alms until the beggar has addressed him in words; and would then God, who is love itself, do so?

First, I say, that just because God's love is the highest, we should not misunderstand Him if He withholds His gifts until we ask for them. Of all that we have, and all that we are, there is nothing that we do not owe to His love, nothing that is not derived from Him. We may therefore consider it as beyond all doubt, that if there are any gifts that He keeps back until we ask for them, the reason of it cannot be assigned to a want of love. On the contrary, if we do not receive the innumerable blessings which constitute our existence quite thoughtlessly and ungratefully, we must be sure that if He withholds certain boons until we have asked for them, the reason of this dispensation can be no other than love, and love alone. Do we not know, from our own experience of human intercourse, that love does not show itself only in granting, but also in denying? We do not speak here of this denying that God so often must practise from love, when human beings ask Him for more munificent mental gifts, or a higher field of labour, before they are capable of making a proper use of the more modest endowments of their minds, or of fulfilling the duties of the humbler vocation entrusted to them. We do not speak now of what God denies; we speak of what He can grant, notwithstanding His love; what He is willing to vouchsafe to His children, but only grants under one condition, only grants when men beseech Him to grant it. God has not established this condition arbitrarily. Before any of us could pray, before we were conscious of life, His loving care and solicitude had united all the forces of the body and the soul, all the affluence of life and experience, the astounding power of will and of liberty to the glory of human nature, into one being. But is there not a law inherent in our very nature, according to which, after so many gifts having been freely bestowed upon us, the granting of holy justice * should depend on this indispensable condition, that man seek it, demand it; that he exert himself to obtain it, that he pine for it, entreat God to let him have it—in short, that he be determined to have it? To grant to man even justice before he has sought it, obtained it by entreaty and by the force of his will, would be nothing short of the abolition of free-will. "God will be entreated," is only another way of expressing the fundamental law of the will, namely, that justice

---

* Justice is used here in a sense similar to that which Plato attributed to it. The word "righteousness," although a good one, is not comprehensive enough. We should not think of speaking of God's righteousness, this term applying more to the outward, i e. human, manifestation of this divine attribute. Here the author, vindicating that which is divine in man, must avoid a term which would imply a difference between father and son in reference to their nature.

allows itself to be known only by those who labour to obtain this knowledge; and "God will allow Himself to be moved by prayer," is only another expression for the power of the human will, that is sure to obtain the object of its efforts. Jesus has truly recognised the nature of man and that of God. We find Him constantly coming back to this point, that among all gifts of God, one must be obtained by prayer; that God keeps it back until the longing of man for it reaches Him. God, in His eternal love, gave you everything except this love itself; and He cannot impart it to you until you pray for it. But "Ask, and it shall be given you; seek, and you shall find; knock, and it shall be opened unto you." Longings, cravings of all sorts, requests and demands, spontaneously rise in our hearts, as independent of our will as the existence of our ears and eyes and all other possessions; but the wish to be made partakers of Divine justice does so originate itself, that, to produce and to maintain it may be called, nay, *must* be called, the most difficult enterprise in life; so much so, that Jesus's appeals to men to re-awaken that desire, which was all but dead in their hearts, led Him to His grievous path to the cross, while many before and many after Him have had to follow the same sorrowful course. For in the eyes of the world, with its selfishness, vanity, and lust of power, there can be no crime more worthy of persecution than the attempt to re-awaken this desire in the hearts of men. Woe to our self-delusion if we imagine that we have prayed for this love of justice, and we have had our prayer granted, because we sometimes feel moved and edified by the elevating thoughts of justice. Justice has nothing in common with what occasionally elevates our feelings, with what causes us delight, and the enthusiasm that carries us away. Justice is not really in us until we have created it as our own work, with heart and soul, with all our mind, and with all our might. Whosoever has even but entered on the path of liberty, knows that Divine love does not yield to our entreaties until the craving of prayer for justice has become so strong in man, through the constant renewal of it, that all common temptations have ceased to be dangerous to him.

Thirdly.—No! I find the error in the prayers of the Church, neither in the conception of God which admits of His being addressed by man, nor in the idea that Divine love does not grant us certain favours until we have asked Him for them. Both, on the contrary, are to me a pure and true expression of truth. What prevents me from praying in the way the Church teaches us to do, is: that, with the mixture of error and truth which forms the tenour of her prayers, the chief condition of every true prayer is wanting. The Apostle James points to this chief condition of prayer in the words of the Siracide, borrowed from the Old Testament: "If any of you pray—let him ask in faith, nothing wavering." Indeed, the soul of prayer is faith and trust; an unconditional faith, an immovable trust, that excludes every doubt concerning the realisation of it. The apostle is right when he requires that we should free ourselves from every doubt; for moral and religious doubt differs from all other kinds of doubt in this, that it depends on every individual, and depends on him alone, whether he succumb to his own contradictions, or whether, through faith and trust, he stands firm in himself. But do not let us imagine that the deliverance from doubt which the apostle requires of us can be brought about merely by isolated intentions and resolutions; it depends on the tenour of our prayer and its character, whether the realisation of it appears to us an indubitable fact, or whether, on the contrary, notwithstanding all our efforts to believe in the efficacy of our prayer, we are hampered by the unwelcome doubt whether it will be granted. And the tenour of the Church prayer is such that it undermines the feeling of trust, and gives us up, over and over again, to doubt and uncertainties.

In order to obtain a distinct view of the tendency in which the Church brings up her faithful children, we must examine the contents of the prayers which she has prescribed for her services of general worship and special festivals. The ideas contained in these prayers certainly refer to the life of self-government; they recall the blessings of eternal life to our consciousness; they direct the longings of the human heart towards the obedience of freedom, the cognition of truth, the self-denial in the lives of the just, the devotion of love, the salvation of the soul, and its reconciliation with God. But besides these, there are other component parts in these prayers. There are other wishes which the Church entertains, other benefits which she mentions, other emotions which she kindles. She certainly prays that God may, above all, bless her efforts in promoting His kingdom, that He may make her victorious in her struggle for truth, that He may grant her power and success, and ensure her the victory over the enemies of the right faith. And as she turns her attention to public life, to the fate of the people and country in the midst of which she is called upon to exert her activity, her prayer also turns to the happiness and prosperity of civil society and the different classes that compose it, and beseeches Heaven to turn away from the people epidemics, failure of crops, scarcity, dangers of war, and sundry adversities. And when the nation has taken up arms, she prays that their homes may be protected, and that they may overcome their enemies. And by making these entreaties part of her public prayers, the Church herself opens the channel into which the thoughts of the individuals will run in their prayers, and thus teaches fathers of families to pray for the happiness and prosperity of their households, women for the affection of those whom they love, husbands for the health of their wives, mothers for the life and welfare of their children. The Church certainly answers to the wishes of the majority of the people by thus entering into the joys and sorrows of civil society; and certainly she owes to that sympathy the influence she still possesses. But it is no less certain that this tendency in the life of the Church makes it impossible to the true followers of Jesus to pray as she teaches them to pray; and further, that such prayers, instead of producing in the hearts faith and trust, produce doubts and infidelity; and that they have not in themselves the blessing inherent in every true prayer.

In prayer nothing can be more important, in the interest of the cognition of truth, than to keep before one's mind the difference between necessity and liberty, *i.e.* that part of our destiny which is not in our hands, and that which it is entirely in our power to shape; to draw the sharpest line of distinction between that which the body and soul of man derives from the divine forces that manifest themselves in nature, and that which the will of God expects from the free will of man. If we draw that line between necessity and liberty in the wrong region of our existence, we at once distort our life, and we henceforth make it a picture of confusion and disorder; we erroneously attribute to ourselves a power of obtaining certain advantages which it is as impossible as it is unnecessary for us to have, and we fall into doubts as to the possibility of carrying out and making true that which depends on us entirely. He, whose belief in the efficiency of prayer is a living belief, perseveres on his path in spite of the wrong and violence which, endowed with all means of coercion and strengthened by public opinion, rise before him like a chain of mountains, impenetrable and insurmountable; he advances on his path as quietly as if these mountains had been dissolved into vapour in the twinkling of an eye. Indeed, for him, they are not there. But only those men can believe in such power in prayer who do not ascribe to it a power that it does not, and ought not to, possess. An ancient Church-writer says: " Joshua spoke trustfully, and God immediately submitted to the voice of that human being and delayed the sun in its course." This writer certainly goes on to assure us that the power of miraculously subverting the laws of nature is not in man; but he is mistaken if he thinks that by this explanation he has prevented misconception and error. Whoever admits that God has, even in one single instance, granted a prayer contrary to the laws of nature, that God even in one single case, be it that of Joshua or anyone else, approves the fond illusion of a man who presumes to act upon nature otherwise than by submission to her laws; whoever admits that God has ever been obliged, even on one single occasion, for the sake of man, to alter the limits that He has established in His eternal wisdom and love, he who can bear the thought of this contradiction of God with Himself, even in one single instance, will vainly try to persuade Himself that it has happened once only; he will insensibly and unconsciously, but unavoidably, make this a part of his view of the human destiny in general. And in considering the course of his own life, he will think:—Perhaps it is possible after all that God will also make an exception with me.—And do not all those entertain this idea who, according to the teaching of the Church, pray that God may turn away death from their children or their friends, or that He may grant a happy issue to their affairs and undertakings? They do not think at the moment that they place themselves in Joshua's position, and in reality have applied to themselves what they meant to be limited to Joshua alone. They do not consider that if the life of a human being were prolonged only an hour longer than is consistent with the course of things and means offered by nature, or that if a transaction were to produce one shilling more than is the necessary profit in the usual sequence of cause and effect, the miracle necessary for this result is in no way different from that of Joshua. They do not consider that the smallest change in their fate, for which they pray, is exactly as much in contradiction to the destiny of man as this word that was to delay the sun in its course. Nothing less than the delay of the sun in its course is expected by them as possible when they pray for deliverance from some danger or misfortune; that is, they say to themselves, "Perhaps God will allow Himself to be persuaded that He will do well to alter the course of nature for my sake." But this "perhaps," by which man ascribes to prayer a power that it does not possess, is a gate of error through which a doubt, the more dangerous from its not being obvious, creeps in and undermines faith in the power which really belongs to true prayer. From the moment man prays with the idea that he can, by doing so, alter the course of his outward life, by turning away misfortune and insuring prosperity, he at once doubts whether the holy law of justice entirely depends on him and his prayer, whether he is not in this, as in other things, subject to circumstances. He will pray for the love of what is good, for the courage that truth requires, but he will pray without the trust of real faith, for a doubt interposes itself between him and his God, and whispers: "Perhaps this prayer will be of as little use as all those I have sent up to Heaven before." Every prayer for material advantages must needs weaken faith in the efficacy of even true prayer, and finally destroy it altogether. That is the conviction which makes it impossible for me to pray in the way customary in the Church. I cannot pray as the Church has taught me to do, without desecrating and weakening the longing of my conscience for God's kingdom of liberty and justice, with the foolish wish that God may distribute good and evil in the life of nations, of individuals, and in my own, otherwise than He has done, or ever will do, in His eternal wisdom and love.

He only can obtain the full blessing of prayer who, when praying, never goes down into those regions that are subject to the frequent changes of personal joy and sorrow, who never leaves the sacred field of liberty, and is therefore moved by no other emotions than those of sorrow for sin and the joy of justice; *he* only knows the full blessing of prayer who, when he prays, beholds this double star of pious feelings in such bright glory of light, that the whole world in which the borrowed light of personal weal and woe comes into being, disappears from his sight.* He who expects prayer to help nature in illness and to assist the efforts of medical men, to heap money about him by a kind of charm, or to protect misjudged virtue and good reputation against calumny, or, again, to assist truth when he wishes it, to gain a speedy victory, does not know that prayer in which every doubt is conquered; he

---

* The reader who would conclude from these lines that the author advocated a religion of mere asceticism would thoroughly misconstrue his meaning. He who, like Dr. Rupp, considers nature as one of the manifestations of God, and one as sacred as any other, and denies that man can realise his vocation if he attributes to himself any other power over nature than that which man enjoys by submitting to her laws, never could deny the joys of nature. But he is perfectly consistent with himself when he keeps distinct the life of liberty which embraces his whole moral and religious life, from his life as part of nature, like two circles, the lines of which contain without breaking one another. To keep these two circles distinct, and to work out within them the plan of God as his co-operator, is man's vocation on earth.

does not know the confidence of the just man, who is as certain that his prayer is granted as he is of the alternation of day and night. The just man knows that honour and dishonour, riches and poverty, illness and health, must, according to eternal order, equally serve that justice which forms the only aim of true prayer; he knows that what is good can be rejected from the heart of man, but that, when it lives, it does not require prayer for its protection; that it has itself an active part in the eternal order and in the fulness of divine power, and that it is itself the power and the victory. Whatever path he may be obliged to tread in the course of events, whether he stand on the grave of his dearest ones, or whether he see his work fall to pieces, he allows no foolish prayer to rise to his lips: but he draws deeper and deeper from its well of liberty, and, at every blow of fate, he gains new strength, until he is able to utter this, the purest and holiest of prayers:

"Father, I thank Thee for all! All that Thou sendest is very good! Amen!"

VI.

"LORD, TEACH US HOW TO PRAY."

WE are told in the Gospel tradition that one of the disciples once addressed Jesus with these words: "Lord, teach us how to pray;" and that Jesus, far from blaming him, granted his request. And we can well understand that He who had said: "The letter killeth, but the spirit quickeneth," in His usual way, readily entered into this wish. It is an undeniable historical fact that the disciples not only retained the Lord's prayer and other expressions of pious emotions in their memory, but that they learned from our Saviour to find something in prayer which they never had sought in it before. And on the other hand, if many among us take exception to this request of the disciples, and still more to the readiness with which Jesus granted it, we can account for their surprise. Their conception of these words rests mainly on the experience of the present age, which offers nothing to their minds but the experience of their own early days, and the reflections suggested by the communications of other people; they can therefore see nothing in this request but a superficial, insignificant, barren, nay, even *injurious attempt*. But is it not unfair to carry into the history of so remote a time, which is perfectly strange to us, notions borrowed from the present state of society? Is it not an indisputable act of justice that we should do our best to explain the events and ways of dealing transmitted to us from the past by the characteristics and the spirit of the people belonging to the period which we study? If we do this in the case before us, we shall see that the circumstances that impress the character of the dead letter, of servility and self-delusion, on the common routine of prayer and the teaching of it, at once disappear. The reason why the teaching of prayer has fallen into such disregard during the degeneracy of the Church can only be sought in the fact that, on one side, those who were supposed to teach others how to pray could not pray themselves; *i.e.* they lacked the intimate communion with all that is divine, this communion which is indispensably presupposed in every true prayer. And again, those who were supposed to be taught how to pray, either had lost the yearning for it, or had never felt the desirability of such guiding and teaching. With Jesus and His disciples the case was the reverse of this in every respect. Jesus, equally free from the Pharisaic spirit and the scepticism of His time, had found again, like a treasure hidden in a field, the costly pearl of prayer in the depths of the human heart, and brought it to the light of consciousness and experience as a glorious testimony of liberty. The disciples, powerfully stirred by the wonderful beauty which enwrapped in a glow of light the intercourse of the Son of man with His Divine Father, but still kept back, enthralled by the superstitious customs and accompanying doubts deeply rooted in their minds, wished for nothing more fervently than to be led by their Master on the paths on which they might find the inexhaustible well from which He drew. When Jesus, entering into their wish, joyfully moved by it to a new outburst of thankfulness, taught them how to pray, what else did He do but give this feeling of gratitude a natural expression? And when the love of truth which manifested itself in His disciples gave Him a new guarantee of the success of His great work, surely the faith, the confidence of His prayer, must then more than ever have made on the souls of His friends an impression so deep that nothing could ever efface it. Even if we familiarise ourselves but faintly with the circle of those described to us by the Gospel as surrounding Jesus, it is impossible to apply to our Saviour's teaching to His disciples the standard which we borrow from the decline of the Church. The more we succeed in dismissing from our minds the narrow and empty views of religion and prayer which such times have left in our minds, the more urgently we shall feel pressed to join in the wish and request of the disciples: "Teach us also, Lord, teach us also how to pray." And it is this yearning alone that incites me now to speak of prayer; this yearning is the only source from which I have drawn the convictions experienced in my last discourses, and from which alone I shall draw what I have still to say. We were following Jesus's leadership, when, in our last discourse, we pointed to justice as the only object of true prayer. In this one word, "justice," is contained everything. Are we sure that the meaning we attach to this word, the feelings and tendencies it keeps up in us, point in the same direction as the channel of thought which he meant to indicate? There is a notion of justice lower than that of Jesus, namely, that consisting merely in securing everybody his own, and notwithstanding its elements of hatred and discord, it is highly praised in the world. But even though we may have raised our standard to the conception of that higher justice that is one with Christian love, are we quite sure we see clearly what it is in justice that can be obtained by prayer? There is something in justice that never ought to be the object of prayer; that something is man's very own doing, and can therefore never be offered as a gift, even by God. I mean the one act of self-determination, an act of volition, the distinguishing between right and wrong, which, far from being the effect of prayer, rather is as the soil and seed without which man never is able to bring about true prayer in himself. The fulfilment of duty never can be spared to us by the granting of any prayer. The only benefits we can consider as the fruits of prayer are the zeal for what is good, the joy in it, the purer conception of it, and the faith in the power of justice. Perhaps the earnest work of the cognition of truth awaiting those who will learn from Jesus how to pray, may be rendered easier to us by availing ourselves of the words of an old Roman Catholic writer, who, during the time of the Church's deepest humiliation, kept up so close a communion with our Saviour, that the spirit of the Gospel has not rarely found in his words as pure an expression as in the times of apostolic manifestations. The words of Fénelon, to which I refer, are these: "*The law of prayer is reciprocity between God and us.*"

According to this saying, man cannot pray in the true sense of the word without having become conscious of the reciprocity which exists between him and God. Indeed, it is a truism that in order to be able to address a request to any one, we must be able to feel that in a certain respect there is an equality between him and us. Men's unconscious acknowledgment of truth, which manifests itself in the formation of language, points to the truth stated by Fénelon in the two distinct meanings of the one word, "to beg," used so differently, that the derivative of one, "beggar," is a term of contempt, whilst "to beg," used in the sense of "to pray a fellow-being," is an expression of daily occurrence in all grades of society. And this presupposes the reciprocal use of it, the one who is addressed with it one moment will be the one to use it the next, and no one hesitates to use it in his turn. "Beggars" we call those who beg, no matter for what reason, without having anything to grant in their turn. This may be a misapplication of the term which arises from our baleful habit of limiting our notions of exchange to the sole possessions of outward life. The world knows only of an outward fellowship among men.

Money is so much the absolute standard by which those advantages which enter into social exchange can be compared, that a gift the worth of which cannot be expressed by a money value, is, according to the prevailing notions, without value at all. Judging by this standard, we call him a "beggar" who has nothing to offer which can be estimated in money, however much he may have to give of those goods that are estimated by quite a different measure of value. Any one who has made himself acquainted with life in an earnest spirit, knows that many of those whom we call "beggars" are considerably richer in moral possessions than those at whose door they stand waiting. The consciousness of the wrong we inflict upon people whom we brand with a contemptuous name lives in most people, at least, as a sort of painful feeling which prevents them from calling them by it in their presence. We must put aside this misapplication of the word in order to make the distinction we want between the beggar and the one who begs in the right sense of the word. We speak here of the beggar with special reference to the true inner possessions of life. In this sense a human being does not become a beggar by any unavoidable misfortune. He may be one, even where chance has assigned to him a considerable amount of those goods that can be estimated in money value. In this case, nature and fate do not make a man a beggar, but his own guilt does, *i.e.* the misuse of liberty. He is a beggar who has none of those truly human possessions, good faith, honesty, diligence, and love of order, cognition of truth and justice, the production of which depends exclusively on the will, *i.e.* he is a beggar who has nothing to offer, or who even, through a long neglect of these spiritual advantages, has become a prey to the fallacy that he is incapable of gaining and deserving them. Only by bearing in mind the meaning of the word shall we use it in the original sense, which was meant to convey an idea of contempt. The difference between "to beg," in a right and wrong sense, consists therefore, to my mind, in this, that he who begs in the wrong sense, has deprived himself by guilt of what he might have offered as a counter-gift; and that he only can beg, in the right sense of the word, who can help in his turn. And from this it follows that we can apply the term "prayer" only to an intercourse in which we can approach God, not as beggars, but as petitioners bringing to God the offering of our talents and their results. Thus even God we can approach with the consciousness of equality. But we can do so only if we are thoroughly convinced of that reciprocity; if our souls are really quickened by this feeling; if our lives and the relative position we take towards God are such that we have a right to believe; that notwithstanding the disparity between us and God in every respect, when we think of it superficially, there is, in one respect, according to the will and law of eternal order, a provision made to fill up this chasm.

This provision is the consciousness that man has a counter-gift to offer God, in exchange for the gift which he receives from Him. In no one was this recognition so strong or so pure as in Jesus of Nazareth; and in no period of the whole history of the civilisation of the world was this faith so completely dead, if we except our own time, as in that in which Jesus entered on His career. He was penetrated with the idea of God's greatness and glory, for He felt deeply and saw clearly that the same divine beauty and perfection, the image of which human nature bears, have chosen everything besides us as their symbols, the bird in the air and the grass in the field. He was penetrated by the thought that everything in and about us, the voice of conscience, like the hair on our heads, is a gift of divine love. But He knew at the same time that man stands by himself, and enjoys perfect independence in his treatment of these things, in the use he makes of them, from the voice of his conscience, to waking and sleeping, to food and raiment, in the way he judges them, manipulates them, and that he remains absolutely free in his will and his actions. And, lastly, He recognised that the architecture of creation was not complete until the kingdom of God, which was to unite human kind into one community of justice and peace, should be established; and that as the founding of it (of the kingdom of God) must be the immediate result of just willing and just doing, man can, if he choose, deny it to God. God requires for the completion of His work the co-operation of men, and receives from them, as a free gift, all they do to the furtherance of His plan.

In this consciousness, Jesus says (John xvii. 4) that He has glorified the Eternal Father on earth, and finished the work He had given Him to do. In this consciousness Paul says, in his Epistle to the Corinthians, that the vocation of men on earth is to be God's co-operators (1 Cor. iii. 9). And, in another epistle, he says that Jesus did not think it robbery to make Himself equal to God. With the awaking of this consciousness begins the age of maturity, on which, according to St. Paul, the followers of Jesus enter. If, in the candour of childhood, a human being lives in this most close union with God; or if, after having left the paradise of childhood, he produces this consciousness in his soul by his faithful perseverance in all that is good, and recognises this law of reciprocity, this loving equalisation between God and himself, then alone is he able to approach God as a proper petitioner; then alone he may be certain that his petition will be granted; then, and then only, he will truly pray. As long as this law of reciprocity—which even unsought by him shows itself to him as a picture of his inward life in the mirror of his consciousness, and there appears to him as a stranger; as long as, in consequence of his own guilt, the thought of such reciprocity appears to him to be arrogance, a sacrilege, and a blasphemy against God, so long is he incapable of praying so that his prayer can be heard; so long must he feel what he is, and must doubt in all that he calls his prayer, like the so-called beggar who knocks at a strange door, not knowing whether he will not be sent away. The whole religious tone and attitude of man depends on this, whether he dare approach God as a good child approaches his father with his request, or whether he feels that he is a mere beggar. We often hear people say that they find it difficult to ask their fellow-creatures for anything. Do not believe them; they do not know themselves, or, if it is, they have perverted their natural feeling. The truth is that they have made it impossible to ask, *i.e.* to entreat their fellow-men for anything in the real sense of the word. For to be able to entreat any one, presupposes that one has given something one's self before, and is ready to give again; but their selfish hearts refuse these truly good and perfect gifts of devotion, and love of confidence and esteem.

He who knows the pleasure of giving and taking, never finds it hard to express his requests. The more benevolent and kind a man is, the greater happiness he finds in helping others; the more devoted and self-sacrificing he is in his dealing, the more gladly will he, by his acceptance and his request, tighten the bonds that unite him to those for whose sake he has, in his affection, made the highest self-sacrifice.

Nothing, on the contrary, can be more humiliating than to seek love with an unloving heart; that truly is the act of a beggar; it is not a request. And as it is in the relations of man to man, so it is in our relations to God. He who, in order to do the will of God, devotes himself more entirely and zealously to obey the law of justice, and in this way makes himself God's fellow-worker, and recognises the reciprocity which exists between God and human beings, will find joy in prayer. But he who sees himself only in the low character of a beggar when he directs his thoughts to God, must feel prayer to be a burden which he reluctantly bears, and tries to shake off under every pretext; a burden which he is pleased to forget altogether, unconscious that he who gives up prayer takes much heavier burdens upon himself. For the eternal order of things never changes according to the wish and caprice of men. Either man recognises the holy law of equality and reciprocity between himself and God, or he comes to the notion that he is a thing of nought, a worthless creature of caprice. In the first case he is able to pray with his whole soul, with inmost confidence. In the other case he feels, even when his wish seems granted, the curse that weighs down every arbitrary gift. The prayer of the free soul, whose love helps God in His eternal work of creation, is elevating and inspiring, whilst the prayer of the wretched one, who, like a beggar, approaches God with his heart full of nothing but fears and cares, continually holds before him a picture of abasement.

These two courses are placed before us for our choice; there is no third alternative. The whole attitude and tone of a man's mind will depend on his way of looking at his relation to God, to whom he prays. Yea, more than that; the whole activity of his life will be moulded by it. All his doings, private and public, will show whether he considers the Divine Being, to whom he prays as a power superior to him, and himself as a mere toy of caprice, or whether his conception of prayer, like that of Jesus of Nazareth and Fénelon, rests on a feeling of equality and reciprocity between God and humanity. The bent which his will takes in prayer will be reflected in broad features in his attitude towards his fellow-men, as well as in the share he takes in the organisation of civil society.

The characteristic features of a Church association and its prayers can be indicated in a few words; but they are like the inscriptions on the walls of the Arabian desert, which now, after thousands of years, bear testimony to the stormy life of a whole nation, which saw its inclinations and its customs, its family habits, and its rights and laws renewed during its passage from Egypt into the land of its fathers. Few as are the words required to describe the striking contrast that exists between the prayer of the man who is conscious of his being God's fellow-worker, and that of the man who bears in himself the slavish fear of a guilty conscience, this same contrast assumes a thousand forms in real life. It is like an echo repeated a thousand times, with innumerable degrees of greater or less intensity. This contrast strikes ear and eye everywhere where the great man of the world meets with his humbler brethren, the rich with the poor, the strong with the weak, the workman with his employer, the happy with the unhappy—in short, in every place where men meet with men.

The same difference that in reality marks the features of a John and those of a Judas, will necessarily show itself in any looking-glass before which two such men may stand; as surely as the same difference which exists between them in reality must exist in the images they reflect, so surely will the real life of two nations reflect the same differences that exist in their respective views concerning prayer. These views will unavoidably determine the character of their life in their homes, their social intercourse, and their public affairs. The notion of reciprocity between God and humanity as the foundation of prayer in one nation, or servile obedience to the Almighty in the other, must necessarily give each an entirely different aspect. For the outward life of a people is nothing but the image of the fundamental religious views that animate and regulate it. The experience of the past exactly confirms this intimate connection between prayer and the work of life. The belief of the pre-Christian heathenism, religious and philosophic, admitted of no reciprocity between the Deity and men, and placed the human race at the mercy and caprice and waywardness of the gods. The expression of this belief was the general condition of slavery.

But when the Gospel spread the consciousness that man is God's helper, the natural expression of it was the conviction of the iniquity of slavery and its abolition. When, in our relation to God, we consider Him as an employer and ourselves as His workmen, the relation of employer and employed among us at once undergoes a transformation.

From the whole attitude the master and mistress of a house assume towards their servants, we can conclude whether they approach God as free petitioners or as beggars. In heaven, as on earth, there is but one alternative in respect to the want and the satisfaction of it. Only he who gives willingly prays willingly; only he who is able to pray receives what he takes with due acknowledgment and respect for the liberty of him from whom he receives it; only he who can pray receives everything with thanksgiving, be it the gift of health which he has received through God's institution, or the contracted work of him who is in his service and pay. He who does not give willingly, and who at last becomes a prey to the illusion that he can offer God no worthy return, must be a beggar; and he who is reduced to beggary does not receive, but snatches away what he gets. He who can approach one superior to him in force, only as a beggar, becomes a robber to those weaker than himself; and deserves this name doubly when he uses what he has seized in such a way that public opinion must be compelled to consider he has a right to it.

Self-government being equally active in work and prayer, religion and life must be incessantly reacting upon each other. At certain times, when the forms of prayer have lost their life and significance, and religion in general has sunk to a dead letter service, the re-awakening to the cognition of truth breaks out in a higher appreciation and new division of work. Then this movement spreads in all directions, and breathes life again into the deadened forms of prayer, and penetrates religion with its renewing and invigorating spirit. At other times the reverse process takes place; the re-awakening manifests itself by a return to prayer; and it is then the renewal of religious life that reconciles men together, and brings order again into a disorganised society, and a purer and more hallowed spirit into the sphere of work, where vanity, carelessness and confusion had reigned before. In the last centuries this work of regeneration began its work.

Work was the means of self-education that opened the road for a purer cognition of truth; its pioneers were science, industry, and legislation, and they broke many of the chains that ignorance and injustice had riveted on men. At the present time, when the general activity has sunk under the dominion of self-indulgence and selfishness, and is degraded to a mere means of making money and securing its enjoyment, the deliverance can only come, as was the case at the origin of Christianity, from religion, from the small communities that are gathered and united together by a common aspiration for self-knowledge and the longing after the communion with what is eternal. If these communities fulfil their vocation; if, led by the Gospel, they work their way through to the recognition of the law of reciprocity between man and God; if they teach men to approach God again as free petitioners, with the childlike confidence that justice inspires, then this new spirit will again consecrate and sanctify the relations of men to men. The more thoroughly, therefore, every one in this community recognises the real wants of society, the deeper our desire will be to go into ourselves, the more ardent our longing to find the Eternal through prayer, the truer our love for every community founded for mutual improvement, the more sincere our wish that the holy character and spirit to which the Gospel bears testimony may "teach us also how to pray" in truth. Amen.

VII.

HOW ARE WE TO RESUME THE WORK OF SELF-EDUCATION BY PRAYER?

Our meditations on prayer have shown so far that it is an error to consider the decline of prayer during the past centuries as a proof of the progressive cognition of truth. And although we reject this opinion as an error, we have seen also why it is impossible for us to go back to the traditional view and treatment of prayer in the Church. And, lastly, we justified our previous statement—that we can conceive no life to be a sound one without prayer—by showing that prayer alternating with work is the healthy action by which spiritual life finds its realisation in self-education (*i.e.* the building up of a moral and religious life).

We now ask, what have we gained by these meditations for the improvement of our lives? If they have caused us to wish for this higher, larger, and more complete life, to which self-education can raise us by means of prayer, if they have ripened this wish in us to a steadfast resolution to seek it with all our might, then they have done for us all that could be expected. But the way that leads from the awakening of a wish to its fulfilment is rarely a short one; and how many wishes never are fulfilled, because the means and ways on which this fulfilment depends remain unknown to us for ever! And they must remain unknown to us for ever, if we either over or underrate our strength, or mistake our goal. So, during our last discourse, the wish may have arisen in many of us to obtain this blessing of prayer, and yet nevertheless have left nothing behind but a vague remembrance of it. Such will be the fate of this wish, be it ever so glowing and sincere, if we do not convince ourselves that for him who has lived long without the confirmed habit of prayer, it will require a careful revision of all his circumstances, a matured plan and serious consideration, to insure his return to prayer and his regular and careful exercise of it. Certainly there is a moral and religious life in which man depends on himself alone at every time and under all circumstances; its demands and laws are binding on us, and it would have been senseless to think that there could be any insurmountable difficulty which might free us from their allegiance. The life of liberty and self-government shows itself every time we bear testimony to truth such as we are able to see it; every time we give a fellow-creature a proof of that unmixed benevolence which remains the same towards friend or foe. It is liberty and self-government again which shows itself in our words, in our countenance, or any other expression of our faith in the uniformity of man's nature and spiritual vocation. In short, all the doings of a pure heart have their origin in our moral liberty, *i.e.*, in the exercise of self-government. This life of liberty and self-government being in its essence one and indivisible, has at all times, independently of all circumstances, the power to be and to remain what it ought to be, and to manifest what it wills even unconsciously and unintentionally, by any means that just happen to be at its disposal at any given moment. But the case is just the reverse when we deal with definite objects belonging either to our own inner or outer life; when we propose to exercise a certain activity, to bring about certain states of mind, and deem it desirable to secure them as a lasting good. There is no preparation necessary to protect myself against any bitterness, when an offence is offered, or to accept the pain as a divinely appointed trial, and to honour God in him who inflicted the pain. Any reflection as to the attitude I had to take towards him would betray a heart estranged from the love of God. But if I intend to dispose of a part of my fortune for charitable purposes, serious consideration and pre-arrangement will be necessary, if I wish to spare myself the humiliating experience of having done harm when I intended to do good. The same consideration will be necessary, if I wish to give such development to certain dispositions and certain tendencies and wants in me that they may ripen into decided inclinations and lasting states of mind. And this is just what I intend when I propose to make prayer again an ordinary practice of my daily life. Any mistake which might arise from a misconception of prayer and of the existing strength and capacities available for this intended undertaking, will necessarily bring about the failure of it. In order to prevent any such disappointment, let us try to find out what prayer must do in order to accomplish its task, how far we are prepared to meet its demands, and what we have to do, according to our position, to resume or begin the work of self-education by prayer.

1. What is the aim and meaning of self-education by prayer? What place will self-education occupy in a

sound human life? Life itself, being considered as the total result of all our conscious aspirations, that alone is properly speaking the human art. Every other so-called art pre-supposes special gifts: music requires different gifts from painting and poetry, and the large majority of men do not possess the talents necessary for producing any work of fine art worthy of distinction. But to mould our own lives so that they may correspond to the prototype of human life which we find in our own reason, to be our own educators—that is an art which it is incumbent upon every man to practise, an art in which every individual being can raise himself to mastery. Here the free will of man is the artist who works and creates. Every age of life, every day, every single activity in itself, any and every definite part of existence, our intercourse with men, our labour for the profession which we have chosen, is destined to become a work of art. But among the instruments by means of which we accomplish this task, prayer and work occupy the most important place. I call them instruments in the same way that, speaking of a poet, we should consider his fancy and his descriptive power, which he must himself cultivate and develop, as the real instruments by which his works of art are produced. Prayer and work are in the art of life the instruments which every one of us must invent, make, and learn to use. Nature has given us nothing for that purpose but the sense of their necessity, and the impelling instinct; she has left us to our own devices as to what we will create and form by their helps. Imagination, descriptive talent, manifest themselves very early in the child, when it invents a tale and forms its first rhymes. But how much care and application, how much practice and devotion, are required, if this fancy and power of representation are to pass from their first dormant germinating state to that of the perfect instrumentality of creative poetical power! These gifts must be brought to such perfection that on a mere beckoning on the part of the artist, they place at his disposal every occurrence on earth, in heaven or hell, like a grand spectacle spread out before his eyes. Then he must possess, too, the fulness of language, with all the depth of reason underlying its harmony, from the accents of the most delicate feeling to the expression of the most violent passions. These innate instincts, common to all men, urging them to inward and outward activity, inviting them to return into themselves, require the same continued efforts, the same untiring patience, in order to be made fit instruments of work and prayer. On the training of these natural instincts it will depend whether we shall succeed in shaping our lives as a master work of art. How much perseverance is required to transform these innate instincts into the perfect instruments of work and prayer in the development and culture and in the connected action on which the success of every individual depends who wishes to make his life a work of art!

Let us now try to realise what prayer really is, what must be its character in order fully to satisfy our expectations of it as a perfect instrument for the divine art of life. Evidently the scholastic subtleties and barren whims of commentators who also make this subject an occasion to argue about the orthodox or heterodox creeds can be of no use to us. From the point of view which we have chosen, it would be absurd to ask whether in order to pray aright we require a church, a mosque, or a synagogue, or (not to forget those versed in sentimentality) the cool shades of the woods, or a fine spring morning with a view over the sea. For us there is no sense in asking whether we must fold our hands or bend our knees, whether our invocations are not blasphemies rather than prayers, when we call the one Omnipresent and Eternal our Father instead of calling Him our Lord, or whether we call Him Mother instead of Father. And surely we shall not seek the essence of prayer in the form under which we address Him. He will not listen to us any more if we say Thou than if we say He or I. This would no more be the test of real prayer, than the fact of *feeling* more closely united with Him in prayer than in work. Nor is it of any consequence whether or not an overwhelming feeling fills our eyes with tears, and whether or not our entreaties are expressed in looks upturned to heaven. Nothing of all this occupies us here, for we ask what prayer is *to be* and to do, but we do not ask in what garb it may appear. If we wish to draw a distinct line between prayer and work, so as to distinguish clearly two most important instruments of self-education according to their special objects, we must direct our attention to that difference only which would exist between the different organs of our senses.

Let us take the organs of sight, hearing, and touch as examples. By means of the eye and the ear a picture of the world is conveyed to us, and the significances of it. Hand and mouth in their turn are the instruments which render the most important services to practical life. Work is to self-education, in the light of a means, what hand and mouth are to the life of the senses and of the soul. What they do for these, prayer as an instrument must do for the art of life. There are no words which express this idea so strikingly as the exhortation of Jesus to his disciples, "Watch and pray." To *pray*, my friends, *is* to be awake, to watch. When we pass from one kind of daily work to another, and from plan to plan, when we have to do our utmost not to slip away from the track prescribed to us by our vocation, when we have to be on our guard against the conflicting interests of reality, the ties and claims of family, of town and country, we then also see the various aspects of life, but we do not analyse them. We see them, as it were, with closed eyes, like the dissolving pictures of a dream. When I say this, I do not intend to speak in a derogatory manner of practical life, for God has invested it also with a sacred character, but work is not destined to reveal to us the very essence of things, to make us find out their real meaning. It is only when we put work aside in order to devote ourselves entirely to prayer, that the mind can open its eyes and take possession of the riches of its cognition, and can reveal to us the depths thereof. The worship of God is nothing less than this act of the cognition of truth and the contemplation of it.

To bring the master work of life to its perfection, it is necessary that besides our devotion to the duties of our labour, we should be in close companionship with this cognition and contemplation of truth. It must become to us a dear friend whose intercourse we seek, whom we joyfully hasten to meet, from whom we never part without the wish soon to enjoy his presence again. The meditation of prayer never exerts over us the power of nature which makes us a prey to the pangs of real hunger and thirst, and the violence of greed and passion. Therefore the longing of the heart after prayer, the feeling of its indispensability, and herewith the feeling of certainty that we never can mistake the want of it, will only arise in us when the experience of years of prayer has deeply impressed on our minds the grateful memory of all its gifts of faith and hope. Moreover, the cognition and contemplation that form part of prayer, must, in order to promote self-education, be able readily and completely to remove the barriers which again and again have to be raised in order to separate the diverse kinds of work in active life. None of these can succeed, unless we devote ourselves to each one specially, as completely as if nothing else existed; we must plunge into it so that everything else disappears from our sight. What power must our soul have obtained if it is able in a moment to raise us from such a depth to such a height of contemplation that, from it, we see the whole of creation spread around us, so that the point on which our heart was but just now fixed, appears to us of no more importance than as the place where our efforts have been interrupted. We were just now combating men who appeared to us to be the enemies of truth; but prayer, if it is of the right kind, fills us with the feelings of the heart of God, who furnishes rain and sunshine to the good and to the wicked without any difference. In short, the contemplation and cognition that are necessary for prayer must make it clear and certain to me, whether the mirror of my soul distorts this picture of creation, or whether it reproduces it faithfully. Our spiritual vision can be impaired in various ways: the desire to confirm and strengthen our ties with our fellow men by trying to satisfy their expectations of us, the undeserved praise or blame of which we may be the object, the vanity owing to which we allow ourselves to be adorned with virtues that we do not possess, and even the fear of the illusions and disappointments of vanity: all this must make our faults appear either greater or smaller in our own eyes than they really are, and thus transform right into wrong and wrong into right, whenever we judge the world according to this unconsciously warped standard of what is good or bad. So, in this respect also, if prayer is to prove a safe means of self-education, its special function, by no means an easy one, is ever and again to free us from self, to re-establish this pure conception of eternal order, so well calculated to make us feel how far short we are of the standard it holds before our eyes, to inspire us with the love and reverence which it deserves, and to show us our humble place in it.

Now, to sum up briefly what we have said, we cannot admit that prayer has fulfilled its task in the life of a man unless he, in the hour of prayer, can free himself from outward restrictions and undeserved blame as well as from his own errors, unless he feels this gift of prayer to be a happiness for which he ever longs. And what else is this freedom that he acquires but wisdom? And what else is this longing for prayer but the love for wisdom? Can we do otherwise than praise the first Christians for restoring to the name of love for wisdom or philosophy, which was so often misunderstood or underrated, its original meaning, and for designating as true friends of wisdom, as true philosophers, those who at least showed an earnest desire to avail themselves of the means of self-education that lie in meditation and in the work of cognition, both inseparable from true prayer?

2. Let us now consider how far we have succeeded in securing these means of self-education. Have we gained a confirmed habit of meditation? Have we given a real development to our faculty of cognition? Have both assumed a definite character, and have they become a power that we can apply to all sides of life, to all our pursuits and interests? Do they prove real means of self-education that can be applied successfully day by day in every direction?

We will first take into account everything that can form a part of this practice, and then examine whether that which we have attained answers to the conception that we have formed of a perfect instrument for the art of life.

Many among us will probably have kept up or revived the old custom of devoting a certain time in the day to pray, either alone or with others. The way in which these exercises of prayer are carried on may be different; the intention with which they are undertaken by those who do not share in them merely for the sake of appearance can only be, by raising their thoughts to the Eternal, to obtain a more perfect knowledge of His will and of our vocation. And this edification recurring every day, is evidently considered to be that means of self-education of which we are speaking. With those who have not kept up the custom of daily family prayers, religious public meetings serve the same object. They expect from the discourses which they hear on Sundays and feast-days that advancement in the cognition of self which they require for the fulfilment of their vocation, or they meet together with friends who hold similar views in order to obtain more clearness of thought by common meditations, and discussions on the religious and moral task of life.

Lastly we might also reckon as an element of prayer, in the sense which we attribute to it (*i.e.* comprising all exercises of religious meditation and cognition), besides the use of books of devotion properly so called, the reading of instructive books by any author who has been able to throw light on the religious tendencies of human nature, and the course and significance of human fate. Why should we doubt that these various ways can lead to the goal? But they can lead us to it *only* if man considers them as ways that are to lead him to *this one* goal, if the holiness of the object becomes manifest in the value which he attaches to this object, if the attitude he takes in relation to this custom of daily prayer, to these religious meetings and this reading destined to help him to know himself better, gives the proof that the gain aimed at in these practises is to him a godly, indispensable gain, which nothing could replace. Can many of us say that we leave our religious assemblies carrying away the impression that we attach the highest importance to the part we take in them, and that we have been occupied with what is dearest and most precious to us? The animation, the zeal of the youth who hastens to meet his friend, or his beloved, leaves no doubt that at the time, he knows no higher happiness than his or her presence. How grievously he feels his disappointment when the opportunity of seeing them again is taken from him; or if he has obtained from fate a few moments for exchanging his thoughts and feelings with his friend, what could possibly take his attention away and turn it to any other object? During prayer, on the contrary, occasions, recollections, and sudden fancies, are rarely wanting to interrupt the meditations and distract the thoughts; and is it really felt as a grievous loss when the moments destined to religious exercises are, by accident, lost for that purpose and given to some intruding occupation? Could we speak of our prayers at all, if—leaving out of our reckoning those which we owe to occasions from without, or to momentary distress, or to our feeling of duty—we only took account of those inspired by an irresistible longing of the soul, and by the demands for our inward satisfaction? It may be that among those people who are designated as superstitious, or as visionary dreamers, we might find some in whose life prayer possesses this power and intensity which everywhere characterises that which is considered as a necessity. But let us turn to those who reject as an immoral yoke, as a submission, a false respect to authority, as a humiliating surrender of our judgment, and altogether as a self-degradation every religious rule that cannot be justified by reason and conscience. Let us turn to those who have determined to free the conception of truth from the darkness in which the dreamy enthusiast enwraps it, and to free life from the illusions created by the mania for miracles. Let us turn to those who would re-invest religion with its truly human character, and who, therefore, must consider prayer as an indispensable exercise of meditation and cognition. Even in the prayer of these men, the human rarely seems to rise to the divine. Rarely does the human element in them seem to be purified by the godlike and transfigured, but more frequently what is godly appears to be dragged down to the level of human weakness, and to be stripped of its imperishable beauty and dignity; and instead of the inmost, intense, devoted love for truth, which ought to be produced by its purification from misuse and superstition, coldness and indifference appear to gain the mastery. With them the vigour they have displayed in their zeal against error seems to have been exhausted, so that there is nothing of it left for prayer. After the work of destruction has been accomplished, they appear to be now distinguished by nothing but their complete incapacity for creating anything, for establishing right and truth. Those who continue to attend religious practices, are rarely otherwise distinguishable from those whose efforts are exclusively devoted to the spreading of the scientific knowledge now so much in public favour. They do not appear to see in these religious conferences and

Self-education by Prayer.

services any manifestations of the seeking, the aspirations, the entreaties and longings, without which all happiness, all honours and power, all science and art, are but the silk and purple, the gold and precious stones accompanying a corpse into its dwelling of death and corruption.

3. Now what are those who wish to resume the work of self-education through prayer to do, in whom the power to pray is so completely gone and paralysed, when the greatness of their loss becomes manifest to them? If the professed conviction that the work of cognition requires daily practice is not a mere phrase, a mere repetition of what they hear from others, they will at once take the necessary measures to gain time for prayer every day. This is an obvious necessity, and we shall not dwell on this point. The difficulties that are to be overcome for this purpose, and which will be absent nowhere, will prove different in the lives of different people. Our discourses are of too general a character to allow us to enter into these details. But whatever we may undertake in this respect, no result can be expected without the utmost care to avoid certain impending errors. And of these errors I will now speak.

First of all, the work of self-education through prayer is of too long a growth to justify far-reaching hopes of immediate result from the beginning. Such expectations would be irrational. The stately tree that year after year gives to us its cooling shade and delicious fruit has for a long time stood there poor and useless. And how long hast thou neglected the soil to which thou must now confide the seed of prayer?

Be patient, therefore, if for a time it appear as if the constraint of prayer to which thou now forcest thyself were vain; as if thine efforts to know God and thyself were powerless and barren in the struggle against thy desires and passions, as if thy prayers were dead words. No less important is it not to overvalue thy strength. Prayer will certainly not prove a perfect instrument for the art of life, until we succeed in remaining so collected, notwithstanding the distractions of all kinds which intrude upon us, that when the labour of the day is over, the images of people and things that have surrounded us, obedient to the call of our will, take their places in the mirror of our minds and show us their ideal meanings, and group themselves as pictures of the spiritual world, under the government of the eternal laws of nature and liberty; until we are so collected in ourselves that, under all circumstances, we are able to perceive the voice of the eternal love, dissolving all grounds of contradiction and reconciling hostile elements; so collected, so continually conscious of our connection with the things around, that we can clearly express all that we hear and see, if not in eloquent language, at least with words of our own, for the benefit of a religious community. He whose prayer has for a long time reached the perfection of which it is capable, may well exact this from himself. But I must speak now of him who has lost this power, and has to create it again. It is one thing to work when you are provided with a perfect instrument, another to have to make it and put it in motion. In this case we are not in a position to refuse any help that is offered. There is much evil in us that will spare no effort to silence prayer, which it dreads as a judge. Let us despise no friend without to help us against this foe within. Let us give anyone living with us the right, nay, make it his duty, to warn us when we flag in this duty of prayer which we have undertaken. Here we are on a level with children, the good that lives in us has no words. Let us therefore not think it below our dignity to use the words of others. It *is* humiliating, we admit it, to have to borrow the words of others to express our own inmost life, but it is a humiliation that we have brought upon ourselves. People who will not subject themselves to this kind of humiliation, often deprive themselves of the only help left to them. Exaggerated hopes and overrated strength can only retard a return to education by prayer, if they do not altogether prevent it, and the wish to advance quickly rather than safely must also render it more difficult. We require the help of others. And again, do not let us mistake the suggestions of our indolence for the wholesome recognition of our weakness; do not let us seek the easiest aid, but rather the most vigorous. Our religious exercises might perhaps obtain for us more feeling of satisfaction from the works of such of our contemporaries as have attempted to contribute to the advancement of religious and moral cognition. But this feeling of satisfaction is rarely free from deception. Their help gratifies our feeling because they all more or less serve the spirit of our time, which has long been our master, and distort our notions of truth by their prejudices. What is necessary to us is the pure word of truth, such as Jesus offers. His language sounds strange to us, sounds hard, incomprehensible, and so it sounded at first to the disciples, who, nevertheless, later announced in His place the liberty and love of the reign of God in the same language. The road they followed is open to us still. Let us follow them, and we shall soon be convinced that even now, as then, one who wishes to learn how to pray can do no better than make that prayer his own which our Master gave to His disciples for this purpose. There are, it must be owned, few words generally repeated so thoughtlessly as those of the Lord's prayer, and we also may have thought with others that there is no life in them, and have turned away from them, as if the words themselves could be the cause of the misuse made of them. If they have fallen into the service of superstition, who is to be blamed? words may only appear to be dead. Many a word, my brethren, has before this been resuscitated! These also will come into life again, notwithstanding all the efforts of those who fear the truth that lives in them, and know how to conceal it. These words will in future take the place which the ten commandments have occupied in the past. The law given on Sinai is the law of the bondman who does that which he would not do; it is the confession of him who is ashamed of the chains which he has bound on himself and nevertheless does not break. The Lord's prayer is the creed of the freeman who acknowledges the voice of his true nature, of the freeman who knows no stronger longing than the thirst for justice and love.

Looking forward to this day in joyful faith, and in

the anticipation of this happy future, let us conclude with the prayer of our Lord,
"Our Father which art in Heaven," etc. Amen!

VIII.—A.

"OUR FATHER WHICH ART IN HEAVEN."

MY FRIENDS! We enter to-day upon a course of meditations, the object of which is to ascertain how far we recognise in the prayer that our Master used with His disciples, the thoughts in which is to be found the living truth. A very simple introductory word precedes the requests which Jesus has bound together in His prayer. "Our Father which art in Heaven." Let us dwell this morning on these introductory words! When one condition or activity of soul is interrupted by another one about to begin, we naturally feel the want of a sort of transition, an announcement of what is coming. And when could we experience this want more distinctly than when such different states and activities of mind as work and prayer are to succeed each other? Certainly these two different states and activities both belong to the same life of consciousness and experience, to the same sphere, in which are united what has been given us, *i.e.* what *we are* with what we *have*. But of all things in the horizon of this life of consciousness and experience, work and prayer are the most distinctly different and unlike phenomena; one excluding the other as entirely as winter and summer, night and day, in the life of nature. Therefore, if prayer is really to attain its object, it is essentially necessary that, before we begin prayer, we should be clearly aware of the change that we wish to bring about. We must be fully aware that the moment we begin to pray, we must turn our back upon all that is connected with the work of the day, be it the duties or the rewards it implies. If we are not fully conscious of this necessity, we shall take with us into prayer the cares or hopes of work, its antagonisms and its friendships, and thus disfigure and foil it, and deprive ourselves of its benefits. For this reason, even the most ancient nations took measures of all kinds at the beginning of their religious services, in order to draw away the minds of men from all objects foreign to, or in any way incompatible with them, and to direct them to thoughts corresponding with their prayers. For this purpose they gave to the temples of their gods a distinctive character of greatness and beauty, so that they might be recognised at once in the midst of all other architectural edifices. For this purpose they tried to attract the attention of their people by inscriptions placed above the gates of these temples, inviting them to collect their thoughts and feelings; for this same purpose they surrounded their sanctuaries by halls and courts, where the worshippers of the Deity had to divest themselves of all that was not in keeping with the sanctity of the ceremony, so as to appear before their gods free from all that might be unfitting and unworthy of them. We know certainly that measures calculated to act upon the senses can in themselves contribute very little to the advancement of spiritual life; and therefore we do not expect from them the results attributed to them by the adherents of religions old and new. And we are convinced that the idea on which all these measures rest, according to which religious practices are supposed to be more sacred than every-day work, is one of the most injurious effects of superstition. We consider nothing as holy but the will of God manifested in reason, nothing as unholy but the ignorance that breaks this law. Divine will can be kept sacred as faithfully in work as in prayer; and again, it can be treated with the same hardness and contempt in prayer as in work. The more we disapprove of the reason why the attempt was made to inculcate in man as deeply as possible the difference between work and prayer, the less can we expect from the means chosen for this purpose. Nevertheless, we absolutely agree with the opinion of all ages, that for the beginning of religious meditations, it is most important to turn away from the earthly interests which most occupy us during work. And that is what the words at the beginning of our Lord's prayer call upon us to do. "Our Father which art in Heaven." These words are for us the inscription over the gate of the temple of prayer. Let us give them our full attention. According to my interpretation of them, they are to bring vividly before us the condition on which it depends whether our prayers will be granted or not. They demand of us that we should examine whether we are not on the point of sending up prayers which God will not fulfil. O my friends! how much might we not owe to these words, as often as we use them, if of all the religious feelings and views we entertain, only this one thought could be held fast, the thought that there are prayers which never will be granted!

Most of us have received with the teaching of our Lord's prayer certain clerical notions which prescribe to us the tendency of thought and feeling which our minds are to follow, as well when we ponder or utter these introductory words, as in prayer generally. In those who use them, without the preconceived notions, in all freedom and ingenuousness, and can give themselves up to the direct impression of these words, the "Our Father which art in Heaven" must produce a consciousness of conflicting ideas and feelings. Much nearer as the name of Father brings us to God, yet much farther do we feel from Him when heaven is made to be His dwelling-place. In those whose religious notions are still dependent on the catechism, this feeling of distance may not be called forth by the idea of heaven; on the contrary, the felicity of the blessed, in that life of which they have been accustomed to think, will awaken in them thoughts and feelings similar to those called forth by the name of Father. But they who have given up those Church notions are at once reminded of what is most distant from them by the idea of heaven. Just as the name of Father establishes a connection between them and God, heaven as God's dwelling-place limits the bearings of this connection to a sort of merely figurative speech. Heaven is indeed a most appropriate expression for that part of the creation entirely beyond the power and out of the reach of man's action. Great is the attraction which even the most senseless manifestations of superstition exert over the largest majority of the educated and uneducated. Superstition, nevertheless, is also subject to fashion. Even those who think they can obtain from the spirits of the dead an answer to any kind of questions, believe neither with the Greeks and Romans that enchanters can bring the moon to the earth, nor with the old Israelites that a conquering general has the power to keep back the sun in his course in the heavens, until he has destroyed the last remnants of the hostile army. For the present, even the superstitious themselves are convinced that the heavenly bodies proceed in their course without any respect for the thoughts and wishes of men. The moon does not veil her face when she rises over a bloody battle-field, nor does the sun lose its brilliancy when a devastating pestilence wields its scourge over whole nations, and when the complaints of widows and orphans fill the air; he lends his light equally to the godless and to the pious for their works. And if we do not give up these considerations at pleasure, merely because they are inconvenient for our theories, we find that these heavens (for the word "heaven" used in the Lord's prayer is after all but an image and a synonym of heaven), which are out of the reach of man's action, are by no means limited to these distant fields of space in which the stars live, but that this life, deprived of sympathy for the feelings of men, also governs this earth, men's dwelling-place, and surrounds us on all sides. The clouds ready to burst do not wait to discharge their floods until the day is over which a whole nation has chosen for its jubilee, nor does the lightning spare the temples. Yet this nature which shares in the heartlessness of the heavens, does not manifest itself in the grand scenes only which take place before our eyes, but it knows how to make its power felt in our own lives. This same nature which, without any respect for our wishes, prescribes their paths to suns, moons, winds and clouds, flows in our veins also with a vivifying power, or bids our blood to circulate no longer, and the beatings of our hearts cease, without caring whether we are weary of life or fond of it, without inquiring as to our hopes and our undertakings. This nature, the thought of which is in the mind of anyone who reflects on the significance of his being, is inseparable from the feeling of his own complete powerlessness. This nature which, without hating or loving man, without feeling for his happiness, without pity for his grief, which interweaves birth and death, growth and decay, above, below, and all round about him, this nature is that heaven in which God dwells. This God to whom thou prayest, has a heart, ears and eyes for the eternal order of nature, for the safe maintenance of its economy which He has established, but not *for thy wishes*. No grain of sand, no dust-atom, no breath of air in the infinite space of the universe is lost or wanders away from its appointed course. God knows how to preserve every single part for the whole. God takes care that everything accomplishes its appointed task. But the words thou speakest from the lust of life and its enjoyments, and thy cry of sorrow over the transitory character of all things, resound in vain under the vaults of heaven;

the God to whom thou prayest has no ears for the wishes of thy heart. He will not allow one hair on thy head to deprive nature of its due, and no prayers can prolong happiness and life one moment beyond the time appointed by nature. When the thought of that God who is in heaven has again awakened in us the conviction that every change which our wishes would prevent or bring about, is as far out of the reach of our prayers as the heavenly bodies are of our hand, then and then alone are we rightly prepared for prayer.

Can we say, my friends, that there is no need for us to be reminded of that? No doubt if there is any fact clearly stated in the book of nature and of fate, it is this: The Eternal whom men seek in their prayers leaves their wishes unanswered. The hopes and fears of men, even when clad in the language of prayer, never are capable of delaying or hastening the course of things. But, indisputable as this fact is, men have from the most remote ages spared no efforts to conceal it from their view, and to invest that which is not, with the appearance of reality and plausibility.

Is there even one among all national religions, the adherents of which have not persuaded themselves that the gods had come to meet their longing for happiness? Is there one, the adherents of which have not attempted to detect the conditions which men ought to fulfil in order to excite the pity of the gods, in order to obtain their favours?. Has it not been the aim of the religious codes in which we have been brought up, to confirm these notions in us? Have we not been

taught by them to pray to God that He may turn
away from us the danger of war, the failure of crops
and epidemics, and enrich our lives with goods that
heighten its enjoyment? These notions that have
been inculcated by the teaching of the Church, and
render every prayer in the spirit of Jesus impossible,
have certainly excited a considerable amount of
opposition. The progress of natural sciences has
rendered men attentive to the consistent cohesion that
closely connects all the phenomena of the world
together, to the absolute reign of law which exists
everywhere in the formation and development of all
things, to the order and inflexible necessity that cause
one phenomenon to follow upon another. This knowledge of Nature and her laws set men's judgment free
from the dominion of their sensations, and considerably
shook the stronghold of the old illusions, according to
which the eternal order of things was destined only to
satisfy the many wants of men. The new way of
viewing the world and the life of men, brought about
by these new studies, necessarily must bear upon the
religious opinions and feelings of the public. People
henceforth began to consider that a God who could be
supposed to interfere with the forces of nature according to the pleasures of men, could only be an invention
of that human arbitrariness which feels the laws of
eternal order as inconvenient barriers, and likes to
imagine that we can free ourselves from them. The
conviction thus gained that our former conception of
God was erroneous, found its expression in the axiom
that *God cannot be a personal being*. We all know
what a sensation these words caused in the nation. It

seemed as if something quite new and unheard of had been expressed; and the men who were entrusted with the transmission of the Church traditions declared that this was a declaration of complete unbelief. We certainly are far from joining in this accusation, for we see in it a new proof that the teaching of Jesus had more and more fallen into oblivion, even among those who call themselves after his name. For Jesus was the first to express this conviction. Or what else does it mean when he says that God has no respect of persons? It means this and nothing else. The value which man attaches to his accidental and transitory existence, and to the personal wishes connected with the preservation of it, answers to nothing in nature, nor to the will of God. It is an error in man to consider and designate himself as a personal being, when he attempts to express what is his nature and the object of his life. And it is an error again when he takes this disfigured notion of man's life as a foundation for his conception of God. Far therefore from suspecting this view of irreligion, we must, on the contrary, rejoice that one of the truest thoughts expressed by Jesus should have entered again into the consciousness of men, after so long a time of oblivion. Nevertheless, we cannot overlook the fact that Jesus came to this view by a very different path from that which led the learned of our time to it. And does not the value of every doctrine and every confession in the field of moral and religious aspirations depend essentially on the way by which you attain to it? Can we say that it was by the right way that people came in modern times to the view that God is not a personal being? We will give an answer to this question through an expression of Schiller, which very well characterises the public feeling that goes hand in hand with this confession of the representatives of the spirit of the time—the leaders of public opinion. He writes to a lady friend, "Oh that the fate of men might be in the hands of a being that would be like men, before whom I could throw myself down on my knees and obtain you from him!"

This is, in other words, what he means:—I know that no prayers can give man the realisation of his wishes, but what would I not give that it might be otherwise!—that is plainly the sense of his words. He *cannot* believe in a personal God; and herewith is his happiness, the value of his life gone. The illusion in which he once lived was to him life itself, and the knowledge for which he has exchanged it is to him death. Thus, in the way in which our age has come to the conviction that there is no personal God, this confession is the expression of a doctrine which does not raise man, but, on the contrary, strikes him helpless to the ground; which, instead of elevating him, bows him down; instead of filling him with the love of life, makes life an unbearable burden. That is to say:—this is what the doctrine means to those who proclaim it as the gain of the present culture; it causes in them the contrary of what Jesus meant and produced by this doctrine.

When those who do homage to the spirit of the time proclaim their adherence to the doctrine that there is no personal God, they at once confess that the idea of God is becoming dim in their soul, and is dwindling away. I do not mean to say that they therefore cease to believe in God, but the divinity is thus transformed into some vague and strange being, with whom man can establish and keep up no communion. For, according to their notions of man's nature, they are convinced that if the Divinity be no personal being, He can have no likeness to man; and that man's nature can therefore give no clue to the knowledge of His. Nothing then is left to them but to seek God in nature; and they unavoidably have to go through the experience of old, that to the man who has not found in himself the word of truth, nature brings nothing but shadows and mist, nothing but dull and indistinct sounds and impenetrable evils. And the same happens to all who persevere in this course. The doctrine that God is no personal being, means and causes just the contrary of what Jesus meant, and what it produced in Him. All those who deduce this doctrine from the consciousness of the time, deprive themselves of the understanding of human life; for them the world only presents a picture of discord, confusion, and perpetual inconsistency, and raises doubts from which men always try to free themselves, even if they find themselves obliged to deny this doctrine again, in order to obtain their end. For if the true life of man consisted in the wishes of his heart, if nature had destined man to nothing higher than the fulfilment of these wishes and the world nevertheless be so constituted that he never could reckon upon the satisfaction of his wishes, life would be nothing but a tissue of disappointments. And this idea that the world altogether lacks unity and consistency, and is only a toy of a senseless hazard, is so unbearable to man, that, sooner or later, he rejects it, and returns to the allegiance of the Church, and puts up with the consolation she offers, that the life hereafter will give him a compensation for the wishes that remain unfulfilled on earth. Here again the doctrine that God is no personal being now means and produces the contrary to what it meant and produced in Jesus of Nazareth.

The fact that Jesus chose the most intimate relationship, the closest tie known among mankind, that of father and child, to illustrate His doctrine that God has no regard for the person, leaves no possible doubt as to the exact meaning which He meant to convey to us by His doctrine. The same God who in His heaven is as inaccessible to the wishes of our heart as the heavenly bodies are to our hand, this same God is our Father. The same spirit, the same will of God, is our own spirit, our own will. God does not fulfil the wishes of our hearts. No. He has given man a spirit which does not require the fulfilment of wishes concerning our earthly existence: a spirit, the aspirations of which cannot be satisfied by the fulfilment of any of these wishes. The divine spirit in man, which recognises the true character of things, their essence, which determines its own course and takes its share in the holy work performed by the invisible force and the divinity of reason and liberty, of justice and love, this spirit of God, dwelling in man, which feels its blessedness to consist in this cognition of things, and in deeds pertaining to self-government, this spirit never can feel it to be a loss or a gain when one of these wishes concerning what is transitory is denied or granted to it. As long as we have nothing better to ask of God or to expect from Him than the fulfilment of personal wishes, a real appreciation of life, a true enjoyment of it, will remain unknown to us. And even a fate, which we arbitrarily interpret as a fulfilment of our wishes, will be accompanied by a feeling of disappointed hope. If, on the contrary, we learn to understand the doctrine that God is no personal being in the sense that Jesus attached to it, we obtain a state of calm founded upon the contemplation of what is eternal, we acquire a peace independent of transitory things, and therefore not to be shaken. As long as man asks God for nothing better than the fulfilment of changing wishes, the old tradition that God resembles man remains an incomprehensible enigma for him. For anyone remains a heathen, even in the heart of Christendom, who pictures God to himself, either as a young man or as a virgin, as an old man, or as a female beauty, or again as the personification of manly strength; in short, under any special attribute and shape of our nature, instead of as the human being who remains the same in every one of us. As Jesus conceived this doctrine, that God has no respect of persons, God never ceases to resemble the human being. On the contrary, it is with this doctrine that He begins for us to resemble man in truth. The conviction that this God who has no respect of persons is our Father, that His spirit, free from all the barriers that limit and hamper the personal being, is in us, this conviction it is that teaches us to understand our nature and our fate. In the light of this thought we can no longer consider it as an inconsistency that there is no guarantee in the condition of this world's existence for the fulfilment of the many personal wishes that rise in our hearts. Are there not many tasks from the beginning of our lives which have for their object, not the bringing about any single result, but a much higher one, namely, to exercise the human being in the use of his divine power of liberty and cognition, to develop and form it? The sheet of paper on which we let little children paint some given outlines, is not destined to appear in any picture-gallery. Through the intermediate object we reach the higher one, without the attainment of *which* all picture-galleries in the world are useless, nay, without which they become injurious. By giving to the child the opportunity of gaining the experience, the knowledge that light and shade and all colours which they produce are means to express and to bring into action the life of his mind; by it we give to the child the opportunity of exercising that power by means of which he perceives the voice of the Eternal, which says to us " Everything is yours." So it is with the wishes that rise in our hearts. They are not intended to lead to any special object that could be considered as the fulfilment of them; they are intended merely to give to man the opportunity of recognising his liberty, and of bringing it into activity, to procure for him the occasion of becoming acquainted with God and himself. How, therefore, could there be any inconsistency in the constant rising up of wishes in every individual, and the evident absence of a provision for their fulfilment in the course prescribed to the order of things in this world? The fate of our wishes, whatever they may be, is perfectly indifferent as regards the end to which this faculty of foreseeing in man has been destined, namely, his education, his rearing in reason and liberty, since the task of self-government is absolutely the same in regard to a frustrated hope, or the satisfaction of a personal wish. For reason and liberty, understanding and reflection, are equally necessary, whether we are to bear misfortune without discouragement, or to avoid the abuse of good fortune.

It is of the utmost importance for us to have a clear conception of what is an impersonal God, to understand why Jesus attached such importance to this question. We therefore recapitulate the foregoing. It was a salient point in His teaching, that, as far as our personal wishes are concerned, God dwells in the remotest space of heaven; and yet, at the same time, Jesus tells us that God Himself is dwelling in the creative power of reason, in the creative power of liberty, both of which together form the true self of every individual man. That is to say, God never cares for any personal wish of men for this reason, and this alone: the essence of the Eternal Father is self-government, this essence rests in Him. But He has imparted to all His children this same divine essence, the power of self-government, which is independent of any fate.* Now, if this meditation is to have any result for us, it must be shown by the answer which everyone gives in his soul and conscience to this question: has this view of the world gained such strength in us, such clearness and such firmness in our minds, that we can resist the scoffing to

---

* What would be thought of a central government who, after having given full independence to one of its colonies, would interfere with it in its decisions and provide for its wants and carry out its plans, and thus annul its responsibilities and duties?

which it may be exposed? Shall we remain faithful to it, notwithstanding the wrong conclusions which other people may draw from it, and turn against it? If there are any among us who can answer this question in the affirmative, they of all people will know that these dangers are not the only ones threatening such faith in the Gospel.

There are many things which we are determined never to let go, which we really defend against all attacks, which we nevertheless lose from want of attention and from carelessness, and there is perhaps among all the goods that we can lose in this way none more exposed to such danger than this result of our cognition. But be we ever so thoroughly convinced that God and nature have no heart for our personal wishes, we nevertheless are tempted day after day to lose sight of this conviction whenever our wishes bear upon a certain kind of activity and its results. By this activity I mean our *daily work*. We may be on our guard against other wishes, but those concerned in the results of our work generally take us by surprise; for they are dearer to us than even their object, and they themselves make us lose sight of the conviction gained of their shadowy character and their nullity before God. The danger lies in this, that we are not prepared to consider our daily work as an obstacle to the cognition of truth. And indeed, work is no obstacle to it, much as it is necessary to be on our guard that it may not become one. It is obviously necessary, in the interest of work, that during the time destined to the affairs of outward life we should bestow our whole attention and our whole interest on the task assigned to every hour. The object in view is to be attained. Certain wishes will always be connected with the object aimed at. The notion that the fulfilment of these wishes falls in with the attainment of the object in view will imperceptibly creep into our minds.* If we allow this confusion between our object and our wishes, the bitterest disappointment awaits us. This world is very seldom favourable to the fulfilment of our wishes, hence the many complaints of its imperfections.† The work of every day being inseparable from this continual temptation, and everyone who falls into it being unfit to go into himself, and to enter into communion with God, there can be no thought more appropriate to lead us from work to meditation than that with which our Master has begun His prayer.

VIII.—B.

'OUR FATHER WHICH ART IN HEAVEN'—*(continued).*

IN order to be able to attain the object aimed at in these introductory words, namely, to dismiss from our minds all personal wishes as often as we turn to prayer or any exercises of religious meditation, we must make sure that we shall detect them under whatever forms

---

* In other words, most people make no distinction between what they think desirable and what may be obtained or not: they desire it; therefore they think they must have it or ought to have it.

† The imperfection is in our overlooking the higher aim intended for our faculty of forming wishes, namely, the incitement to work and to think, the practice in planning, striving, and the practice in bearing.

they may assume. We have, therefore, still to answer
the important question why it so often happens that
we unconsciously warp our aspirations after the knowledge of truth by our desire to obtain the fulfilment of
our personal wishes. And we have to discover what we
must do if we will avoid this danger of self-deception.
The cause of it lies in the supposed connection between
our wishes and the just interest in our work. Now I am
anxious to show that there the connection between the
progress of our work and our personal wishes is an arbitrary one, against which we ought to be on our guard.

It is in the nature of work to promote a feeling of self-consciousness and self-confidence. Even
before the division of work which takes place at
the earliest beginnings of civilisation, before the
various trades and professions become distinct from
each other, everyone finds himself obliged to ascertain what are his own peculiarities, what in him is
different from his fellow-creatures, and what advantages or disadvantages distinguish him from
them. Even in the most simple and primitive condition, in which man knows of no larger association than
that of the family, work demands that a difference be
made between the child and the full-grown man.
Work incumbent upon a man is different from the
work natural to a woman. And as a society fixed in
one locality grows and develops, as the united forces
of its members venture upon more complicated and
difficult enterprises, the more earnestly will their attention be attracted by the differences of dispositions, of
talents, and by the manifold gradations of similar
faculties, the more also will the peculiarities that dis-

tinguish man from man come to the front. Yea, in a certain sense the observation of the best and most zealous worker will become the keenest for what concerns his own self. The indolent man may not care particularly whether he or somebody else does the greater part of a work which is carried on in common. But the better and more efficient worker will instinctively compare his share of the labour with that of his companions. For him it is not enough to know that the work is progressing; he wants to know by whom it is done. He will not remain behind the others; he enjoys what is done in proportion to the share that he may justly take in the praise that will be bestowed upon it when it is done. He wants to be certain that when the work can be looked at as a complete whole, his diligence, his exertions, and his perseverance have not a little contributed to its existence and its perfection.

But besides this self-consciousness in a large number of people in every organised society through work done in common, the feeling of self is awakened and developed through work, even when the differences of merit are not striking—yea, even when the stimulus of comparison with others entirely fails. For man is naturally anxious to know that he does not work in vain. Be his exertions great or small, he demands that they shall have a result. Even when there is no opportunity of ascertaining that he has advanced more than others, he at least wants to make sure that he has really advanced; that what he thought ought to be done and ought to give him the opportunity of showing his power of enterprise has succeeded according to his expectations, and justified his efforts. An

inner voice tells every human being that he is expected
and called upon to justify his existence by his actions
and his work in general. Everyone feels that his relation to life is that of a debtor, and that the produce of his work, his labour, his deeds, alone makes
him competent to pay his debt.

If work thus favours the growth of our self-confidence and self-respect, by bringing the consciousness
of our own self prominently before us, the danger also
arises of extending without due consideration the importance and significance which cannot be denied to
that self and its fate to things that are not necessarily
connected with it, but which easily assume the appearance of pertaining to it. If we do not avoid this
danger we allow hopes and expectations, desires and
entreaties, to arise in us which neither God nor nature
does anything to realise, and these vain foolish hopes
and expectations fill our souls so completely, that at
last no place is left in us for the hopes and longings
that are always satisfied, for the prayers which are
always granted.

If we do not take a shallow and merely external
view of the object of work, of that which ought to be
accomplished from day to day, it stands to reason that
the results will correspond exactly with the amount of
force spent upon it. The true result and produce of
labour are in exact proportion to its inner worth; that
is one of the firmly established facts of the psycho-
logical history of the world, one of those living laws
which of necessity fulfil themselves and must become
manifest in all cases to reason and conscience. Each
single piece of work may certainly be performed at
some given times rather than at others, in this or that

special way, in preference to any other, for some special reasons; but the sole aim of work as work is the training and practice of power. The result or produce which ought to be striven after in every case alike, is the growth of power, and the influence which our progress in goodness may exercise over others. What the grapes are to the wine, this result and produce are to human work; just as impossible as it is for the vine to produce thistles, just as impossible is it in the course of nature that a failure in the result of his work should await man. That a work performed lazily should produce an augmentation of power, that one performed diligently should miss its results, would be one of those wonders in which man can absolutely not believe. At the outset he draws a very sharp line of distinction between the various standpoints which he may occupy when he considers and values his work. He knows as well when a work which brings manifold advantages for civil life remains fruitless for the growth of the inner life of cognition and liberty, as when, on the contrary, a work which is exposed to blame on many sides, and which really may be considered as a failure as far as its outward object goes, has considerably increased and developed his strength. He knows that the real result of work depends on its intrinsic, *i.e.* its inner value, that the faithfulness and conscientiousness in which this inner worth consists is the only thing that can determine this result. What kind of work may be allotted to your vocation, and with what inborn faculties you may be endowed for it, is, as regards the result in the life of spiritual liberty, absolutely indifferent. The days when St. Paul was working at his tents were no less fertile for his inner life than those in which he preached the Gospel; and the same may be said of all occupations to which we devote ourselves faithfully with our whole hearts. Nor will the increase of our cognition of God and of our own self, which constitutes the result of labour, be any greater for all the wit or amiability, the quickness of understanding, or the erudition which one of us may bring to bear upon his work. Neither will it be less for the want of all these advantages with which another may begin his task. And as the growth of our own power corresponds with the inner worth of our work, so also does the saving and conciliating activity of a free, just man correspond with the influence that he exercises on all who seek his help. Only people whose interest is limited to novelties, to things that make a sensation, will think it possible that honest efforts on behalf of the sacred cause of truth and right, could be deprived of the result due to them. In a history written for inquisitive people, the most important circumstances, the events most rich in results are left out. The Christian communities of old knew very well that the action of their work did not cease when they were not allowed to be spoken about in public, and were then considered by the great mass of the higher and lower classes as a sect that had long ceased to exist. In short, the determination of man that his work shall succeed and have a result, is perfectly justifiable; and this act of volition on his part is always unfailingly crowned with success, if only in every one of his enterprises he keeps its real object in view. What he seeks, he finds; what he aims at, he attains; his prayer is granted, his wish is satisfied. That it is so, man knows. He not only hopes and believes it in a certain way, but he *knows* that it is so. As long as he is faithful in his work, he finds his happiness in being confirmed in his own experience that in this field also the harvest is of the nature of the seed, and so long as this experience lasts, he finds his joy in this consciousness. And not he alone comes to this conclusion; the indolent man also, who, owing to the inevitable sequence of cause and effect, has brought down shame upon himself, and who willingly would, if he could, justify himself by an interpretation of his doubts favourable to his weakness, cannot conceal from himself that what he reaps is the fruit of the seed he has sown. No, he cannot conceal it from himself, for it is the very essence of our nature that manifests itself alike in the preference that we give to what is good over what is evil, and in the demand that the result of our work shall correspond to the amount of exertion spent upon it.

As long as the feeling of our own self-consciousness, intensified by work, manifests itself in *this demand only*, there is nothing in it that could distort the character of our prayer, or cause the meditation intended to promote our cognition to deviate from the right path. But how rarely is our ambition limited to the expectation of the sure results of our labours! Side by side with this expectation, how many wishes are there, the object of which concerns our personal existence, the outward form of our being and its ever-changing wants and enjoyments! There are times when man is not satisfied to know in a general way that his work is not superfluous; he wants to know exactly what results may be attributed to his own work. He is not satisfied to know that the results of his work must exist; he wants to see that they belong to himself. He wishes that it might be granted to him to obtain a palpable assurance, to convince himself by his own eyes of the beneficent changes that have been wrought by his own activity. He wishes to be able to distinguish the special plants that have grown from the seeds which he himself has thrown with his own hand in the field that he has ploughed in common with others, and wishes to see the special fruit that these special plants will produce. This palpable certainty of the good result of his work is all the greater, if his observations on the share of the success attributable to his own efforts are confirmed by others. If in the beginning he only wishes to see with his own eyes the results of his own work, the other wish very soon springs up that they may be seen by many others besides. He is glad if his well-meant aspirations obtain the approbation of his friends, if public opinion pronounces him to be the originator of results worthy of public gratitude. He wishes that the whole world could witness what he has accomplished. Herewith a new and unforeseen wish arises. The share which I have taken in a work can only be recognised easily, and with certainty, if it can be proved that the plan of the work was mine, and that the means which have been used to carry it out were those I proposed. If we aim at the approbation of men, we shall frequently occupy our thoughts with the conditions on which such approbation depends; and we shall no longer be satisfied with a general aspiration for justice and liberty, be it conceived in ever so sincere and self-sacrificing a spirit on our part; we shall then require that, in order to attain this object, the path be chosen which *we* think will lead most rapidly to the goal, that the interest of all should be extended to such undertakings as *we* think ought to take precedence of others, that our notions of justice and liberty should be the common standard; in short, that, whatever is done, it should be carried out in the very way *we* think right. The wishes which the individual entertains for himself easily extend to this united general personality which is formed from the aggregation of many, from their forces united in view of the attainment of one object; they extend to the fate of the party to which we belong. It is not enough for us that this party should contribute its share to the realisation of what is good; it must be known, it must be seen by all, that it excels all others. And how can that be made manifest, if it does not spread ? if it does not obtain general consideration ? if it does not grow more and more influential ? if the power which it exercises over public affairs by the embodiment of its principles does not increase ? Thus our personal wishes lead us to desire that we should see our party crowned with glory and victory. The palpable certainty of the results of the work towards which our wishes are directed, consists not only in *being seen;* they must manifest themselves to our feelings; they must make us happy. The impulse natural to man, born with him, one with his earthly existence, which contracts the heart at any sensation of pain, and again dilates it with joy, goes further still, and creates in us the notion that it depends on our actions how joy and sorrow will be mixed in our individual life, and that ultimately unmixed happiness is to be the reward obtained by diligence and faithfulness in the exercise of the vocation God has given us in life. This happiness, with which our thoughts are engaged, may assume various shapes: one limits his hopes to his own future; another connects his expectations with the fate of the human race, or that of his nationality; a third puts off the harvest of his good deeds beyond the grave; a fourth prophecies that humanity will, even in this world, be freed from the evils that oppress it by the dominion of man over the forces of nature, and that here on earth we shall reach a state of perfect well-being. The various people whose wishes and expectations we have been describing, all have one thing in common, and it is this—the manifold wants and enjoyments of the life of the senses form in their minds a picture of what they conceive to be an insured welfare, and they think they have, in the contemplation of it, a foretaste of what they consider to be the most important and ultimate result of faithful labour.

The personal wishes of which we have been speaking concern now one kind of human activity and now several at once. They arise in us independently of our will, as often as we have to deal with the concerns of active life which fall to our share, whether a man tills the land or follows a trade, whether he is a scientific man or an artist, whether he is engaged in teaching and education, or whether he is called upon to judge or govern his fellow-creatures. The more zealously he pursues his work, the more food his personal wishes derive from it, and the louder their demands will be. When we now interrupt our work in order to turn our minds away from the many distractions and occupations of outward life, in order to consecrate our often very distracted thoughts to the contemplation of the one and eternal, of which all things are a manifestation, by retiring into ourselves, and so resume the work of cognition which we call prayer, what becomes of these personal wishes? Does our experience prove that these wishes, to which the business of the day has given rise, have become silent, or have disappeared when work was put aside? On the contrary, these wishes are by no means prepared to make room for other thoughts. They will be our companions even in prayer, and demand nothing less than to be the objects of our religious aspirations, and to determine the contents of our prayers. If we yield to these pretensions, our wishes will undergo a complete transformation. A healthy mind remains conscious that wishes are nothing but wishes, fantastic creations of broad daylight dreams, which can just as little substantiate themselves as the soap-bubbles with which the boy is playing can become solid bodies. Men must consider their wishes as a play of the imagination, which ever manifests anew the spirit's independence of the outer world. Fancy will not allow herself to be disturbed in her airy building, castles and bowers of a moment adorned with all the brilliant colours of hope; no, not even by the most heavy and gloomy realities of a miserable present. But if we allow these personal wishes to have their place in our prayers, and to assume a religious character, we thus invest them with the sacredness that the name of God gives to everything which we connect with Him. They thus assume a character of necessity; their fulfilment appears to be the most important thing in our lives; a duty for the fulfilment of which all powers in heaven and earth must be set in motion. At last man feels convinced that the whole creation has no other object than to realise these airy phantoms created by the activity of his fancy. Generally it is only certain wishes which religious superstition thus surrounds with the halo of sanctity, those especially that refer to the support of our own church through the power of the Almighty, to the victory of our own soul-saving belief, to the welfare and safety of its adherents. But as soon as man begins to believe in the necessity of the fulfilment of even a few wishes, these wishes being all more or less connected with each other, he is exposed with all of them to a similar illusion. The greater the importance we attach to our personal wishes, the more discontented we grow with reality; and who does not know by his own experience the paralysing action of discontent upon our strength and our love for work? But the worst effect of this giving way to our own wishes and inclinations is that our religious exercises become artificial and a means of self-deceit, that our prayers, which ought to be consecrated to the contemplation of cognition of what is eternal, chain us with new ties to transitory things.

If we wish not to deprive ourselves of the blessings of prayer and of the benefits of cognition, we must listen to the voice of reason and of conscience which tells us that eternal life and our personal wishes have nothing in common. What can the love of God, which acknowledges the manifestations of His holy will in the various forms of existence as well in life as in death, have to do with these personal wishes which never allow us to enjoy any gift of our eternal Father without being themselves a reproach to some other of His gifts? What can there be in common between the invisible deed of self-government, our obedience and our faithful adherence to the law of justice, which always remains true to itself with the ever-changing phenomena of outward life, and the feelings and sensations inseparable from them? What can the purification of the heart and the sanctification of the will have to do with flesh and blood, for which there can be no distinction between good and evil? How could the eye of the body and the sense of hearing inform us whether the love of what is good, or the pleasure in what is evil, will ripen in us fruit unto eternal life or fruit unto death? He who listens to the voice of reason and conscience will learn that neither reason nor conscience wishes the course of nature to be different from what it is, that nature, and the God that lives in her, have no ear and no heart for the wishes of the fool who is dissatisfied with his fate. Man has not been created without some understanding for the eternal order of things; he knows that their laws must have their course. He knows therefore that effect and counter-effect keep the balance, that the seed and its fruit are always corresponding to each other, according to their kind, and that nothing in heaven or in earth can deprive him of the result of his work. But have we this same certainty when we demand that our work should bring us happiness and enjoyment, or that the cause which we espouse should attract the attention of the world by its outward results? We know that nature herself refuses this certainty and this assurance to everyone so far as his personal wishes are concerned. If such a certainty or the assurance of it were possible here on earth, would men have been obliged to go to the priests in order to have the promise of felicity in heaven? Would men have found it necessary to have recourse to persuasion, to cunning and violence, in order to secure the victory to their party? No! whatever man may do to deceive himself, in spite of his own knowledge, and to present the fulfilment of his personal wishes as a necessity, doubt haunts him, and incessantly reminds him that the heaven in which God dwells is inaccessible to the changing wishes of our hearts, that no prayers which demand a change in the course of nature can reckon upon its fulfilment.

May we therefore, my friends, never set ourselves to the holy work of the cognition of God and man, never begin our religious exercises until we have asked ourselves what we seek from God, and what we entreat of Him. If we have nothing better to tell Him than that the ways He leads us do not please us, that we want health, honours, pleasure, and consolation, when He sends death, humiliation, griefs, and doubts, our prayer can be but the expression of foolishness and absurdity. We can therefore earn by it nothing but the fruits of foolishness; namely, more anxious cares, more feverish desires, an imaginary fulfilment of our wishes without inner satisfaction, and when hope after hope has been frustrated, the doubt whether there is a God at all that can help us. But, if we have at last become aware what are the prayers that never are granted, then we may rejoice, my friends. Then we raise ourselves to that prayer which never can remain unfulfilled, to that prayer which requires nothing less than God Himself, His Spirit and His love. Then we recognise our Father in Him, we get free from the feeling of alienation; then we feel that also in our human nature, in our life, His love and His Spirit are at work. In this blessed feeling of our communion with Him, we see the changing scenes of our transitory existence as He sees them, when, unveiling the inner coherence of all things, He speaks and says: "Behold, it is very good." If we then turn from our solitary prayer back again into the throng of life, and we again meet with grief and ill-success, we yet know the divine mission entrusted to fate, we know that this fate also is a help which the eternal Father has prepared for His child. Pain does not cease to be pain, but we cease to fear this pain; we do not ask to be freed from it, but we are full of joyful courage to try ourselves, and to prove what precious fruit of cognition and freedom even the seed of frustrated hope and grievous ill-success may produce in those who love God! Amen.

IX.

"HALLOWED BE THY NAME."

The first request, after the introductory words of the Lord's Prayer, is that the name of God may be sanctified. These words do, no doubt, appear as a sort of repetition of one of the commandments promulgated on Sinai, which enjoins us not to misuse the name of God. It is very probable that the Jewish sect of Essenes, among whom the Lord's Prayer was in use even before the time of Jesus, according to trustworthy information, may have attached to these words the same sense as that conveyed in the commandment. It was considered as one of the most important duties towards God, that the greatest respect should be paid to the words used to designate the Supreme Being. One was not to pronounce them without the feeling of respect and awe, which it seemed natural that man should feel when he thought of his Maker and All-powerful Lord. The whole attitude of the body, the tone of the voice, the gestures and expression of the face, were all to indicate, in an unmistakable manner, the difference between these words and those used by men in their intercourse with each other. The word Jehovah was the object of special veneration, being, according to the popular belief, the name by which God had called Himself when speaking with Moses; and the old Israelites thought they rendered to it due honour by abstaining absolutely from using it in ordinary circumstances.

And who among us does not remember the exhortations and warnings addressed to him in his youth when he pronounced the name of God thoughtlessly? This misuse was represented to him as a desecration of the name of the Almighty, and as a breach of the second commandment, to which a threat of special punishment was added.

The early notions which men formed of God were more or less under the influence of the senses. He was generally spoken of as being either absent, and therefore far away from men, or as being present, and therefore near to them. It is on the ground of this sensuous conception of God that the sanctification of His name, has both in ancient and modern times, been prescribed to us as a duty; this command was supposed to be obeyed under special circumstances and under no others, *i.e.* whenever this word—God—or any of its equivalents was to be pronounced; nor could it be broken under any other circumstances. Such was the limited extent of this commandment.

But what did Jesus understand by the sanctification of God's name, when he used this old expression in the religious language of the Essenian sect in His prayer? It is obvious that He could not attach to it the notions current among his contemporaries. One like Jesus, who stamped as a superstition the idea that God could be nearer to us in the temple of Jerusalem than in any other place, could not believe that any special connection of sounds, any special word, could be dearer to the Eternal than any other word. He who stamped as a superstition the idea that the essence of what is good or evil could be sought in special or isolated acts, recognisable only in their outward shape, could not possibly admit that piety or morality could set forth as a law to men, how they should pronounce certain words.

Many will ask what else can be understood by the sanctification of God's name save these very notions which Jesus rejected? Does the sanctification of the name of God, in itself, not point to a superstitious worship, to a religion of sense offered to God? Was Jesus right in directing the moral sense of men to such purely material and outward things as words and names, when His object was to promote the worship of God 'in spirit and in truth'? Those who put these questions start from the notion that the world of our moral aspirations and the life of sense are two sides of life, between which there is no connection and no reciprocal action; a notion which does not consider the world of matter as of equal nobility with the spirit, and as a creation manifesting divine reason simply in a different manner; but looks upon it as a fall, a derogation of the spirit from itself—a notion under the influence of which we consider the human body as a trammel, as the burden of the spirit; a notion according to which the invisible character of the spirit is to be so conceived, that one cannot perceive whether man is good or bad. If we shared this view, we should certainly be obliged logically to blame Jesus for mentioning the sanctification of God's name. But we consider the spirit and the body to be united in the closest manner, although differing the one from the other, the body serving the spirit as readily as air, light, and metals receive the electric fluid and conduct it farther. In the same way we consider the soul to be embodied in the eye, the ear, and all the senses. This union of body and spirit seems to be expressed most pointedly and ingeniously in these words—sanctification of the name of God. And now what does Jesus mean by these words?

Let our thoughts go back to the time when God had as yet no name, when men had not realised that point in the structure of language, when the name of God was created; (for we speak here of the name of God in the sense only which it has as the production of free and conscious aspiration).* And as such it is a creation of human thought and reflection. In the same way the author of the first book of Moses represents language to us, when he says that all plants and all animals on earth, in the sea, and in the air, were brought to Adam to see what he would call them; and whatever Adam called every living creature, that was the name thereof. Thus progressing from one point of their experience to another, extending their horizon, men formed out of the breath of their mouths an expression for everything, until they at last came to create a name for Him also, through whom they themselves and all things have their being.

We do not know how late or how soon they reached that degree of development; nor do we know on what spot of the earth, by what race, in what language or dialect, the name, which among us has this particular

---

* The reader must remember that these discourses were delivered in a country where the rationalists and skilled critics of the materialistic school are numerous, and that the speaker is as much opposed to that school as to that of a crude orthodoxy.

form—God—was uttered for the first time in the world. But anyone who thinks must find this, that all those who have distinguished themselves as the greatest discoverers in the realm of spiritual life during the last centuries must appear small indeed, compared with this unknown author, who, not satisfied with imitating in the sounds of human language that which is to be seen or heard, undertook to open, by the help of these sounds, the unseen world to our consciousness, and to overtop the limits of all that comes under the perception of the senses by creating the name of God. If we consider of what kind was the life of thought that arose with the introduction and use of this word, if we consider that the creation of the name of God was in its germ one with the awakening of the moral and religious consciousness, we must see that the change was a progress, beside which, taking into account its vastness and the importance of its results, very few others can be placed.

The progress did not consist in the ultimate achievement of a work, fraught with difficulty, begun ages before, and left by one generation to the perseverance of succeeding generations, and at last successfully accomplished; no, the progress which one race accomplished with the creation of the name of God, consisted in the new task which began with this new acquisition, an idea never conceived before. After having given names to all things, *i.e.* after having assigned a proper place in his consciousness to each picture that earth, sea, plants, animals and all that was on or under the earth formed in his mind, he at last discovered a life beyond the limits of this world, and with the word—God—endowed with a name this life and being, which reaches beyond all earthly existence. But so far, this word did no more than point to a new sphere of action for the mind of man; this word remained *empty* as long as man did not venture to enter this newly-discovered life beyond the world of matter; as long as he did not take his starting point in it, and did not become conscious of the new aspect which the now old world of sense must present to his eyes from the point of view newly gained. Now if this—for a time empty—word is to keep its promise to men, if men receive its messages, and are able to read aright the contents of the name of God, they must put it into connection with every being that formed a part of this old world of sense, and see in what relation they all stand to that life beyond theirs, which is their common centre.

Men could attain this result only by taking one by one all the things that form part of this old world, and ascertaining what aspect they presented when viewed as objects of meditation for the life in God, under the light streaming over them from this newly gained life beyond them. In this way everything belonging to this old world of sense must form a part of the meaning of the name of God. Thus the name God was in a certain way to be considered as containing all the names of every single thing, of which the old world of sense was composed, in such a way that all those names became enriched by the new significance now attached to them by their connection with the life beyond them. The name of God therefore remained an empty sound as long as it indicated a

God outside the world. In order to enter into its full substance and meaning, this name must unfold itself into the innumerable names which compose the language of men; in order to give its full meaning, it must take up into itself the names of all things in the world, the names of the earth and of the air, of animals and men, of phenomena and of all changes in nature, as well as the names of all the productions in the domain of art. The name of God must take up all names in order to determine the significance of each of them, so far as it has its roots in the world beyond the world of sense, so far as it lives in and for God, as it lives and has its being in Him. Whatsoever word you may choose in the whole store of human language is a contribution to the substance and meaning, yea, even, so to speak, a part of the all-embracing name of God.

Is the presentiment of this thought, and an attempt to embody it practically, not expressed in various words of the Bible, such as "God, Thou hast the name that Thou livest"—"God, Thy name is Lord;" and elsewhere, "His name is love," and so on? Certainly from these isolated expressions, which sound like accidental inspirations arising in the minds of the sacred writers, there is a long way to pass before we come to the consciousness that what is true of the words Lord, Life, Love, is equally true of, and can with equal propriety be applied to, every word; and that all words are names of God. Certainly it will be long before the generality of men are able to overcome their spiritual narrowness sufficiently to hear us ask of every object without exception, what its name implies, when used as one of the many names of God. Many people would be alarmed at such a question, and many more would turn the attempt into derision. But long as this road may be, it is the only one which those can tread who are animated by this inward feeling, this insatiable desire to know, this pious longing, this holy yearning which cannot bear that the name of God should remain empty and meaningless. We cannot therefore help thinking that as God is for us the inward unity, the common root and the eternal order of all things, His name also embraces the names of all individual beings and phenomena in the world, which are united in this eternal order.

But then what is the sum total of these names and words but human language in so far as they serve as an exposition of the eternal unity of all things that are manifested to men? The name of God is therefore in truth the human language itself, in so far as it is designed for this exposition; and no one can sanctify the name of God otherwise than *by sanctifying His language*. In giving this meaning to the sanctification of the name of God, we prove and ratify that man is the image of God. As soon as we thus recognise the sense of this petition that the name of God may be sanctified, we clearly see that this sanctification of the name of God must necessarily take place in every sound human life; and that it indicates a spiritual striving which need not wait for rare and isolated occasions; but, on the contrary, must every day of our life become a fact, and ever must accomplish the work committed to our care.

As in nature the most different objects are attained by one and the same means, so is it with the wonderful instrument which man creates in language. What has the question, how many feet and inches a fence has in length, in common with the forgiving and forgetting of offences? And still the eye, which answers the question, brings also the message of peace, love, and reconciliation. The same sounds form the names of numbers in calculations of profits and expenses on the last market-day, and the names which express the essence of things, which in itself has nothing in common with any kind of calculation or computation. The same sounds are required by the workman, the student, the art-critic, the huntsman, the warrior, in the language proper to their several kinds of work, as by the apostle of truth for the language of the Spirit and its cognition of truth.

In the perfecting of this language of the Spirit in man, of the language in which he expresses his cognition of truth, we all are concerned; it is our common interest. It is in so close a connection with the distinction of good and evil through the link of our will, that is, our self-government, that to purify it, to develop and cultivate it, so that it may correspond to the noble task to which it is destined, justly appears to be a process of sanctification. This sanctification of the human language can, therefore, be nothing more and nothing less than a steady effort, at every word which we use, to call into consciousness the connection and internal unity which exist between the beings and phenomena indicated by these words and all others. It can be nothing more nor less than to have present to our mind, at every name and word which we utter, the place in the eternal order of things to which it points when well understood.

Now, whence arises all spiritual narrowness and the endless prejudices which manifest it? Certainly from nothing else than the indolence which shirks the effort of thought and work of cognition. The longer man allows himself this thoughtless use of words, the more he estranges himself from the things which he designates. By repeating certain appellations and expressions of others, without knowing their meaning, he becomes the more incapable of recognising the things with which language is meant to acquaint him, and the less capable of remembering that none of all these names point to anything that he would not find in his own mind. Every name that remains foreign to him in spite of his frequent use of it—every word that does not give him an insight into his own nature—is a barrier which hinders the free action of the mind. The way in which this want of freedom in the action of the mind, this thoughtlessness and narrowness of the individual, manifests itself, depends on his own disposition and on accidental circumstances. Now, he will declare one part of creation to be ugly and repulsive; at another time he finds the most absurd habits beautiful and amiable. Now, a man will appear to him of a low order, because his skin is black; now, again, a person decked with purple and gold and precious stones, impresses him as being an apparition of superhuman power and loftiness; what is most rational will appear ridiculous to him, and the most senseless things will inspire him with respect and devotion. He does not perceive that he practises the same idolatry to-day which yesterday he derided in others; that here he flings away money, and elsewhere he is miserly; that he alternately throws a thing away as worthless, and craves for it as his highest happiness; that he alternately worships it and treads it under his feet. His language has become the mere expression of countless prejudices, which, like the innumerable rings of a chain, fetter and shackle him on every side. But only let him remember that language is meant to be the manifestation of God's Spirit in his reason and conscience; only let him make up his mind to render this word and that word to its sacred destination, finding the place to which it points in the order of things; only let him make a real beginning with the sanctification of his language, and every one of these memories, decisions, and actions is the destruction of a prejudice—is a step in his spiritual enfranchisement. The more words and names he thus sanctifies, the more freely his mind will move. Yes, my friends, the hallowing the name of God is the hallowing of our language, and the sanctification of our language is spiritual enfranchisement, one of the two foundations on which rests the establishment of truth in human life.

If this be the hallowing of the name of God, then we must admit that Jesus shows deep understanding of human nature in teaching us that the request for the sanctification of the name of the Eternal must necessarily find its place in every life that is truly human in the full sense of the word. The nature of man is founded on liberty. There is no human breast without some strong instinct of liberty; a decided craving for a consciousness of the fact, and an impetus to make it grow. To cultivate it, to penetrate life in all directions with the spirit of liberty, and to make sure that one is one's own master in face of all the powers in the world—this is the yearning of every human heart.

That man who, we are convinced, will and can help us to this liberty, may be sure that we shall acknowledge him as our friend, our teacher, and our master. Truly we also know how frequently it happens that, in consequence of the delusions into which men fall in their aspirations after liberty, they hate and fear those who are their surest friends as much as if they were their most dangerous enemies. It is therefore most important to avoid these misconceptions. What will protect us against them? Nothing, it seems to me, so effectually as the resolution to enter upon the path indicated in our prayer, and earnestly to set to work to sanctify *our* language, the language of every day. I repeat it, the way to sanctify your language is to sanctify the language of every-day life, for that alone we can call our own.

In all ages an attempt has been made to persuade men that there was another language, one specially holy and consecrated to the service of God, which it was not only possible, but necessary to learn. The history of reigning religions is, in a great measure, nothing else than the history of the efforts made to teach men this sacred language. This language had its own character everywhere; it differed in the temples the ruins of which we now find on the banks of the Euphrates and Tigris, from what it was in Syria and Egypt. The priests who offered sacrifices to the Olympian gods, did not utter the same words as those used in the mediæval cathedrals, or in the Arabian mosques. But as we study these sacred tongues, we find in all of them the same substance and the same spirit. These, like all the languages that have had dominion over the world, all are a collection of expressions for one and the same thought, namely, that man cannot reach unto God; that he cannot know Him. The corollary of this thought forms the rest of this vocabulary of sacred tongues, and leads us to this natural conclusion, that the sum-total of precepts and commands promulgated in the name of God, is not to be tested by reason and intellect; in other words, that they are not meant to be, and cannot be, understood; and therefore, that what is unknown and mysterious to men, is worthy of reverence and holy, whilst the language of every-day life, which represents that which is knowable and familiar to men, is common and bad.

Now, whether this so-called sacred language be introduced by insinuating words or by threats, it must remain strange to men. Its use is forced, and must have a paralysing effect on the mind of those who use it. If we were to deduce historical facts from the old tradition of the tower of Babel, and the confusion of languages that broke out then, we could only refer them to the invention of these unnatural languages. Wherever they were accepted, man became a stranger to himself; his language became the expression of untruth, a means of deceit, a source of misunderstanding. Man has received from nature *one* tongue and *one* language. The duplicity of language, which arose with the introduction of a second tongue,* is the mother of all moral and religious prejudices. Therefore, if we are determined to sanctify the language of man, and lead him back to the safe path of spiritual enfranchisement, we must take a firm hold on this, that the language of every-day life which contains that which we know, that on which we have to decide according to the standard of reason and conscience, is the only one which we can call our own.

It must be admitted that the undertaking to *sanctify* it, is so strange to us that we find it difficult even to prepare the way for it. A task, an undertaking in the sphere of moral and religious life, can be seen clearly and grasped confidently, when it is possible to refer to cases in which it has been fulfilled. And how poor is the past and present in experiences of this kind! May I be successful in choosing among the few at our disposal such as are most likely to lead us in our search after others! Also in this respect the picture presented to us by the life of Jesus is the most instructive for us. Let us try to realise, as far as it is possible in a single case, how He proceeded in view of this attempt which we propose. The language to be sanctified comprises as many names and words as there are things that we perceive about us, on, or in us. The sanctification is then only complete, when every word which men use has become a name of God in our consciousness. Word after word has thus to be stamped anew. With which word shall we begin? Jesus began with the word

* The second language here meant was in ancient times a separate one; now it is, in Protestant countries at least, a sort of dialect within the language, or what is familiarly termed "cant."

that distinguishes itself from all others in a double
respect; first, by being more frequently used than any
other; and secondly, by indicating that which concerns
us most clearly; that is the word *I*. In daily intercourse at least, man uses it almost every time he opens
his mouth, and at the same time it is the word in
using which he ever and again transforms the world
into a mirror of his own form; it is the word in using
which he can least escape himself. This *I*, this self of
mine, is one of God's many names—God is in me and
I am in Him. Jesus makes this *I*, this personality of
His, one of God's names in the same way that the
word tree is made to designate innumerable beings
composed of roots, leaves, and blossoms. It is meant
to take all that together which you put into the name
of God, eternal and infinite, necessity and liberty,
intelligence and perfection, unlimited power and love.
On the other side, take altogether all that of which
the word *I*, the name of your own personality, reminds
you, thought and feeling, will and deed, birth and
death, eye and ear, hand and foot, in short, mind and
body, and all this is, in truth, a name for the first. As
in answering a child's question "What is a tree?" one
would show him the first tree that comes in the way,
so when Philip said to Him, "Show us the Father,"
Jesus answered with perfect simplicity: "See Me,
Philip; he who sees Me, sees the Father."

I will not, my friends, dwell on the different ways
in which these words may be pronounced. They may
come from the lips of an unfortunate man who has
lost his reason; they may come from one, still more to
be pitied, who scoffs at eternal truth; or they may be

the words of one who uses religion as a cloak. But when we hear them from Jesus, they are the granting of our prayer that the name of God may be hallowed; He does what this petition demands; He brings back to its original meaning one of the words of life, which has been most thoughtlessly abused and has served as a resting pillar to the most baneful prejudices; He brings it back to its original meaning; He recognises and declares truly, that if God is really God, and is all in all, the word also, which designates the personality of man, must represent a manifestation of the omnipresent; and that word—like the word God—must thus be a name of the Eternal.

Let us now turn to the picture which the present time presents to us. However far the present attempts remain behind the pure, consciously elevated and resolute efforts of Jesus, in the way of sanctifying the language of every-day life, these beginnings of spiritual liberation touch us closely, for the very reason that they arise out of our consciousness, and may therefore reckon upon a general understanding. This so-called sacred language, which our forefathers bequeathed to us, had made the word truth, along with other words, to be the expression of the unknown and incomprehensible, and had robbed it of its moral and religious signification; so much so, that of truth we had nothing left for every-day use but the notion necessary for the life of sense, a husk without a kernel. Veracity, which was limited to the accuracy of statements concerning things to be seen or heard, was so far considered indispensable, that the traffic and affairs of life could not flourish without it. That it was used only as a means to an end is plainly shown by the fact that it was considered as a duty, to the fulfilment of which people could be brought by force, through the menaces of secular or ecclesiastical power; as a duty which ceases when deception is useful; as a duty from which grown-up persons feel free towards children, and the learned towards the unlearned. We know how at last it came to this, that the majority of those who discovered the systematic fraud determined to imitate it, and unhesitatingly to profess that which appeared to them to be foolish and contrary to reason, and, if necessary, to affirm it by oath. But there were some who found it impossible to follow such a course. They did not deny that it may often be useful to minors to be deceived; but they could not help asking themselves whether it be good for minors to remain in their infancy, whether it be good for them to be kept in their ignorance, through special arrangements for that purpose; and especially if this be the case when this ignorance concerns no one and nothing but their own and innermost selves. They convinced themselves that by deceiving others they deceived themselves, that veracity is not a means to false ends; that the love of truth, that the harmony of man with himself, requires no outward stay; but that, on the contrary, it is one of those foundations of life on which the whole life of phenomena rests. They regained the consciousness of their true selves; they made a vow to break with the old hypocrisy, and remained true to their vow. However steep and full of dangers its narrow path became; however much they were flattered or threatened with being brought back to the broad and easy road, they

remained faithful to the truth and to their true nature
they could not find it in themselves to do otherwise;
the truth had again become a name for what is necessary and unconditional, a name for what is eternal and
omnipotent, for that the presence of which is indestructible, the want of which makes life unbearable.
Truth had again become for them a name of God. And
this truth, with regard to which such a change had
taken place, did not belong in their eyes to any particular language, was not set apart or consecrated to
any special purpose, and used only for baptisms or the
communion service inside the walls of a church; it was
again a word of the language used in every-day life.
In everything they see and hear, this truth makes itself
felt; and amid the experiences of their every-day life
the question is heard again and again whether this
existence of ours is founded on truth. They see
their brothers of the large human family struggling
in bitter need; they see them succumb because no
help is given; they see honours and power lavished
on vain objects; they hear of free work where they
see a wild turmoil, and the incessant efforts of men
to snatch from each other their respective advantages;
they see life borne with disgust, or time wasted as if
it were superfluous, and with all that, death feared as
if it robbed us of the highest good; and in this and in
all around, the question resounds, as from a thousand
echoes—is this an existence that bears testimony to the
truth? Certainly we often hear in our desecrated
language the question asked, "Is this true?" But in
this language it is a question without heart and without
reason, the question of a curiosity empty of thought

and feeling, which considers as all-important some most indifferent thing, whilst some really important consideration is set aside even without a thought. Has this fact, which forms the subject of conversation, taken place just here or just now? That is in the eyes of merely inquisitive people the all-important matter, whilst this question, is this story—fictitious or real— a manifestation of human life in its divine character or a monstrous disfigurement of it?—this, the only really important question, is so indifferent, that if in a gathering of people anyone is ill-bred enough to direct attention to it, a dead silence follows. If once our own language is sanctified, then he who questions—is it true?—expresses his remembrance of eternal justice and will no longer offend against what is considered the good tone of society. If we find it difficult clearly to illustrate by isolated examples from the past and present, what is meant by the sanctification of our language, how can we hope to draw a picture of that future time when the languages of nations in general will no longer serve superstition and vanity, but, on the contrary, will fulfil their holy object, that is, represent to the senses under a tangible form what is eternal and divine. One thing only we know for certain, namely, that this time will not come until everything that has a name in every-day language, *every one, without exception*, is recognised as a name of God. There was a time when the language of life indicated more distinctly that it had its origin in the spirit of the Eternal than is the case with our present language, deprived as it is of its soul and its divine character. The faith of the ancient Greeks hallowed the name of God more truly than the fanaticism that succeeded to it, which considered it as one and the same thing to sanctify the name of God, and to hate and despise reason. The faith of the ancient Greeks was, that as the earth and heavens, the sun and moon, the nascent life of the early morning, the rainbow and the evening-star, the altar of the gods, the life of man, were all the work, the dwelling, in some way the manifestation of God; so also the earth, the fire on the hearth, the love and friendship in the human breast, the sleep of death, the heroic games, the juvenile dance, the wine and its joys, were also full of God's presence and God's love. Had the teaching of that ancient faith not begun to sanctify the name of God by teaching its adepts to honour all these things as the many names of the Deity?

And how beautiful and glorious were the proportions of human life as it shaped itself under the influence of this faith, and this sanctification of language! Nevertheless, this glory has fallen, could not but fall into decay, because the faith of the ancient world did not in its teaching recognise a name of God in every word, because according to it, only what was beautiful, great and powerful was holy; because this faith prevented man from recognising also in what is weak and impotent, in what is ugly, in toilsome labour, in the slave who performs it, in illness and death, names of the Eternal God; because this faith could only direct the people who held it to an unknown God, without a name, as Paul reproached it with doing.

In the presence of that unknown God, the glory of

that life must sink into nothingness. As long as there is one word left, the significance and sense of which do not remind men of Thy presence and Thy creative power, Eternal Father, man does not understand Thy spirit and Thy love!

Teach us above all to consider this, when we pray, that Thy name may be hallowed! Amen!

IX.—B.

"HALLOWED BE THY NAME."

WE tried in our last discourse to find a clear definition of what is meant by the word—the sanctification of the name of God. At first this name seems to lead our thoughts to distances out of our reach; but in our efforts to realise the meaning of this expression, we convinced ourselves that men whose devotions are animated by feeling and thought, must necessarily acquire the habit of connecting the name of God with what is near to them, with all that they perceive round about them and in them, and with everything which forms part of themselves, or is in any way connected with them. The name of God thus unfolded itself into an innumerable variety of words. We found them all to be the words used by men to indicate anything they see or experience, and, taken collectively, they form a complete picture of the language of men so far as it represents the totality of things and their coherence. In this way the sanctification of the name of God became the sanctification of human language, and this sanctification was not found to consist in extracting a small number of expressions from the whole stock of words consecrated to general use, in order to form a sacred language to which an exclusive privilege is granted in order to express what is divine; but, on the contrary, this sanctification consisted, according to our conviction, in making every word and every name that expresses the phenomena of nature and life, remind us of the eternal order of things. We made this sanctification to consist in making the every-day language throughout, besides the use everyone makes of it, in his special vocation, serve to help everyone in the same way to realise the thought and presence of the eternal God. The petition that the name of God may be sanctified, will be the more perfectly fulfilled, in proportion as men learn to use the language of every-day life as an instrument of the cognition of eternal truth.

This explanation of the sanctification of the name of God will always prove to be one of the meanings which we can consistently attach to these words of the Lord's prayer, according to our way of thinking. Viewed in this way, they remind us of the worship of God in spirit and in truth which fills us with the feeling and thought of the omnipresence of what is the divine element; viewed in this way, they teach us how to bridge over the gulf between this life and the life to come,* in which the guilt, the division of man

---

* On the first reading, we may be tempted to ask how this statement can be justified, how the promise can be fulfilled, but the thoughtful reader may soon perceive how a man who has accustomed himself to live in this world as amid as many mirrors of God as there are things about him and in him, must

with himself is reflected; viewed in this light, these words show that religion and morality are not separated

---

feel that all that is spiritual, the thought or the action it has brought about, is the only reality of life, and that the continuity of it is a necessary certainty which no syllogism can take from him; the *scenes* and things of life are to him like the manifestations of a fluid that itself escapes our grasp, but is as well-known as its manifestations themselves. To such a man eternity does not begin in the hereafter; his present life is part and parcel of it, and he lives amid a thousandfold reverberations of the divine element. Anyone who has ever observed nature and life must sometime have been struck by the reflections of objects placed near any current or expanse of water: the observer may have found a parallel in this feature of creation to the manifold reflections of life in art, in poetry, and in literature in general. He must be conscious that all art, all poetry, and all literature is either an effulgence of divine thought or a reflection of life reproduced by the vivifying mind of man, itself divine, ever imparting a new originality to these scenes, thus reproducing life *ad infinitum*, like the objects he saw reflected in the water, or, to use another comparison, like the pictures that many mirrors placed around a room reflect again and again from each other so often that the bewildered looker-on scarcely knows which is the original and which is the refracted shadow, even when the original figure is himself. Anyone, I say, who has been struck by this wonderful action and reaction of life upon itself, and knows how to distinguish the cause from its effects, may form an idea of the state of mind of a man who views life as the author does; such a man, in order to be sure of his own identity, has gained an intense consciousness of the essence of life both in himself and in others; he absolutely requires the consciousness of the eternal unity, the first and immutable cause of these dioramic apparitions which we call the scenes of life, of which he takes a second, a bird's-eye view.

But nothing could be more erroneous than to draw the conclusion that such a man is a dreamer and lives in a state of inaction; on the contrary, living in the closest union with the source of all life, gaining an insight into it, he has all the impetus of a brook descending from a height; he has a clear view of the course to follow: in a word, he is the prophet that has an insight into God's will, and cannot rest until he has used all his energy and power to carry out all that he has seen in his Father's will. If he is not at once little Samuel, saying, "Speak, from the outer world by any insurmountable barrier, but that real life is one in its essence and destination with religion and morality, that religion and morality permeate, renew and transform it; viewed in this light, they give us the certainty that prayer brings no petitions that can or cannot be granted according to the arbitrary will of higher powers, but that true prayer is the expression of a yearning, the realisation of which the Eternal Father has made to depend directly on the seeking and striving, on the volition and deeds, of his human children. In short, the result of our meditation, according to which the sanctification of the name of God and the transformation of the language of every-day life into a perfect instrument of cognition are synonymous, is in perfect harmony with the convictions from which we always start, and in so far it gives us satisfaction.

Lord, Thy servant heareth," he must either, like Jonah, be tossed by the tempest, and ultimately be obliged by his conscience to do what he knows to be his duty, or like Balaam, act against his conscience; for there is no peace for him, and ultimately he will not be able even to discern his own voice from that of his beast of burden. Nay, this man, if true to himself, is and must be conscious of this immutable cause which is at work in his thoughts, in every fibre, every muscle and nerve in him, and which will remain so in its fulness even when these fibres, muscles, and nerves will be at rest for ever. For this man, therefore, there is no break between this life and the life beyond, for his body is not his permanent self, and in spite of those men who are such strangers to their own consciousness, such strangers to what is everlasting that they laugh at the idea that their persons are not their true selves, as well as in spite of those who, in order to retain their individuality, require the resurrection of the flesh; this truth, I say, that the present life is part of, and no break in, eternity, is as simple to him as to a child the notion that it cannot remain what it is now, neither in stature or mental development, and that yet he will be the same person as a man that he was as a child.

But if we compare what our language of every-day is, with what we demand of it, the result of this comparison can only bring humiliation and shame upon us. We feel keenly that our language does not reflect the picture of eternal thoughts as in a clear looking glass. Then what must this language be in order to fulfil its destination? What will be its form, and what impression will it create, what effects will it produce, if once it answers to its destination? Nobody is able to say what it will be. In this case, as in all others where the life of liberty and self-government is concerned, we know in what direction we have to turn; and that is all. A visible goal that you might show to others there is not, and still less a prescribed way that would lead to it with certainty. Everyone has to break his own path. No one knows how to describe the goal until he has reached it. Seek, we are told, and ye shall find! No one knows a name for what he seeks. And how could he name it, since it is a thing that is not in existence yet? Our moral aspiration is a seeking like that of the poet after his poem, before it is ready to be read; the painter seeking and forming his conception of the queen of heaven before he realises it on the canvas; and the musician his choral song before anyone can hear it. Also the seeking of our moral aspirations is a creative power. Let us therefore put aside the question what the language of men will be, when it has become a perfect instrument of cognition! Let us give our attention to the next question, namely, what it is that hinders us from sanctifying our language, as we now are, and what can help us to do it.

What hinders us? It is this: whenever thought has taken a new tendency which has to be followed and kept steadily on its proper track, the old social habits form a dangerous obstacle to its progress. The effects, which these old habits leave behind them, are most dangerous when they divest themselves of their former garb and re-appear under a new form which conceals from us their incompatibility with our new tendencies. There are therefore two deceptions against which we ought to be specially on our guard: the first is the new varnish with which the old sacred language has learned hypocritically to condescend to the affairs of daily life; the other is the religious varnish with which the desecrated language of every-day life, assuming a religious colouring, again and again deceives so many, and conceals from them its really irreligious tendency.

In order to recognise with certainty the old sacred language, often so unlike its former self, under its new garb, we must first ascertain on what foundation rests the difference so long observed between an ecclesiastical and a civil, a sacred and a common language. This distinction is not due to any religious faith; on the contrary, wherever the thought of what is divine reaches a state of consciousness, it protests against this wrenching and dividing of the one human language into two languages opposed to and excluding each other. The religious ideas only form the stuff out of which the tendencies underlying this division of language know, under certain circumstances, how to make a cloak for themselves. Now, are not pride and the love of power by their own nature always bent on using the means most easily adapted to the spirit of the time for their own purposes? And is there anything that under all circumstances is more pliable, more easily used and misused, more adapted for substituting at will truth for untruth, than language? And when have pride and the love of power not attempted to destroy and succeeded in destroying the unity and the harmony of language? The only thing these old enemies of the human race require in order to exert their influence, is some one peculiarity of nature, some special state of things created by circumstances, which distinguishes some people from others to their advantage, and which appears to establish some claims to certain privileges. If general handling of religious affairs and the dignity of priesthood be not used in this way, the privilege which was formerly attached to the language used in divine service is easily transferred to some one of the technical kinds of language pertaining to the various small circles of society created by special circumstances, in the midst of one nation or born of the collective life of different nations. It is so natural that the so-called cultivated classes, distinguished from others by the possession of a certain knowledge, should adopt, in consequence of it, a special language. It is so natural that every special profession should have its special technical language. But, as soon as pride and the love of power take hold of this accidental advantage, immediately the prejudice arises that this language of the higher classes is the only language truly worthy of humanity, that the clever man alone possesses a language which fits him for the cognition of divine and human questions; and that, on the contrary, the large mass of the people speak a language in which it is impossible to express the statements of reason without producing the grossest and most dangerous errors. And this popular language is treated like a soiled vessel that would contaminate and corrupt the best and noblest things entrusted to it. There we have again, albeit in another shape than under the dominion of priesthood, two different languages separated from each other by the power of circumstances, as well as by natural causes, of which one is designated low and common, and declared to be the language of the "eternally blind man" to whom the heavenly torch of light can only serve for destruction and devastation. As long as this illusion is kept up—and what disease of the mind is more far spread in the present day than this?—as long as this error is maintained, there can be no question of the sanctification of the general human language. As long as this goes on, the divine name remains profaned.

The greatest surprise is now often expressed that, in our so-called enlightened times, the superstitious fear of God—that fear of God which has no other meaning but the worship of the unknown—not only does not lose ground, but spreads triumphantly. The fact is undeniable. In this respect the change of feeling and of views in the public may well be considered as one of the most remarkable of our time. If we go back sixty years, we find that the dislike for that prejudice that demanded a special and sacred language for divine service was so great that in the Roman

Church the Latin, and in the Protestant Church the obsolete words in the mother-tongue, were gradually supplanted by what was intelligible to all, and expressed the religious wants of the community at large. Now the counter-movement takes place; everywhere we hear of the efforts made to introduce again the old mysterious character into the songs, into the sermons, and into the prayers, to reinstate the old sacred language which seemed before to be doomed to gradual extinction. And in very rare cases only these efforts meet with any vigorous resistance. But can this last change surprise anyone accustomed to watch the inner connection of events and their causes? At the time when the notion of a sacred language specially reserved for divine service met with no approbation, the prejudices founded on pride and the love of power remained in full force; they only changed their outward appearance. These prejudices themselves were not changed by the fact that the old ecclesiastical language had been replaced by the refined language of cultivated society; therefore no change could take place in the effects produced by these prejudices. The old evil which undermined the unity and harmony of human language had gone on as before. The language of men, destined by the will of God to bind the whole race into one large family, had unnaturally and craftily been transformed into an aristocratic and a plebeian language, and become again what it had been before this temporary movement, a tool of discord, hatred, distrust, and fear. As long as the change does not reach the depths of our inner life, as long as the knowledge of self does not take the place of error, there will be no guarantee whatever against the reinstatement of forms of speech which were supposed to have been set aside. As long as the root of the old evil remains, the prejudice itself, the same caprices of fashion which determine the shape and colour of the raiments with which we deck our persons, will determine the forms under which our prejudices alternately change their appearance.

The first illusion which prevents the hallowing of our language in every-day life, is the produce of pride and love of power, which combine together to have a privileged language; the second—self-deception, which renders fruitless the efforts made to sanctify the name of God—is originated by the thoughtlessness which sees a progress in the gloss with which our desecrated language of every day is invested, by giving to it a certain appearance of religion, without changing its old nature and tendencies.

It sometimes happens that two human faces appear at first sight to have a striking likeness to each other; and nevertheless, when we look at them more attentively, we find that, in spite of the similar lines, the eyes and all else in these two faces lead us to conclude that the characters are diametrically opposed to each other. This experience will repeat itself often when we compare the features of social conditions and social changes. Two phenomena of the spirit of the time may at first sight appear to be produced by the same spirit, but, if we look at them more closely, we find ultimately that one of these phenomena is a decided progress and the other a decided step backwards. The progress of the culture such as we conceive the

hallowing of the name of God to be, consists, according
to our view, in recognising that the words and names
which form our language do not represent things without coherence, unity and order, an inconsistent existence forming a contrast to what is divine; but that, on
the contrary, all our words and names are, in truth, so
many expressions of what is in itself good and perfect,
so many names of God, designating beings, forces, and
phenomena of a divine origin. If we now consider the
change which the opinions of the cultivated classes
have undergone in the last few generations, it appears
as if this same progress of culture had been brought
about by the new opinions that have come into honour
and prominence. The old faith in a God who reigns
above the world in solitary height falls into decay;
the divine element seems, according to the newer faith,
to have come down upon earth, to embody itself in the
nature of things that surround us; it seems to live in
flesh and blood, to manifest itself in its thought and
feeling, to awake and become conscious in the reason
of men. The world beyond the grave, to which humanity used to look up with awe, exists no longer;
such imaginations are mocked as the inventions of
superstition of times gone by, and combated as an
error which estranges man from himself. The doctrine
that, beyond what men see in themselves and all
around them, there is no existence, no life, no supreme
power and wisdom—that doctrine is proclaimed as the
last word, the ultimate conclusion of all aspirations to
knowledge. But then, if the work of thought is thus
to be considered as having reached its ultimate conclusion, there is one question which cannot be shirked,

and it is this: What changes in the life and actions of men have occurred in consequence of the awakening of thought and change of opinions which have taken place among them? What guarantee do these changes, this progress in their lives, this improvement in their actions—what guarantee, I ask, do they give us that this new heaven and new earth, praised by the poets, are not a dream which vanishes when we awake, and leaves us nothing behind but disappointment?

Where is the new strength of life, the manifestation of justice, the peace of Heaven, the victory of reason, the creation of liberty, the power of love in which this human incarnation of God shows itself and gives its living proofs? Instead of being able to show the object of our search, those who take the other side of the argument tell us that our question is a new suggestion of the old superstition, that the responsibility of man for his actions is a delusion as well as what has been called evil and sin; that there is no such thing as a difference between what is and what ought to be; that the contradiction between right and power rests on a delusion, and that the love for what is good and the hatred for what is wrong is a mistake, since the divine in man requires both evil and good as conditions of life; that it both wills and practises them equally. This revelation made to us concerning the true sense of this new wisdom, may sound well in the ears of those whose God was nothing but power, whose religion was nothing but fear. We, whose belief in God entirely depends on our belief in love and justice, we can see a progress in culture there only where we find the conviction of the unity of this life and the life to come,

the conviction that every word in human language is a
name of God; and where these convictions both manifest themselves as the expression of a pure heart, of a
free soul, of its courage, of its holy love, of its devotion
to what is good, as its holy hatred for arbitrariness and
wrong. We cannot help turning away in disgust from
the thoughtlessness which would consider as progress
the religious gloss given to the inner life, as well as to
the language of men, by declaring what is evil to be
equal to what is good. Men never are further from
the realisation of their petition that the name of the
Eternal be hallowed, than when, in order to get over
their shame, they pronounce to be divine that which
debases them in their own eyes.

Certain as this is for us in the hour of reflection, as
certain is it, nevertheless, that the false wisdom which
is always ready to make amends for the guilt of men
at the expense of their liberty, has not remained without influence on our volition and our feelings. In our
lives also, although we may be unconscious of it, it is
the habit engendered by pride and thoughtlessness that
has prevented us from hallowing the name of God and
our own language.

What can we do to weaken the influence of the old
habits which we have just mentioned, and to ensure
success to those of our efforts that tend to make our
language an instrument of cognition? The whole
world, the society in which we grow up and live,
favour these old habits, draw us in the same direction,
confine us in the old mould through which we wish to
break, in the fulfilment of our task. The simplest
means would, therefore, be to create a counterpoise to

act against this unintentional oppression of society; we must unite our forces to work in the opposite direction, form an association whose object must be to create a language that will really express our aspirations to the cognition of truth.

Nothing is easier than to bring people together to form an association, whatever its object may be, but nothing is rarer than for such an association to attain the object for the sake of which it has come into existence. Everything depends on the character of the members. I say the character; for it is a matter of course that their talents, gifts, and natural dispositions, necessarily different in all of us, are not to be drawn into consideration in a case like this, where the point at issue is a religious and moral question. That which alone will determine the success of the task they have undertaken is the spirit which animates them, the course upon which their will is bent, the notions of the vocation of men as moral beings dependent thereon, and what they expect, and have a right to expect, from this new association. That is all-important. This society has for its object to bring into recognition the omnipresence of God in nature and in the life of men, and thereby to restore to its full significance the name of God, which has been deprived of its meaning and reduced to an empty sound by a belief in a God dwelling outside the world. But the efforts to rise to this conviction would soon evaporate in vain professions and phrases if the members of this society did not themselves see evidences of the presence of the living God in the lives, of at least a few, of those who share their aspirations, evidences of the working of the divine Power and divine Spirit. What brought our friends to found a new association was this : that the whole world, forgetful of the one eternal object, appeared to pursue only single and isolated objects ; all the pursuits of men bore testimony to that which is accidental and transitory only ; the holy name of God, the name of what is necessary and everlasting, was as the designation of beings and forces whose life and known only action were out of men's reach and beyond the limits prescribed to their activity.* Everywhere around them they saw nothing but a life from which the divine was banished ; the spectacle of a society resigned to the belief in a God unknown and inaccessible; *this*, and this alone, incited them to form this new association. But there is one indispensable condition to the success of their enterprise which the world has forgotten to look for, namely, the features of what is divine in human life. This they must find out, and evidence it in their own being. They must practise their spiritual eye sufficiently to see the divine features, the living likeness of God, in their own community ; and not there alone, but in any society of men. Unless they succeed in gathering, in uniting these features of the godlike into an evidence of an indisputable order, all-powerful, rational, and indestructible, anything they may deem necessary to do besides, to attain their aim, will be vain and fruitless. All speaking, all zeal and eloquence, is useless, if they do not succeed in making a living reality of their faith, of that faith

* These forces and beings out of men's reach and beyond the limits prescribed to their activity, are, no doubt, the angels which were supposed to be the only agents of God's will with whose existence a lazy belief lulled its own conscience.

that God's very life is active in the minds of men. And if not everyone in a community attains at the same time to this degree of religious progress, a few, at least of those who share this conviction, must at all times give the others the evidence of its reality in life.

We therefore again repeat the question : What must be the character of people in order to fulfil this condition, without which they can make no progress in the cognition of truth and sanctification of our language ? Our answer is this : They must recognise as false the imaginary knowledge which in them takes the place of a real knowledge acquired by their own exertions ; they must convince themselves that all other knowledge is a presumption and a proof of their ignorance. In all conversations concerning our moral and spiritual life, this moral and spiritual life is constantly mistaken for that which can be taught, and mixed up with the knowledge according to which we know what others have to do to carry out their intended work or their plans. We certainly have it in our power to know, by means of what we have learned, what others must do either to work out a problem correctly, or to make a garment that will fit, or to build a house; but it is a different thing to judge of the way in which others have to fulfil their duties. In all conversations concerning moral questions the experience is renewed that people think they know how other people ought to live and to act in order to fulfil the law of righteousness according to its nature. Everyone thinks he knows what is amiss with his neighbour, and why he is not, and does not, what he ought to be or to do.

Everybody in every class of society knows this of everybody else in every other class, profession or trade; the husband knows it of his wife, the sister of her brother, the citizen knows it of his neighbour and of his sovereign, the parents know it of their children—yea, this knowing has made such strides, and gained such an extension, that even the children are now convinced that they know in what their parents err. In short, everybody professes to know what is wrong in everybody else. Everybody wants to see *that which does not exist*. See that which does not exist! Who could help seeing the absurdity of it? Well, this vain want of seeing what is not there and can therefore not be seen—that is the false knowledge which embodies itself in our conversation—that is the thing which desecrates the language of men. Can there be anything more fatal to our object than to take with us this false knowledge into the new community, and perhaps to consider this new community as the proper place to bring it into honour, and the proper sphere in which to work with one's whole might, to make it as quickly as possible the perfection of a school for moralising, for blaming and proselytising? Would *that* have required the foundation of a new association? This old vicious habit is practised in every house and in every street, and it certainly therefore does not require our commendation. No, my friends, in order to be fit for this new community, we must, on the contrary, learn to despise this false knowledge. Only when we succeed in forgetting what is wanting in our neighbour, according to our yard-measure, before he can be the perfection of a god to our taste and shape, then only will our eyes be opened to see what in the lives of our brethren is a manifestation of God and of His eternal order. I do not speak here of certain isolated and so-called praiseworthy deeds and charitable works on the part of our neighbours, for there could be no worse exchange if, instead of the old vicious practice of blaming and judging, we introduced the new and vicious practice of flattering one another. No, what I would that we should open our eyes to see is that which, under all circumstances of human life, is and ever remains the unchanging manifestation of the Eternal, and which no doings of men can destroy. I speak of that divine beauty, of that holy order pervading nature and the whole being of man, and which, just because it belongs to God, is indestructible. I speak of the inexhaustible fulness of divine beauty and holy order, never more nor less in degree, though always different in its way of manifesting itself in every human being, according to his peculiarity. In order to be able to take our share in this work—*i.e.*, to contribute to the sanctification of the language—we must recognise that this presumptuous knowledge of other people's duties has darkened in us the conception of the divine prototype, we must feel that the ignorance in which this false knowledge has kept us captive is a deplorable misfortune; we must resolve once for all to part with it. We must study with love those differences which exist between our fellow-creatures and us; we must put our whole devotion, our whole power of self-denial into that search. Unamiable or even repulsive as those differences may appear to us at first, we must not only respect them, but honour them as divine features which, as such, have their right to live, their right to embody themselves in actions; we must honour these distinctive features as much as those which strike us as most dignified and beautiful. Such a way of thinking, such a spirit alone, will justify us in having wished to be members of a community which, with the help and the united forces of many friends bent on the same purpose, has resolved to cultivate and restore to its original aim the human language which has been deteriorated and degraded by being applied to the life of sense chiefly, and desecrated by pious deceit. Animated by such a spirit, such a way of thinking, we may confidently hope that we may succeed in purifying our language, and make it again a means of recognising everywhere the features of the omnipresent One, and thus to reinstate it in its sacred vocation. Amen.

X.

"THY KINGDOM COME."

My friends! Upon the petition for the hallowing of the divine name follows that for the coming of the kingdom of the Eternal. Are we not on the point of doing something very superfluous when we set to work to examine the exact meaning of these words? Can there be any doubt as to the meaning to be attached to the words—The kingdom of God—in the minds of those, at least, who consider the Lord's prayer as a true rendering of the life and consciousness of Jesus? Has He not expressed as clearly and positively as possible all that can be uttered on that subject when He said, "By this shall all men know that ye are my disciples, if ye have love one to another"? And yet it cannot be denied that these plain words have been misunderstood, when we consider how many have thought it necessary to have recourse to fire and sword in order to carry out this new law of love on which He wished to found His community. It would be an unbearable repetition for this audience, at least, to dwell upon such errors. It would indeed; and we will therefore pass on to an important and unavoidable question: On what ground is our conviction founded, when we say that fire and sword are means which love never would choose? We all agree to that, but not on the reason why such means are incompatible with love. Many people will see a contradiction in it; they say that fire and sword give pain, and that love never chooses to give pain. Is it really so? Is it contrary to the character of love to give pain? Is it inadmissible that a person in whom love is active should wound the feelings of those with whom he is bound by the ties of love? If so—if that is incompatible with our views—then our craving for love prepares a pitiable fate for us; for in this case we are seeking something that not only our fellow-creatures cannot grant to us, but something that even God Himself will not grant to us. This something is not to be found; there is no place for it in the order of human life which manifests the holy will of God. Whoever thinks himself convinced that it is contrary to the nature of love to give pain, deceives himself in an unwarrantable manner, if he professes to believe at the same time that God is love. In him, this belief is a blind one, the belief of a man for whom that, on which he has established his confidence, can last only so long as he arbitrarily suppresses the natural instinct of his eyes to see and refuses to see. The moment he opens his eyes, he must recognise that he has believed in a God who does not exist. The moment he is sincere enough with himself to see things as they are, the features of God in whose gracious love he had been sunning and enjoying himself according to his previous notions, will show him nothing but a merciless inflexibility and a heartless cruelty. For who does not feel pain, when he sees his brethren in bitter need, or when death takes away from his side his beloved wife or child? And has he any other answer to the question, Whence comes the failure of crops which makes thousands of people a prey to death—whence the destroying epidemic which has devastated his house?—any other answer than that they come from God? Either God is not love, or it is not incompatible with the character of love to give pain! It appears unavoidable for anyone to say otherwise than that only one of these alternatives is possible; but we know that when the distinction between right and wrong is concerned, there is nothing that can coerce men to see otherwise than they like; we know how inexhaustible are the resources of deceit and cunning in the human mind, if there is any disagreeable truth which we want to disguise from ourselves or from others. And so the large majority of people have, until now, refused to give up the prejudice that it is impossible that love should choose to give pain and affliction. And as long as we start from this prejudice, there is no possibility of recognising what the kingdom of God is. And our prayer that the kingdom of the Eternal may come, necessarily remains unfulfilled. Certainly we should not come any nearer to a right understanding of what is the kingdom of God, if we gave the preference to the contrary opinion, according to which suffering is the infallible sign by which the elect can be recognised. The objects which divine love pursues in its continual process of creation are holy and eternal, and have as little in common with the vicissitudes of good and ill fortune as with the contrast of light and darkness. If we earnestly wish to enable ourselves to recognise what are the fundamental principles of the kingdom of God, it is essential to dismiss from our minds all the changing scenes of joy and sorrow; and in order to avoid everything that could remind us of them, we will choose as a starting-point for this meditation some theme not connected with love, most men being unable to keep the notion of love distinct in their minds from the feeling of weal and woe. We will therefore take as a subject the first strophe of the hymn beginning with the words:

'In His kingdom all is right and all is equal.'

1st. Let then *equality* be the first fundamental principle of the kingdom of God of which we speak. The position of anyone who announces this fundamental law is, in relation to the world, a very different one from that of Jesus of Nazareth, who first proclaimed it. Even the few men who lived close around Him found it difficult to rise to the height necessary for faith in this joyful announcement. On the contrary, anyone who now proclaims this law of equality, is sure that his words will find an echo in the hearts of millions of men. He is sure, if circumstances present no obstacles, that the mass of the people will receive his words with loud acclamations. The first duty incumbent upon a disciple of Jesus who now wishes to proclaim the equality in the kingdom of God, is to protest against these acclamations; for what he aims at has nothing in common with that which the great crowd seek under this name except the name itself; let us, before all things, accomplish this duty which sincerity enjoins upon us.

The equality that enjoys the favour of the spirit of our time takes nothing into consideration but the outer side of human life, namely the circumstances that constitute our fate. The whole world now is interested in the claims which human beings have upon the advantages that life can give, considering all as having equal rights on them. The conclusion drawn from these rights is the necessity of an equal division of property, the only thing which can satisfy the man whose spirit knows nothing beyond what belongs to the world of sense. The equality of right claimed in this sense has no other object than to serve as a guarantee for the equalisation of the rights of all. But as experience has proved that these rights do not belong to the living rights which maintain themselves, a necessity has made itself felt to have recourse to laws and institutions which must be enforced by material power. This means of enforcement is the corner-stone in the edifice of the equality which our age erects with its fancies and theories, and which never will exist anywhere except in the imagination of men. We all know that in the large deserts of Africa there are airy pictures which bring, as if by magic, flourishing landscapes and magnificent towns before the eyes of the exhausted and thirsty wanderer; the brains of men create similar magic pictures, when their lives have been transformed into deserts by self-love and thoughtlessness. It is the fundamental law of human life itself which is opposed to the realisation of this vision of equality. Human life is no clockwork, the mainspring of which can be wound up from outside by a mere pressure, in order to bring the desired phenomena to pass upon the face of it. No! it is life itself, a creation, the changes of which have a reality only as far as they proceed from the inner forces that scorn coercion. The advocates of the equality which is founded upon the outside of human existence are often reproached with the fact that their desire for equality has no other root than a wicked covetousness. This accusation is unfounded, and shows the prejudiced judgment peculiar to lovelessness. This sensuous belief in equality really only arises when hunger and misery of all kinds are coupled with the oldest and most widely-spread error concerning the vocation of humanity. Although most of the advocates of the belief in equality boast that they have freed themselves from all the old religious prejudices, they are the very people who have unconsciously brought again into honour and rendered most influential one of the worst tenets of superstition; for the idea from which they all start, the notion of the supposed claims upon certain advantages of life which men, they say, ought to have, is evidently nothing else than the thought underlying the old Mosaic tradition, but in a new dress. It seeks the proof of the divine origin of man in the dominion of man over nature with which he is supposed to be endowed; and thus misuses the feelings of Religion herself to direct the attention and aspirations of men to the changing phases of fate, and limit them to the narrow sphere of the life of sense.

The faith in equality which forms one of the fundamental laws of the kingdom of God, keeps itself free from this spiritual narrowness; it does not limit itself to the sensations of life experienced by the hungry man, or by him who is satiated with the pleasures of life. This faith takes no more notice of the complaints of those unfortunate people who nowhere find their love returned, or think that it is not deservedly returned, than of the delight of those who find themselves loved just as they wish to be, with tender or passionate love, or who think that they are so loved. That feeling, and all feelings of that kind which change with the hours either in character or intensity or otherwise, lie, perhaps, not beyond the horizon of the faith in the equality of the kingdom of God, but they certainly lie on the very outside circle of it. That which remains the same in life, which is to-day as it was yesterday, and which will be in the most distant future as it was from the beginning, that forms the centre of the picture in the contemplation of which this faith in equality concentrates itself. He

who has found in himself that eternal equality, will
surely find it in all those whom he meets in life. Now,
then, what is it that we find in the conscious human
life to be the same yesterday, to-day, and to all eternity? First of all, it is the creative power, which in
the midst of all that exists, forms, by means of the
distinction between right and wrong, a new world
absolutely its own. We all proceed in our own manner
in this modelling of our own lives, the youth differently from the old man, woman otherwise than man, the
servant differently from the free man. The worshipper
of Buddha in China, the Christian in our part of the
world, each has his peculiar method ; he who entangles
himself in the nets of error, not acting according to his
true nature, in his way of dealing with what is right
or wrong, proceeds differently from him who, following his nature, adds a new stone to the edifice of truth
every time he chooses the one and rejects the other.
But this creative power itself, through which it is
given to men to have life in themselves, and which
makes them fellow-workers with the Creator of the
worlds, is the same power in all of us, and in everyone
the same at all times. It is ever present in all our
actions ; it is the soul of all our deeds ; it is this power
which stamps its peculiar character upon our action,
whatever it may be, working, eating, playing, praying,
hating, or loving.

Besides this creative power there is one side more
on the contemplation of which the faith in equality
has to dwell. It is the arena and the materials which
have been given to our volition, that it may embody
itself in deeds—all these given circumstances taken

together called fate, not those feelings of which we have been speaking, and which men give as companions to their respective fates. But here, where can any harmony, any equality be found? What is alike in the varied fate of different men? This will be the first question that we shall be asked to answer. Is it not just in these unaccountable destinies of human fate, cast hither and thither by an inexhaustible capricious chance, subject to no law, that it is least possible to detect even a trace of equality? Truly, the first impressions we receive from these ever-changing phenomena of human existence are an uninterrupted succession of changes and differences that never repeat themselves, and that present to our astonished gaze an overwhelming variety. And with what pleasure do not just the most thoughtful of men dwell upon this picture of human life, upon this only perfect poem, upon this only divine comedy, in which the fancy of the Eternal Himself allows us to wander through heaven, earth, and hell? But man does not live upon fancy alone; and to be just to human nature we must not overlook the fact that in one respect the very outside, the drapery of our lives that binds together this apparently incoherent motley crowd of impressions, is marked by a character of rigorous equality. Often as the well-known adage, that there is nothing new under the sun, may have been a sign of the morbidness, of the satiety of life, we must nevertheless acknowledge that these words convey at the same time one of the deepest observations founded upon the most mature experience of sound human reason. Whatever circumstance we may take out of the long chain of events that form the fate of our inner or outer life, be it the loss of a friend, or the gain of a first prize in a lottery; be it the applause we have obtained without deserving it, or the blame that comes with as little justice; be it our musical talent, our good memory, our lively disposition, or the absence of any of these advantages, and the contrary mixture of the vital elements in us, in *one* respect they are all alike. As certain as it is that under all circumstances and everywhere, twice two are four, so certain is it that the same relation, without any exception, exists between these circumstances of our fate and our determining will. This ever-recurring relation consists in this, that all turns of fate are without exception of such a nature that we can, by an act of volition, use every one of them to any given purpose that we choose, and that we can, by our attitude, make every one of them an expression of our true distinction of right and wrong, or an expression of self-deceit and guilt. In this respect all gifts which are cast in our lot, every call upon our self-denial, and all our experience, partake of that property; they all equally prove men to be the masters of their own fate.

The consciousness that there is an indestructible power inherent in our nature to use fate and whatever it may bring as we choose, is itself a creative power. To see, to love, and to honour this glorious power of the Spirit in others as we do in ourselves, that is the homage we pay to the Eternal manifesting Himself in man. Not before we fully recognise that this power of manifesting the divine Spirit is given to every human being (however he may use or abuse it) in his self-determining will, in his power of self-government—not before we acknowledge that this divine power constitutes our humanity, can we recognise equality as one of the fundamental principles of the kingdom of God. The more purity and strength this consciousness of innate divine power over fate and of its equal diffusion among men acquires in us, the more fully will our prayer for the coming of God's kingdom be realised.

2nd. In Thy great kingdom all is equal and all is right. *Equality* is the first fundamental law of God's kingdom. Righteousness, or rather *justice*, is the second.*

---

* Justice is more comprehensive than righteousness, which refers rather to the outward conduct of man as a sign of the existence of justice in him. Justice is the state of the mind which has made its own all that is just before God, or rather *in* God ; in other words, it is the purely divine life freely flowing into man through the closest communion between God and man—that state of purity in man's life which allows him the clear vision of God's will. Man will be righteous rather than just, as long as his affections are still divided, adhering to God to a certain degree because he knows that in God dwells his true nature, but still clinging to what is earthly as if there could be an opposition between that inner and outer life which, in the order intended, are but soul and body to each other. The man who overlooks this unity and perfect balance between inner and outer life, unconsciously creates an artificial opposition in his own heart ; and thus, by making two of himself, he may present to men and to himself the aspect of that righteousness which may scrupulously avoid wrong-doing, and even do a good deal that is praiseworthy and useful, while the dualism in which he lives considerably curtails his true life. The action and exertions, which require his whole energy, being twofold, and tending at once in two directions, are so neutralised that this righteous man becomes almost a nullity, and would seem to justify the accusations of those who prefer a man entirely given to the world, to the man who is always in barley with the world on one side and with his conscience on the other, and thus brings nothing to completion. Justice

Also in the exposition of these words we must begin by rejecting the meaning generally attached to them. How firmly established and how widely spread would be the reign of justice on earth if all who profess to act in its name did really work for it! But many of those who most frequently have this word on their lips are the very people who oppose the greatest obstacles to the recognition of justice in human life and human institutions. We do not mean only those people who, in their own personal interest, attempt to pervert moral feeling, but also those according to whose opinion justice should consist in granting rewards and in inflicting punishments. Men always play a poor part when they presume to support, by their plans and arrangements, the living and almighty law of equilibrium which is destined to keep the balance between cause and effect, and to maintain the unvarying homogeneousness of seed and fruit. "To everyone his own!" are grand words. But to bring this law really into effect, so that it never may favour one at the expense of another, requires the never-erring impartiality, the perfect self-forgetfulness, peculiar to Nature in her whole activity. Human

---

makes him a complete man, working for that which henceforth possesses his whole mind. All narrowness of judgment proceeds from such a divided state of mind and affections, which are nevertheless perfectly compatible with a generally righteous life, as far as may appear to outsiders, but which never can give a man the feeling of a perfect union with God. Hence the opinion generally entertained of man's weakness and fallen state, of his incapacity of ever knowing God. Justice, on the contrary, possesses that roundness which, similar to our planet, comes under the light of the sun on every one of its meridians, and ripens its fruits fully in its proper time, and being what it is wholly in the full light and radiance of the sun.

dealing absolutely lacks this character, not only when man presumes to reward and to punish, but also when he thinks himself called upon to interfere with or care for the proper division of property; as if nature could not accomplish this work without the help of human wisdom. Man, no doubt, helps also in this respect to the realisation of the thoughts regulating the eternal order, but without ever knowing how and by what means he does so. As soon as he acts upon the considerations which prompt his conscious action upon the outer world, he inevitably fails to attain the aims of nature. When we presume to set up the standard of what is to be the share of property of every individual, the usual way of proceeding is this. Although, thanks to God, there are times in everyone's life when, without being a child or a thief, the distinction between mine and thine slips from our consciousness, yet when these exceptional moments are over, we begin again to judge of the individuals and their relation according to this distinction of what belongs to one and what belongs to others; then I, the umpire, never lose sight of what is to be mine. I set to work to divide among the others what is left, after having reserved, as we just mentioned, what is to be mine. We all know the result most easily and usually brought about for everybody by the dealing of men under such circumstances: anxiety and distrust, hatred and discord, lawsuits for individuals, and wars for nations. On this road, no justice is to be found.

In order to find out what is the justice of the kingdom of God, let us go back to the words by which Jesus opened a road to the ambition of some of His disciples, a road on which everyone can attain to the highest honours without molesting any of his neighbours: "Whoso is greatest among you, let him be as he that doth serve;" he who will serve all, that is the common weal, the general interests of human society, he is the greatest in the kingdom of heaven. Such justice is founded upon the law of reciprocity in nature, by which all individuals are connected together like the members of *one* body, by which the natural gifts and talents of every individual are calculated for the benefit and welfare of all. If our mind's eyes are still as little practised to see of themselves, as were those of the apostles who were too prejudiced to be able to see more than the one side of things, and consequently the other side always remains hidden to us, we may nevertheless make a beginning with this law of reciprocity. Did not the very people, before whose spiritual narrowness the harmony of creation seemed destroyed by the contrast between what is great and what is small, between strength and weakness, power and impotency—did not these same people, notwithstanding their narrow-mindedness, incited by the feeling of truth that never can be destroyed, and that so often works in us without our being conscious of it, did they not create the word magnanimity? Let us follow this impulse of our hearts which makes us stand still before the mighty tree that does not deem itself too lofty to serve as a prop to the ivy that clings to it. Let us follow this impulse of our hearts as did those rude ages that, endowed with strength, could conceive nothing else than the use of the fist and the sword; in which the knight in his steel armour, the perfect picture of middle-age feeling, was nevertheless clearly conscious that the vocation of the strong is the protection of the weak, and who, when taking his place among his compeers, made a special vow that he would always be the protector of widows and orphans and oppressed innocence at all times and in all places. The more readily we follow this impulse of our heart, the sooner we shall see that the power to help is not given to one in virtue of his birth and the favour of circumstances and refused to another by fate; that nature, as far as the help which one can give to another, knows nothing of the division of men into strong and weak, but that everyone, as he may be looked at, is now weak and now strong; that the same person who can help in one way, needs help himself in some other way; and that the law of reciprocity, of giving and receiving, is, in the sphere of our humanity, omnipresent. To recognise this reciprocity of giving and receiving; to recognise that he also who commands can give no more than he receives from those who carry out his orders, that the tutor himself can give no more than he receives from the child—to recognise this all is to recognise the law of justice of the kingdom of God. That this holy law of justice should appear so strange to many is easily accounted for; for indeed, according to this law itself, everyone will be conscious of what he receives, and will be able to avail himself of what he has received, in proportion as he himself fulfils the task this imposes upon him; *i.e.*, in proportion as he is able himself to serve and to give. And how small is still the number of those friends and disciples of the art of giving simply and genuinely and of serving freely! With the superficial reigning notion according to which giving can always be brought back to pounds and shillings, it is impossible to understand anything concerning the reciprocity of giving and taking. Arithmetic is of no avail for this knowledge, in which what is all-important cannot be paid. Altogether there is no question here of the single gifts for which accidental circumstances give occasion. If an employer chooses to raise the wages of his workmen, we will not think little of it, even if he does not do it entirely of his own accord, and is driven to it by the force of circumstances; every contribution to the alleviation of misery has its value, even if it have been obtained by the attractions of a concert or a bazaar. These things have their value, but they are not the characteristic signs of that goodwill to give, of that art of giving in which the justice of the kingdom of God consists; else we should be obliged always to investigate beforehand whether he whom we wish to remind of this justice has enough to practise it. The justice of the kingdom of God has no appreciation whatever of the value of anything which, like money or money's worth, or special faculties, rises and falls according to the pressure or laxity of demand for it; justice refers to that alone, the worth of which depends on no change, small or great, in the demand; on the contrary, justice fixes the real worth of all individual manifestations of life according to their relation to what a man has made of himself by his distinction between right and wrong. In proportion to the work which a human being accomplishes in himself, is he faithful and trustworthy, free from the prejudices of his class and of public opinion, proof against the temptations of vanity, proof against the snares of happy or troubled days, spirited and full of a joyful courage in all enterprises for any good cause, convinced that even the worst society cannot prevent him from working for the cognition and spread of truth, indefatigable in detecting evil, however it may disguise itself, and inexhaustible in his power of turning evil to good? This is man's godly character; and in manifesting this, his godly essence, in everything which he undertakes, in every work, in his intercourse with others, in his way of thinking, in his aspirations and feelings, he yields and gives that of which we are all equally in need. This sincere, faithful character, this spirit of freedom and security, this indomitable courage, is the only true service that an individual man can render to the interests of human society. To strive to have that to give, that is fulfilling the law of reciprocity; he alone who is just in this sense, is able to help his brethren indeed.

According to the law of equality, everyone is provided with the same power of self-government; the fate of everyone is so ordered that this self-governing will can maintain and prove its existence: *according to the law of justice*, between giving and receiving there is a perfect reciprocity and balance. The more purity and dignity there is in that which alone we may in truth call our own, and can therefore give, namely the life of our spirit, the more we receive of the gifts of eternal life, the more we grow in the knowledge of God, and the richer we grow in His peace. To him who has, more is given, until he has plenty. The

Church of the present is in need of a reform that may secure the liberty of teaching. Let us strengthen ourselves in the cognition of the kingdom of God which leads men back to their own inner life, that we may join our efforts to those of others in order to accomplish this great object. But let us beware lest these efforts themselves, and the foundation of the independent community which has brought us together in order to gain a common and free arena for the cognition of truth, lead us also into the temptation to forget the inner life whilst we try to secure its outward liberty and growth. The outward changes in ecclesiastical matters to which we have contributed, have taken place from a wish to part with an ecclesiastical association in which we were not allowed to order and govern our own spiritual concerns ourselves; as well as from a real want to further our aspirations to the cognition of truth by the connected action of those who think and feel as we do. But well founded therefore as is our enterprise, it will bear its desired fruits only if our efforts are directed with more and more determination towards the fulfilment of these laws of equality and justice which constitute the kingdom of God. The mere instinct to bring about and organise a new state of things, and the words, gestures, and movements of all kinds coinciding with that instinct, are of very little or no use to the spread of the kingdom of God on earth. Notwithstanding the greatest efforts, no one can give a thing that he has not—*i.e.*, in this case, what does not live in him first; but what lives in him cannot remain hidden. Let this be the only object after which we strive, that there be light in us, enlightening us on those things concerning which we are still in darkness, and that what is dead in us, at last may break forth into life. Amen.

XI.

"THY WILL BE DONE ON EARTH, AS IT IS IN HEAVEN."

The beginning of the Lord's Prayer helps us to answer the question: What is truth? The sanctification of God's name considered as the cognition and emancipation of self, and the efforts to realise the kingdom of God considered as the fulfilment of the law of equality and justice are to us the essence of truth. The next words in the prayer of our Master are, "Thy will be done on earth, as it is in heaven." These words take us into quite a different field of reflection from the first part of the prayer which has hitherto engaged our attention. After having answered the question what the will of God is, our thoughts are led to the other question where this will of God is done. We are called upon to realise in our minds where is the sphere in which truth is manifested and carried into effect, which is, if we may use the expression, truth's place of action.

We may consider this question as a test to which is submitted the knowledge we have gained of the essence of truth. The words and thoughts by means of which people are wont to come to an understanding with each other on the essence of truth, easily obtain acknowledgment; but this acknowledgment is by no means a sure proof of a perfect understanding. Justice, love, and liberty, order and peace, in which the essence of truth is generally sought, are words which in themselves appear clear enough; but if we go into the details, and the where? and when? and how? are taken into consideration, the result soon proves that the agreement of those who thought they understood each other thoroughly was delusive. So it was with the disciples, when they thought that they understood, in the same sense as Jesus, the idea of the kingdom of God to which their Master so often came back, when he conversed with them on the meaning of truth, until this question, on the last day they spent with Him, concerning the realisation of it, showed them how very deeply their notions differed from His on that point. When will these things happen? *i.e.*, when would He establish His kingdom; when will justice, the laws of which Thou preachest, be realised and become a power, and influence the forms of public life? This question proves that they had supposed this change in the history of the world which they looked for with impatient expectations to be fixed for a certain time; that the year, even the day, could be determined. And no doubt it took them by surprise when Jesus told them that He did not know it, and that no one could foretell in what spot, nor at what time, the outward reform of society would begin. When He justified His answer, reminding them of the real character of truth and of the community founded upon it, and pointing to the absolute line that separates the creation of liberty * from that of necessity, and showed them how eclipses of the sun and moon could be foreseen and calculated, and how many things that must be accomplished by the doing of men could be considered as certain as if they were written in the stars, and how nevertheless the most accurate knowledge of the laws of nature at work in men and out of them, never could contribute in the least to such changes as must be brought about by this self-determining will, by this will in men which is entirely independent of the sequence of causes and effects, then the disciples must have convinced themselves that not only Jesus did not think as they did as to the time and place of the kingdom of God, but also that their notions of truth required a rectification.

The same thing repeats itself everywhere. Clearly and steadfastly as we may think we have seen that the essence of truth does not consist in mysteries and miracles, but in liberty and justice, in order and peace; deeply satisfied as we may feel with this doctrine, however we may be spurred by it to new aspirations, the old superstition from which we strive to free ourselves may nevertheless be harboured in us under these words and ideas. The next step which we must take

---

* The author calls the creation of freedom the state of things which arises around us in consequence of our inner life. The meaning which we give to everything which happens in our life, the bent we impose on our will and its determinations, necessarily give a character to them, and greatly influence the combination of things that come independently of us and those determined by the Spirit in which we live. The accidental will always fall under the influence of a will trained by the habit of looking up to God, and determined to make the best of the gifts of fate, be they pleasant or unpleasant.

to protect ourselves against this delusion, is to examine whether we, who think that we agree about what truth is in itself, can agree also about the time and place of its manifestation and realisation. If we do not agree on this last point, our agreement on the first is an illusion and nothing else; in this case, some among us must be guilty of confusing liberty and necessity in this way of viewing the essence of truth, and the rectification of this conception is absolutely necessary, if our efforts to recognise truth are to lead us to the desired results. This retrospective glance at the issues of our former meditations will be easier for the frequent hints given in them, concerning the way in which I think the petition, that the will of God should be done on earth, is to be understood.

First.—We will begin by examining what relative position the reigning opinions assume in respect to the spirit and the realisation of this prayer. Of all notions which men connect with the name of God, the most ancient and the most general is that of a higher power. As soon as men convinced themselves that the intentions attributed to their gods were not realised, the faith in these gods fell into discredit; the government which now dropped from their hands was henceforth attributed to a fate that stood above these gods. When men rose to the belief in the one God, the highest power was attributed to Him: He spake, they said, and it was done; He commanded, and it stood fast. When at last it was understood that the will of God could aim at nothing *less* than truth and justice, therewith came the conviction that within the pale of creation there was a kingdom in which nothing happens that does not bear clear testimony to the reign of justice and truth, i.e., a community of beings who were subject to these laws not by the iron necessity of fate, but in virtue of willing obedience. And accepting the religious traditions of pre-Christian times, which ascribed to God the heavens as His dwelling-place, this realm of goodness was supposed to be the community of the heavenly hosts, a community of spirits who shared with God the heavenly mansions. As to the relative position of the earth and of the human race, the views were taken from experience. Even the prophets, who were charged with the messages of heaven, spoke according to experience, which teaches that the will of God was not done by men. But far from entertaining the idea that it was not possible that the will of God should be done on earth, they considered the reign of evil as a falling away of men from God, they held men responsible for it, and upon their denunciations followed promises of blessings, prompted by the hope of men's return to their allegiance to God.

Thus they always started from the opinion that the will of God could be done on earth as it is in heaven. It was not until men had become accustomed, under the influence of ecclesiastical teaching, to consider their race as excluded from communion with God by an inimical power, and to consider Catholic Churchdom as the only means of reunion with God, that, with the declining faith in this Church, sprang up and grew the now generally reigning view of the relation between man and God. The powerlessness of the Church has been since the time of the Reformation a fact not to be doubted; the hope of the realisation of the kingdom of God in the Church which had been considered as the only possible one, proved a fallacy; all that outlived the faith in the Church were a few of the doctrines, amongst others that concerning the exclusion from the communion of God to which men were condemned by their birth. Special expressions in which the fall of men and original sin were clothed, indeed, were objected to, but only the expressions; the idea itself remained. And in the new garb in which it was dressed, it was so difficult to recognise it, that the most violent opponents of the ecclesiastical faith proclaimed it as theirs, without in the least suspecting that their ideas of human narrowness and imperfection were nothing else than a legacy of the superstition they had so much hated, and that by spreading this idea, they only confirmed this antagonistic influence. The prejudice of the *necessity* of the imperfection of human nature has become the fundamental view to which most thinkers always come back, on their various paths of thought, although starting from the most opposite points of view. It is now the only article of faith on which even those join hands who, with regard to all other opinions, consider each other as irreconcilable adversaries, the only article of faith on which the man of the world, the religious dreamer, the rationalist and the pietist, completely agree. Let us now ask those who do not entirely give up a religious tendency of feeling, what notion they can entertain of these words of our prayer, that the will of God may be done on earth as it is in heaven, in conjunction with the view of life that we have just been stating. Heaven is for them the image of the divine presence, a manifestation of divine perfection which nothing can disturb; the earth, man's habitation, is not a place in this heaven, but one outside it; it is destined by fate to be, and to remain, an image of imperfection. If they think that they can, with their notions at least, reach beyond reality and trace a true picture of what is good, they must add that this conception of good is superhuman (*i.e.* if they do not play with words), that it is in contradiction to the nature of men, and that at the utmost it could only by a miracle be clothed with a human form; that the nature of man in itself is of necessity bound to error and evil. The prayer, which forms the subject of our discourse, springs from the belief in the reconciliation between Heaven and Earth. They, on the contrary, are convinced that this reconciliation is impossible. If they nevertheless join in these words, and try to blend them with the life of thought inseparable from their conviction, they will not escape the dangerous deception which attempts to conceal the discord of the soul with itself under unctuous words and gestures. Whilst their lips speak, "Thy will be done on earth as it is in heaven," an inner voice speaks in them: " It cannot be." And even when their soul, in a vague remembrance of her relationship with the spirit of faith and love which breathes in these words, rouses itself and attempts to follow it, the hope to which the soul clings is nothing for them but a passing shadow; and the thought of the separation between God and what is earthly, into which it sinks again, will only be the more grievous and confusing. Whatever men may do to take from this feeling of exile and misery its bitterest pang—by the consideration that there are different degrees of imperfection, that it is granted to them to tear themselves away from this abyss of evil, and to approach goodness and perfection more and more, and that the earth may at least be considered as a preparatory stage for heaven—it nevertheless remains true, that even that which is least imperfect is entirely out of the domain of perfection, and that if man is walled in within the limits of imperfection through fate, it is after all as impossible to him so to fulfil the will of God on earth, as it is the privilege of the inhabitants of heaven to do.

Secondly.—We have repeatedly pointed out as a prejudice the notion that human nature is of necessity imperfect. We shall be asked what gives us a right to do so. The refutation of this opinion demanded of us only requires a recollection of the unmistakable differences which exist between things. If the prejudice were as easily given up as refuted, people would soon be set right. What is the kind of perfection and imperfection of which there can be any question when the fulfilment of the will of God is concerned? Does the will of God require proofs of greater strength than that which the muscles of men are able to produce, according to their respective conditions? Does the will of God require that we should deny our feelings, that we should laugh over the death of our friends, and cry when love and confidence are shown to us? Does the will of God require knowledge and science beyond the limits of our present horizon? Does the will of God require the youth to view life as does an old man? In one word, the will of God requires of no one that he should become something different from what it is his nature to be; every man in a sound state of mind will see that. The will of God appeals to the will of man alone, and requires him to determine upon that which man himself considers to be right; and that of the two courses which are, on all occasions, at all times open before his mind's eye, he never should enter upon the evil one. That perfection which God demands of us consists in our obeying our conscience. Imperfection consists in contemptuously rejecting its advice. Wherever there is a living will to determine what is good or evil, God never exacts more or less than that it should decide according to its nature. Now are there any special places or times favourable or unfavourable to this determining will, and which render its work hard or easy? Is day-light necessary to pass a just judgment on our neighbour? or does the night save us from evil thoughts? Is it more difficult at the point where the earth is more distant from the sun to follow the law of justice? or is the will of man more disposed to piety when the earth, in its course, has taken him to the point nearest to the sun? No one will think of answering these questions in the affirmative; and everyone knows that neither time, nor place, nor the changes which the laws of time and space prescribe to our flesh and blood, to our imagination and to our feelings, can make the will of man just or unjust. We all know that the will which chooses between good and evil never can be influenced in its decisions by a difference of size or weight in the body in which it dwells. And we all are aware that the two parts which constitute the human being, on one side the determining will and on the other the body and soul, each have their special laws to govern them and keep them distinct from each other. Of which of these two parts of the human being do we now speak, when the difference between earth and heaven is taken into consideration so far as man is concerned? Death has been represented to us as the boundary between heaven and earth. Death is a change which takes place in our body, and is never brought about by anything but by the action of the laws of matter, be it an illness, a knife, or a bullet that brings it. The effects necessarily are of the same character as the causes. Some find the earth too narrow a sphere for their speculations, and cannot prevent their thoughts from wandering from earth to heaven in search of answers to their questions concerning the changes that take place in us after death. If they must do so, let them at least, in the middle of their speculations and day-dreams, not lose sight of the fact that the effects of death, the changes which it brings, can never overstep the limits prescribed to the world of sense, organised according to the laws of space and time. As it is, the effects necessarily are of the same character as their causes. Death and the change consequent thereon cannot fill an unloving soul with the love of God, any more than it can deter anyone from this love for the eternal. You may picture heaven to yourselves as you like, but neither heaven nor earth can endow the will with a perfection which the will does not acquire by an act of its own volition. Remember that this contrast between heaven and earth never can give to man that which the will of

God requires of him; remember that this contrast cannot by any means touch in any way the character of the will which befits it to satisfy these demands on men. The will of God can be done on earth as perfectly as it is in heaven. As far as the fulfilment of the will of God is concerned, there is no difference between heaven and earth. There is no more compulsion in the fulfilment of the will of God in heaven than there is on earth.

Thirdly.—But simple as are the arguments by which we may convince ourselves that the perfection which God requires of men lies outside the sphere of phenomena which men call heaven and earth, most men are nevertheless incapable of securing this conviction, and making it a part of their spiritual life. Why is it that most men always forget again the limit that reason and experience draw between freedom and necessity, and always relapse into the prejudice which supposes the will of God to be fulfilled in heaven more easily than on earth? The reason of this fact is that men never can come to a rectification of their moral and religious notions by arguments that captivate their reason; that they require for that purpose the testimony of their own lives and their own actions. As long as a man acts wrongly, and denies justice,* as long as his will is not steadfastly directed towards goodness, so long must he look for goodness, which he does not perceive in himself, at a distance, out of his reach. The vault of heaven is, for him, the most telling

* It is to be remembered here what has been said of justice in a previous discourse, and that the mathematical justice current in the world finds no application here.

image of such an unattainable distance; and being forced by his conscience to refer to himself that goodness which his guilt distances from him more and more, he transforms heaven, the picture of local distance, into a futurity which certainly means his own future, but which, as long as he lives on earth, remains to him an unknown future. However obstinately man may reject the advice of conscience, however far he may carry the abuse of freedom, in his conscious acts, the gift of self-government in him is indestructible; and even when man consciously and purposely breaks its law, he will unconsciously and unintentionally give the evidences that self-government in him cannot be set aside. For the wicked man, the distinction of right and wrong is an inexhaustible source of disquietude, of cares, fears and anxieties; he cannot, even by the inveterate habit of doing wrong, get rid of this distinction. Nothing is more disagreeable to him than the thought of the limits in which his arbitrariness is circumscribed, and he cannot forget that there is a higher power against which his efforts are vain; that there is a God who is against him, and who carries out his own will. The belief in the power and reality of goodness is a burden to him, and he cannot flee from it. In this case the only difference between the good and the wicked consists in this, that the wicked sees everywhere, except in himself, the power of a God as a distinct power outside himself, as the power of a positive and individual will that he recognises most distinctly in the things farthest from him, in the heavenly bodies, in historical records of the fate of nations; whilst the good, on the contrary, chooses as his starting-point for the cognition of this divine power his own feeling and perception of it, the point where alone faith becomes vision, where guessing and surmising can become an irrefutable experience, namely, his own self, his own self-determining will, which manifests its divine power by embodying the law of justice in the creations of his inner life, a world that has its origin and its being in his own mind, a creation in which reigns the same unity, harmony and order as in the world that surrounds him.

The same peculiarity characterises the spiritual and physical vision. The eye of the body only needs to open itself in order to perceive the infinitude of forms which are displayed before its sight in earth and heaven. But to see one's self requires a looking-glass; and many a mirror yields to the vision only the most strange distortions of the object it reflects. In the same way, the eye of reason recognises the presence of a higher power and eternal order in all the phenomena of nature, as well as in the casual events of human life subjected to the same laws; but the eye of reason must also gaze into a looking-glass in order to see itself; and the mirror given to it for this purpose is the invisible world of self-government. Our judgment of the nature of men depends on the picture that meets our gaze in that mirror. If a man finds here contradictions, disorder, discord, he is led by this distorted picture to the fallacious idea that the nature of man is incapable of presenting a correct manifestation of unmixed good; and as long as he continues to distort his nature by the misuse of his freedom, so long will he, in spite of all counter arguments that his reason may put forth, fall agein and again into the fallacy of the unavoidable imperfection of the life on earth, and expect from the life in heaven a perfection for which there is no yesterday nor to-morrow, no difference of times. Only those, who have found the reflection of the love of truth and faithfulness in its service in the mirror of their inner life, will carry away with them the conviction that this God who gives the power to will, will not refuse the power to do, and they will therefore ever be filled again with confidence, when they say in their prayers, "as Thy will is done in heaven, Father, may it be done on earth."

Now, before we conclude, let us dwell for a few moments on a parallel which we cannot help drawing between two different points of view. Take, on the one hand, this notion, as erroneous in itself as it is widespread, that earthly life is necessarily imperfect. Take, on the other hand, the conviction, or rather cognition, so vivid in Jesus, that the self-determining will in man is able to accomplish with equal perfection the holy law of justice in any part of the endless space, and in any point of everlasting time. Compare the results following on each of these two views. According to the first, earth is not the proper arena for the realisation of divine will; and life on earth, compared with life in heaven, can only be considered as an outer court from which the gates of death lead into the sanctuary of truth; this world of ours can only be considered as a preparatory institution in which our love and seeking for truth must needs have error for its inseparable companion; and, again, in this poor world, a love free from all selfishness is impossible.

If so, heaven must be considered as the only part of creation on the inhabitants of which the goodness of the Eternal can shower the whole store of its blessings.

What, then, I ask, must be the feelings with which those who hold this view consider the time of their earthly pilgrimage and the future which death opens for them? Their predominant mood ought to be the longing for heaven, and they would consider every shortening of their sojourn in the place of privation as a boon, and every prolongation of their present life as a chastisement; death would be their best friend. Nor is it quite rare to hear words fall from their lips pointing to such feelings. But if we consider their lives as a whole, their wishes and their efforts and their consequent activity, we find all round the very opposite of that which we were led to expect. What they call preparations for heaven have to yield precedence to a thousand more important affairs; whenever death may announce itself, it always comes too soon for them; and the severance from this imperfect earthly life is so hard that nothing is left undone that can put off the dreaded hour as long as possible. Palpable as is the contradiction with themselves, it is unavoidable for all who have fallen into the error of the imperfection of earthly life. The mind of man is always directed to something whole in itself, his soul is attached by nature to whatever proves to be a living present and reality; nothing has a charm for him which he knows or thinks that he cannot do thoroughly. If he once gets accustomed to the notion that goodness belongs to the category of things which admit only of half-and-half doings, his joy in goodness and the power of doing it is soon stricken with palsy. Is goodness too good for life on earth—then he can, according to the laws of his nature, only feel a hypocritical reverence for it; he cannot satisfy the longings of his heart, and so he turns his love to those good things the comfort of which does not refer him to a life beyond the grave. Under whatever form evil may approach him, be it gold, honour, or pleasure of the senses, he is ready to serve any one of those idols, if he only knows, or only thinks he is sure, that the advantages they promise are fruits ripening in the present world.

The lame effects produced by the fatalistic notion of the imperfection of men, in the development of the individual, is reproduced in public life. If we try to trace back the origin and cause of the awful power in the service of the material interests of our time, we shall find that the change in public opinion, which betokened the advent of this power, took place at the very time in which the most popular writers promulgated the doctrine that a life really responding to the holy call of duty was too much to ask from the weak nature of men.

When will the time come when men will begin to feel ashamed of their indolence and return to the conviction which incited Jesus to pray thus: "Father, Thy will be done on earth as it is in heaven." His faith was this: God is a spirit; He therefore is not only not nearer the temple in Jerusalem than any other spot on earth, but quite as present on earth as on any other place of infinite space. His presence manifests itself everywhere equally, in the eternal laws of the universe, which are the same in the drop of water and in the ocean, in the crystal and in the eye, in the grain of sand and in the light of the sun. What can the words better and worse, in which the changing feelings of the hour seek an expression, have to do with these eternal laws? And wherever there are beings to whom the Eternal speaks: "Ye are to be holy as I am holy," there is at work in all of them the same freedom with its possibility of error and the necessary self-condemnation of error. And what can signify the words strong and weak, which serve as an epithet for the outward ever-changing phenomenon when applied to the power of freedom, to which is assigned the creation of the invisible world of thought, which never is called upon to do anything but to discriminate, to judge, to choose what is right, to reject what is evil, and for which there never can be a *more* or a less, whether it errs, or whether it accomplishes the will of the Eternal.

Whatever one may mean by the word heaven, heaven never can be, for the power of will in man, who is to apply the law of justice in the world of liberty, anything but his dwelling-place, never anything else than the earth. The conviction that the race of men is not too insignificant to be a fellow-worker of the Eternal in His work of creation, this conviction that man is not inferior to any being in his vocation, and in his power to manifest God, and to carry out His holy will, this conviction that all that is one by man on earth, if it is good, is done for eternity; this conviction is the fire which Jesus came to kindle on earth, the fire which glowed in the enthusiasm of his disciples, in their joyful ardour of victory, and inspired them with a courage unto death, that carried them over the world like godly forms; a conviction which, in the breath of their mouths, like the creative spell of the Almighty God, called to a new life the dormant forces of liberty and love in a world sunk in sordid avarice and voluptuousness, condemned to decay and ruin by servility and self-contempt. They were able to do that, and they did it because by faithfulness and conscientiousness they made their way through all the superstition of their time, and raised themselves above it, to the conviction that earth is as near to God as heaven; and when men have raised themselves to the belief and faith that the holy will of the Almighty can be done, and is, in earth as it is in heaven, then this faith will again be the victory which overcomes the world. Amen!

XII.

"GIVE US TO-DAY OUR DAILY BREAD."

We never could agree with those who would have the decline of prayer during the last generations considered as the proof of the religious and moral enlightenment of our time. Nor can we agree any better with those who consider this change as a manifestation and effect of the growing power of evil. We have always been convinced that this change, like almost every other phenomenon of the time, arises from the concurrent action of old prejudices which must and do pass away, and new ones which supplant them. The prayer of the Church could not fill man with trust and assurance, for it was founded upon the fallacious idea that the human will and reason were subjected to a God not only unknown, but unknowable, and it gave to divine decrees an appearance of caprice and arbitrariness. As long as this notion of God prevails in the mind of men, they never can know whether their prayers will be granted. When men renounced that kind of prayer, the fulfilment of which must be a matter of chance, they freed themselves from the dominion of a prejudice; and it was a proof of an awakening to self-cognition. To go back to a kind of prayer given up for such a reason is impossible. Our lips never will utter again a prayer which is not founded on the conviction that the demand it expresses, being independent of mere chance, must be granted. Our conscience once for all rejects every thought in which we do not find the fundamental thought of all prayers of Jesus expressed in the words: "Ask, and it shall be given you;" our conscience for ever rejects every prayer which is not accompanied by the certainty that we cannot be denied that which we seek.

But is this conviction compatible with the words of the Lord's prayer, which form to-day the subject of our meditation, with this petition: "Give us to-day our daily bread?" The sense commonly attributed to these words is based on that old prejudice which, instead of giving to the mind a feeling of firmness and assurance, a consciousness of unity and peace, on the contrary fills it, during and after prayer, with self-doubts and contradictions. If by "daily bread" *that* is to be understood which belongs to the "food and requirements of the body" we certainly cannot apply to a prayer, which has these things as its object, the words: "Ask, and it shall be given you." For, on one hand, these goods are granted to many who remain through life strangers to the aspirations after the knowledge of truth which we understand under the word prayer. As Luther says: God gives bread daily, certainly without being petitioned for it, to most wicked people. On the other hand, these goods are denied to many who sincerely and eagerly strive after the cognition of truth. If by prayer we are to understand something pertaining to the essence and manifestation of truth, it must not be limited to certain turns of fate, it must embrace equally all forms of human existence. Luther says: "By this petition we ask for our daily bread, that God may open our eyes to the goodness that feeds us, and that we may receive our daily bread with gratitude." But this kind of recognition is limited to the days on which our hunger is satisfied. Could that be the right prayer which ceases when hunger and misery begin? He who, according to this interpretation of prayer, has trained his mind to see the eternal order in that only which fate grants to him, is not likely to recognise a consequence of this eternal order in a turn of fate which imposes privation upon him. Such thanksgivings for daily bread sound very pious; but who could deny the impiety of a soul that is disposed to thank as long as it enjoys the benefits granted, and ceases to be thankful the moment these benefits cease to flow? In short, the usual interpretation of the petition for daily bread is incompatible with what we understand by *Prayer*.

But how was it possible to those who have introduced this interpretation to think that it is the true expression of faithful adherence to Him from whom we have this prayer? This fact undeniably proves that *the* Christianity of which Jesus is called the founder, has been in itself one of the greatest hindrances to the right understanding of his teaching. However scanty and contradictory the traditions preserved to us in the Gospels concerning His life may be, the most complete traditions, the most consistent reports, could not show more clearly than they do what Jesus understood by food and drink, by hunger and thirst. Every word in the Gospels in which He has used these figurative expressions proves that nothing else can be meant by daily bread than that which serves to feed thought, to nourish its vitality, and to advance its development and culture. For us, nothing can be more certain. Under this hypothesis these words lead us, taking up the thread of our last meditation, to consider that for those who hunger and thirst after righteousness, an essential part of our daily bread is the conviction that the will of God must be fulfilled by us individually, and cannot be fulfilled otherwise. When in our last discourse we attempted to show that the heaven which men generally put off to a future after death is no more an appropriate place for the fulfilment of the will of God than the earth; that all conditions necessary for this fulfilment of God's will, and for the realisation of truth, are given on earth, we were conscious that we were putting ourselves in opposition to public opinion. The view entertained of the nature of man under the influence of literature during the last two centuries starts, on the contrary, from the idea that a pure manifestation of goodness, a perfect realisation of the will of God, is superhuman, that the dualism of man (*i.e.*, his power for good or evil) keeps him in a state of contradiction with himself inherent in the fatality of his earthly existence. When we thus designated the conviction of the unavoidable imperfection of human nature as the purport of a belief in which all parties of our time agree, it may have appeared to many as if we had overlooked the very view of human nature which, though a product of the most recent time, has nevertheless obtained a rapid and very considerable influence, and has, like ourselves, attacked as a dangerous error the prejudice which decries life on earth in exalting a super-earthly heavenly world. There certainly is a party who think they have spoken the last word on religion and Christianity, that they have at last redeemed the earth from the degradation to which the fanatic enthusiasm for heaven had condemned it, and that they have brought into honour again the indestructible right of the human mind. But we are far from finding in the doctrines of that party the rectifications of the prejudices which have so long hindered the self-cognition of men. Far from it; we are convinced that even the isolated features of truth which had survived in the religious belief of former times are obliterated in the form which the old prejudices have assumed in the teaching of this new party.

For centuries together the creed that the essence and will of God were indwelling in man himself had been attacked and hunted down, and the contrary creed that God is outside man had been set up as the only correct one. Now this new school, starting from the opposite view, as if error only need be turned inside out to lead to truth, taught that God was strictly confined within the pale of humanity. But as the name of God has been created purposely to express that for which there is no pale and no limit, this school, in order to be consistent with itself, declares that the conception of God, far from being, as we take it, the result of self-knowledge, was, on the contrary, the result of a complete misconception of human nature on the part of men. Now those who consider the belief in God as a self-deception on the part of believers, are naturally not exposed to the temptation of making heaven a picture of superhuman perfection. They do not allow the old question to trouble them, whether the life of the body and soul, which is known to us on earth only, exhausts the nature of things, or whether it be only one side of the collective life in which the Eternal Spirit embodies itself. The question of the whence and whither of human existence, with its besetting doubts, has at all times awakened in men the painful feeling of a blank in human knowledge; and this feeling is of the greatest importance for all those who take the consciousness of knowing nothing as the safest starting-point in the search after truth. For such inquiries after the whence and whither of men must necessarily be set aside by the school of which we speak, if its adherents are not to be disturbed in the enjoyment of their imaginary knowledge. The life of body and soul, such as earth shows it to them, is in their eyes the substance of all conceivable perfection.

Whatever one may think of this doctrine in general, all will admit that, according to the foregoing remarks, it ought to protect its adherents against the prejudice of the imperfection of human nature. This at least seems so. But the following question cannot be avoided. What is this human nature which, according to them, presents the substance of all conceivable perfection ? Let us take human life as it is in reality, place before them a human being, and ask them whether this human being is what they mean by human nature; they will say, "No, certainly not; this human being is only a fragment of it." And now they begin to enumerate and give us an account of all who belong to our nation, and to those on our borders, and to all the nations in the other parts of the world ; and not satisfied with these millions of living beings, they will remind us of all those of past ages, of all the multitudes whose bones rest in their graves, and ultimately they will tell us of all the unborn generations which will live and die after us ; then they say : Now take all these human beings together in your conception. All these taken together form human nature. All truth, all justice, all liberty, and all love is in this human nature; outside that, there is nothing. We will not argue at present, but we have a question at heart which may already have been answered indirectly in what precedes; nevertheless, we wish to have it answered specially. This question concerns the relation which we all bear as individuals towards this sum total of perfection. What can that relation to perfection be? If this perfection is supposed to include goodness, how shall we satisfy conscience, which in what it demands of us individually puts goodness foremost? Shall we prove it by going through the above-mentioned enumeration of the generations of men? Is all that it can require of us accomplished by human kind *en masse*? Will our conscience accept such a commentary of our duties? If you ask the representatives of this school how men will characterise themselves as individuals in respect to goodness and perfection, they will tell you that a difference between one individual and the other is not conceivable, that in this respect no one can really assume an attitude different from that of others. If human nature is to share goodness and perfection only in as much as it embraces all individuals, it is a matter of course that every individual, taken by himself as a fragment, a part of the whole, necessarily is and remains imperfect. The human race is the substance, the sum total of perfection. It unites in itself all that is great, beautiful, and sublime; but the relation of the individual is that of the drop of water to the ocean, that of the grain of sand to the mountain; the individual of necessity is and remains as far from perfection as the notion of the grain of sand from that of Mont Blanc.

If we must, as for the sake of our conscience and responsibility we cannot help doing, if we must by human nature understand the real human life in the individual, according to this new doctrine, goodness and perfection also become something superhuman. Then, as far as human nature is concerned, we can detect no difference between this new doctrine and the old superstition which, in order to honour heaven, decried the life on earth. Instead of the old notion of heaven, we have here the notion of the collective human race. Is this new barrier, which separates us from the perfection attributed to the humanity that spreads over all the earth through endless ages, not just as insuperable for us, as individuals, as the old barrier that rose between man as the citizen of earth and the perfection of heaven? As we rejected the old superstition, according to which goodness was too good for life on earth, so we reject the new superstition, which would make goodness appear as too great for the living reality of human life in the individual. We consider the notion of the necessary imperfection of the real human being, whichever form it may assume, whether it oppose to him the perfection of heaven, or that of the race, we consider and reject it as an invention, as a prejudice. We take the experience of conscience as a test; and conscience admits of no dissecting or taking goodness into parts, and as far as the responsibility which it imposes upon us is concerned, it does not inquire what kind of perfection will result from the computation of all the millions of men living, dead, or not yet born. When I ask what is the sphere in which the will of God can be done, on what ground the edifice of truth is to be erected, what is the power through which this creation of liberty can be, and is to be carried on; experience has but the *one* answer. This power, this ground, and this sphere is *our own self*. Wherever such a self, such an independent will lives, there also lives a power which neither past nor future can diminish, and from which nothing can be withheld: a power which at every point of time is in possession of all conditions on which depends the pure manifestation of goodness, the perfect realisation of the will of God. This power finds in all that intellect and reason bring before it a picture only, a mere phenomenon which serves as the material and occasion to embody itself in action, whilst such a transient picture or phenomenon of life is the one and sole reality in which the wicked believes. How were it possible to consider this free will of mine, this, my very self, as one of the phenomena in which consist these species and generations which to-day are born and to-morrow are no more, no matter how many thousands of years there may be between this to-day and this to-morrow? You may speak of the world of phenomena as of a *whole;* you may call a *whole* also the shadowy existence of men over which life and death wrangle together, but do not let us forget that this word "a whole" is but a metaphor when it is applied to this play of shadows, composed of seeing, hearing, digesting, imagining, feeling, of having seen, having heard, digested, imagined, and felt and the like. Do not let us forget that in truth nothing deserves the name of "a whole" which is not simple and indivisible, unique of its kind, self-existing and imperishable. It is well known that in all that pertains to *nature*, in all that is subject to the inflexible law of *necessity*, the autonomy is not to be found by putting together the single parts of the things that grow and develop, attain a certain strength and lose it again, gradually dwindling away by decay. There is no entirety to be found (and we are well aware of it) in any of all the species of plants, animals and men tending to become a complete whole, and which only attain this end when they again sink into destruction. We know full well that this whole, consisting of stones and plants, animals and men, which comes into existence by parts, and attains its completion in parts, never is seriously spoken of as a whole by any really thinking man. That in them which really deserves this name is *anterior* to all these parts. Knowing all this, why do we forget it, when our thoughts are concerned with the *creation of freedom?* Why forget, when speaking of goodness, that this human existence with its single actions, circumscribed by birth and death, even when it is extended to the unknown duration of the human race, with all its deeds and its whole history, is nothing but a shadow projected by this self, by the self-determining power of the will? Every one of these shadowy phantoms in which alone the wicked man sees a reality, every one of these shadowy pictures produced by free will, as it passes before the mirror of the eye and of consciousness, can be taken apart from other pictures of the same kind; it can be compared with them, and consequently be considered as great or small, and in this respect be called more perfect or imperfect. All these pictures can be considered as parts out of which the collective picture of human history is composed; they can be arranged so that what belongs to one series of events can by no means be placed elsewhere. All this is easily understood when applied to transient scenes and pictures; but when applied to free will, which has, in union with eye and consciousness, brought about these scenes and thrown these shadows, this analysis, this dividing, is *senseless.* They are produced by free will, but they have no determining power over it. Just as little as men feel the footsteps of their fellow creatures walking on their shadows, just as little is free will affected by the affairs of outer life, which only indicate the place that the shadowy form of its manifestations occupies in the history of the world. The dew drop which you see in the chalice of a flower owes what it is to the night that gave it birth, and exists only as long as the sun in the heavens allows it; but who would be foolish enough to think that the elements, the forces which it manifests, did not exist previously, or will cease to be when it is gone? Does such foolishness become wisdom when, speaking of the will, we show ourselves incapable of making a distinction between the temporary phenomenon and the eternal essence of it? The distinction between the eternal essence of the will, which is not even touched by the tide of hours and years, which is every moment that which it is, entirely and solely, between thought's creation of good and evil, and the sum total of all phenomena of the outer world, which become what they are only by what precedes and what surrounds them; this distinction, I say, is the only firm and safe starting-point for the answering of this question: Where is the will of God to be done? This distinction will be overlooked as long as men think it necessary for the cognition of truth to divide the world in such a way, that a part of it of necessity remains for his present life, a life beyond the grave ; be it that he conceives it as a heaven relatively to the earth, or as the collective human race, which he never can take in himself or contain, in relation to which he never can be but as a drop in the ocean. It is no doubt important for us, in order to understand nature *in* and *around* us, to see clearly the contrast that exists between things that lie in our actual horizon and those things which are concealed from us by an obscure futurity ; it is important for that purpose to see the difference between the single individual and the whole race ; but *for the cognition of truth*, these contrasts are meaningless. The cognition of truth only begins in us, and becomes a living reality for us, when we perceive that heaven and earth, the individual man and the whole race, are formed, so to speak, from one and the same stuff ; but that there is *another creation* in us, distinct from this natural process, and that for this other creation it is indifferent whether we live under the equator or in the everlasting winter of the poles ; that for this inner creation it is absolutely indifferent whether our contemporaries are Moses or Joshua, or those in the midst of whom we now live ; whether we exist in the time which precedes or follows death. We shall never be sure what is the place in which the divine will (*i.e.* the law of justice) can be fulfilled before we detect this *other creation* in us, the creation of liberty. In order to see clearly what it means, and what it is, we must be able to draw a sharp line between free will itself and its transient manifestations; we must be able to see that this word—phenomenon—(*i.e.* the passing sight of a thing, its appearance) is equally applicable to the heaven and to the earth, as well as to the existence of the individual man and that of the whole race. Before this clear insight into the world of liberty, as distinct from its manifestations in our own actions, is gained, and the danger is thereby overcome of confusing the creation of liberty with the creation of necessity, there is no hope of our realising what the sphere is, in which the will of God is to be done (*i.e.*, where the law of justice is to be fulfilled and perfection attained. Let us dwell for a few moments on the effect of this view of freedom on the life of those who have grasped the thought of it, and made it their own. How will the conviction that neither the limits of space nor the flight of time can hinder us from fulfilling the will of God perfectly manifest itself in all that we do or avoid doing? To see clearly the effects of this view, compare the life of him who considers the whole race of men as necessary to present the realisation of perfection, and who, in consequence of it, thinks that the individual, taken singly, is unavoidably condemned to imperfection, to error and sin. We shall find that the paths of these two men diverge in every respect, whether we consider the tendency of their way of thinking, or their source of cognition, or their judgment of their own selves.

He who seeks perfection only in collective humanity will necessarily try to embrace as many individuals as possible in one glance. He will direct his attention to whole classes of men, whole nations, whole centuries,

and to what has been done in them; the rise and
decline of their national wealth and industry, wars
and revolutions. The more he limits his attention to
what is great, the more indifferent he grows as to the
more circumscribed interests that compose the history
of his house between every morning and every
evening. The more he accustoms his sight to what is
conspicuous and distant, the more indistinct becomes
what happens under his own eyes and through himself. It is as if what is nearest to him, his own real
life, were removed to such a distance that it appears
to him as a mere point in which nothing is distinguishable. He knows a great deal of men; of man
he knows nothing.—On the contrary, *he*, according to
whose conviction there is place for the perfect fulfilment of God's will in the smallest space of time, will
apply the highest amount of diligence in order to recognise the fulness of life, the inexhaustible riches
and variety of forms which are always found to exist
under the words good and bad, if we only know how
to detect them. Every moment is in itself for him a
magnifying-glass, through which he perceives a new
world which remains hidden to him who thinks little
of the moment. The more diligently he uses this new
instrument of vision, the more distinctly do all the
things which used in former days to run together
into an indistinct mass divide and present themselves
to his sight as distinct units; and he soon discovers
that this inner creation of liberty is as incommensur-
able as the picture of nature that surrounds him.
He then perceives how all the forces of this inner
creation ever act together, in his feeling, in his deci-

sions, and in everyone of the deeds of every moment. To him everything is alive that to the other is dead; for him everything expands into a world of itself; whilst for the other, the whole life of every individual, as such, shrinks into an insignificant nothing.

Secondly, he who is under the illusion that perfection is to be found in the life of collective humanity, must, in order to be consistent with himself, consider it as an impossibility to recognise truth; for this picture of whole humanity, from the contemplation of which alone he thinks that he can obtain this cognition, is never complete. But in order to approach this notion of truth as much as possible, he will seek instruction wherever human life presents to him at least a certain resemblance to that of the whole race; *i.e.* he will honour *that*, as right, in which the majority believes, that which is most highly valued by public opinion. What the majority wills, that is for him the voice of God; what the majority, or he who governs it, does, that is right in his eyes.

When men hold themselves cheap, and consider themselves as a mere herd, the opportunity has then come to represent what they consider as the right and the truth; *i.e.* to exclude the breathing air of liberty, so that no germ of life can develop itself, so that everything decays, rots, and turns to a swamp. This swamp it is from which the superstition of the necessary imperfections of man means to draw the cognition of truth. Only he is protected against this slavery of the spirit who is convinced that, on the contrary, everyone can hear the voice of justice through the voice of his conscience and through it alone. He knows that whenever the great crowd, standing face to face with the just, have a presentiment of what he really aims at, of what he wills, they needs must cry their "Crucify Him, crucify Him!" whilst as often as the great crowd hails the just with their "Hallelujah!" it is because they misunderstand him. He knows that, and he says so without fear, whenever the opportunity occurs, for he thinks too highly of himself to complain of the loss of honours bestowed by a blind power. And how differently must the man judge himself who is occupied exclusively with external transitory matters, and he who, seeing how all events, all changes that compose the history of mankind, belong to the *transitory* world of *phenomena*, is convinced in his mind and conscience that every man, without exception, has been endowed with a power which enables him, through the perfect fulfilment of the will of God, to do his share in bringing the creation of nature to its perfect completion and harmony by another creation, that of freedom. When Protestants indulge in the Pharisaic feeling in which men form a high opinion of themselves at the expense of their neighbours, and thank God that they are not like some other people, no words appear to them strong enough to brand confession and the absolution of the confessor and its effects as demoralising. But what is the difference between that treatment of evil which we blame, and the kind of self-judgment which is so prevalent amongst us? Is it not that we treat evil even more lightly? I mean here, the easy act of forgiving one's own sin, brought about by the superstition of human imperfection. I mean the new kind of absolution which everyone grants to himself, on the ground that perfection being a property belonging to the whole human race, and to no one in particular, everyone convinces himself easily how very little the individual can contribute to it, as he is here nothing but a drop in the ocean, and of how very little consequence therefore it can be whether he does this or that. When once man has given himself up to the fallacious idea that fate and the gods themselves have caused him to become guilty, he no longer hates evil as evil : he only fears it in so far as its effects injure his life and his property. His ideal of a human community is no longer the reign of God, but an insurance society against burglary and manslaughter; the prophet being superfluous in his eyes, the place of the prophet remains empty for him; he knows of no saviour but the gaoler. In a society influenced by this conception of perfection, personal interest becomes the only standard by which men judge of their actions. And that is the case with all but those who know that they can find no higher judge than the voice of their own conscience. If a man appears before what he considers as a foreign judgment-seat, and is going to be judged by a law of perfection which his reason cannot conceive, one cannot wonder that, full of fear of this unknown power which sits in judgment over him, he has recourse to evasions, to denials, to excuses, and tries to conceal that which he knows to be wrong in him. If a man, on the contrary, rises to liberty and becomes his own judge, every deceit ceases. He recognises that goodness is conformable to his nature; his struggle against his errors becomes a self-defence against them, so that he allows no hiding-place to his enemies, but drives them away as a sound constitution throws off bad humours. Let us do the same; and, above all things, let us banish the superstition which attempts to comfort us about the necessary imperfections of collective humanity. Goodness is as little inborn in the whole human race as it is in the individual man. If all men are once to present the picture of a perfect community, there is no other way to that goal than the conviction that free will in me, as in every other man, is able at any and every moment to fulfil perfectly the law of truth. This conviction is the food which maintains the mind in health, and gives to it the power to work at the holy edifice of justice. Let our lives be a testimony to this faith. Then we shall have done what the Father gave us to do in this existence. Then, also, we shall have helped to establish the reign of God on earth, to establish here the union of men for the eternal reign of order and peace! Amen.

XIII.—A.

"FORGIVE US OUR TRESPASSES."

OUR meditations on the prayer of our Master directed our attention foremost to *what truth is in its essence*, to the question, What is the perfection to which the will of God leads us? The answer was: The sanctification of the name of God, the establishment of God's kingdom; self-knowledge and the fulfilment of the law of equality and justice. On the question: What is to be done to fulfil the will of God? follows as a logical sequence the question: What is the place where truth is to be carried out? We convinced ourselves that this place, this heaven, is not beyond the gate of death, any more than it can be the transitory manifestation of liberty in collective humanity which had to spread itself over the earth through endless series of thousands of years. We came to the conclusion that the sphere of the realisation of the will of God is man himself, *i.e.*, his self-determining will, which is a whole in itself, in every individual, in every moment of his life. The following words of the Lord's prayer concern the third and last question, in what manner the essence of truth manifests itself in free-will. According to our prayer we have to consider three points in this petition. The task which we have to fulfil in our intercourse with our fellow-creatures is hinted at in the words: "Father, forgive us our trespasses, as we forgive them that trespass against us."

"Father, forgive us our trespasses." In this wish, in this craving, religious life manifests itself always when man is at variance with himself. May these words ever be the expression of our longing for reunion with the spirit of goodness! May we never desecrate these words by using them with a desire to have the punishment remitted; which, according to our notions, is supposed to be coupled with the breaking of divine commandments. To be freed from evil—that is what we have to strive after—and that is all these words are meant to convey to us. All religions have intended to reconcile man with God, and to free him from the consciousness of his guilt; one prescribes for that purpose sacrifices and prayers, the other offerings to the Church, and gifts to the poor. But whatever way men choose, their lives do not show that their aspirations tend to self-education and purification of the will, but that they seek to free themselves from actual evils, and to turn away threatening dangers. The privations which fate imposes upon us, the need which may befall us in the future, the illness, the pains of which are aggravated by the fear of worse sufferings, the ill-success of our enterprises, the failure of our hopes, the distrust, the disdain, or condescension, with which people offend us, and hundreds of such things, form the horizon that encircles the world of our thoughts. But our guilt and our errors, the untruth, vanity, selfishness—all that makes us so sensitive to these evils, and adds to these experiences the bitterness of after-taste—the evil in us, to conquer which requires the joint efforts of all our energies, an uninterrupted perseverance and faithfulness, and an undivided attention, that is the thing of which the majority among the few who do not forget it altogether only think perhaps for a few minutes on Sundays. It is natural that this rare retrospective thought of our errors should not lead us to the cognition of self. The only results that can be expected from this reckoning with our conscience, opened and closed, merely to have done with it, are new errors and repeated complaints of the weakness of human nature.

And even when, at last, we turn round to put a stop to this thoughtless whirlpool of distraction in which we have been absorbed, when we gather all our strength to see every one of the errors of which we are guilty, to free ourselves from all egotism, even then, we must be prepared to find, after all, that in the ways and means, which we have chosen, the power of evil, by the suggestions of which we have allowed ourselves to be led so long, will often make itself felt. If, in order to secure ourselves against these new errors of self-deceit, we seek advice from those who appear more experienced in the work of self-education, no doubt we enter on a path which our nature prescribes to us; for the instinct of fellowship, which manifests itself in this seeking, is a feature deeply rooted in us. But good advice will remain fruitless if he who seeks it does so only in the hope of sparing himself any exertion; nothing short of independent thought will be of any avail. The same danger will attend the advice received, if he who gives it falls into this error himself, and imagines that he can secure to his client immunity from error by rules and prescriptions, the breaking or keeping of which can be ascertained. Let the advice be limited as much as possible to general principles. The clearer they are, the more easily understood are these indications as to the whither towards which to tend, and the better able will he be who is advised, while keeping in this direction, to trust to his own judgment and break the road to his destination for himself. If you agree with me so far, you will admit that we can wish for no better advice than that which Jesus gives us in his prayer. To this petition, "Father, forgive us our trespasses," he adds, "as we forgive them that trespass against us." The combination of these two ideas teaches us that we can

see best our own relative position to evil, *i.e.* that we
free ourselves most safely from it by conscientiously
observing how we judge of the guilt in our neighbours,
of the evil in others. Learn to forgive! That is the
best way to free ourselves from evil. No one who is
required to forgive them that have trespassed against
him, will pretend that he does not know what these
words require of him. Moments which impose this
duty on him will at once become present to his mind;
the image of such or such a person to whom he has
something to forgive will at once rise before him.
One has damaged his interests, another has wounded
his feelings, a third has betrayed his confidence, and
there are many other people, of whom he thinks he
could tell how they have trespassed against him.
That he is angry with all of them, because they have
done him wrong in some way, that he bears them a
grudge in his heart, he is well aware; and that they
who are in need of his forgiveness make it a reproach
to him that he has accused them to others, and that
they blame the feelings which accompany these accusations, is quite clear to him. He knows what Jesus
means when he requires him to forgive. But his
understanding of this requirement often stops there.
Whether he acknowledges it as based on reason,
whether he feels the reproach made to him of his
accusations against others as a reproach of his own
conscience, whether he be disposed to give up the
proceedings in which he has indulged so far, whether
he has convinced himself that he, on his side, has done
wrong in reference to this or that person, by his
accusations against them, that is another question.

Generally it is just the contrary. People usually maintain that they have been wronged, and that it is natural to entertain different feelings concerning our enemies, and to treat them otherwise than our friends. Far from blaming themselves for the harm they have wished and done to their enemies, many will maintain that this command to forgive one's enemies can be deemed a duty by no one but a fantastic person; that in truth it is an immoral expectation; that the prosecution of wrong is the only barrier against evil, the only protection of human society; and that if the readiness to forgive injuries opened a chance of impunity to every malefactor, passions would break all the bulwarks of society, and that the work of thousands of years of culture would be buried in their ruins. Jesus would certainly never have thought of refuting the arguments of such prophets; for it is a well-known fact that fear knows no arguments. We will follow his example, and only call upon these prophets to consider our subject from a side which cannot possibly cause them any anxieties. Let us observe the relationship in which every one stands to his friends. These can make themselves guilty towards him in many ways. Perhaps he happens to feel it incumbent upon him to give advice to one in reference to household management, to education, or on business matters, the expediency of which no one can deny; but the good advice remains unnoticed. He asks another friend, for the sake of friendship, to oblige him by a service; his request is not granted; some one else has concealed something from him, although even strangers have been made acquainted with it. The change in the manner of this man to his friends shows that he means to make them feel that they have offended against him. Now if he is reminded that it is a duty, at least among friends, to forgive injuries, he will perhaps not deny it absolutely, but he will find that this or some other possible case must be an exception. For just because he entertains so high an opinion of friendship, he is so painfully affected; just because he treated this friend with such special confidence, it is impossible for him to forget the wrong he has met with at his hands. In short, the difference between friend and foe is not so great as may appear to most people. As long as any one considers a part of his fellow men as his enemies, it is impossible for him to treat even a single one of his fellow men as his real friend. Most people think that they *ought* not to forgive the harm done to them by their enemies, and also maintain that they cannot forget what they have suffered from their friends, much as they wish they could forget it.

It surely is no vain pretence when they affirm that they wish they could free themselves from the remembrance of their friend's offences, for the enjoyment which they used to find in friendship no longer flows from this source, when the sight of a friend is enough to renew these painful impressions. And true it is also that they cannot forget the wrong they have suffered, if by that they mean that the feeling of vexation and estrangement continues in spite of the repeated resolutions and efforts they make to suppress it. This fact requires further and thoughtful investigation on our part. In order to recognise why such repeated efforts must remain fruitless, it is necessary to ascertain what it really is that one thinks one cannot forgive to the offending friend. Is it any special acts on his part which cause our accusations against him, any isolated actions, respecting which we can prove that he knew at the time that he was depriving us of an enjoyment, that he foiled our intentions, that he crossed our plans, that he trespassed on our right, or that he caused others to distrust us? Such isolated facts can only cause a little excitement, irritation, and anger, which pass away with their causes. If these isolated acts were the only causes that disturb the peace between friends, the ill-feeling would pass away as well as its momentary causes. There may be individuals here and there who must nourish the ill-feeling longer than others, because, with an unusual degree of irritability and sensitiveness, they combine an excellent memory intensified by a lively imagination; but these are rare and exceptional cases, which do not explain the general and ever-recurring experience in question. The common and lasting estrangement which keeps us apart from so many people, the unconquerable prejudice, the dislike which we feel for them, whenever we meet them, and which makes it impossible for us to judge and appreciate their aspirations and their labours impartially, that is no experience of this exceptional kind. In such cases, special offences on their part may be considered as an occasion on which we show our dislike for them even more distinctly than usual; but the cause of the lasting enmity will not be found in what they occasionally do, but in what they are, or appear to us to be. Indeed, if we earnestly strive to account for our attitude towards our fellow beings, we shall always find that we easily forgive them what they do, but that whenever we find it difficult or impossible to forgive them, it is because our judgment of them bears, not upon what they do, but upon what they are. That this or that person has hurt our feelings is soon forgotten, even when we are convinced that it was done purposely; and if the circumstances largely contribute to remind us of it constantly, it is a remembrance mingled in our understanding with the cares and business of the day. But in our hearts this feeling is very soon supplanted by new occurrences that concern us more nearly. How different, on the contrary, is the impression that the whole individuality of the offender makes upon us! It creates an unyielding feeling that he is repulsive to us, and that it is his own fault! The characters which are described to us in novels, or with which we meet in history, or in the reports that reach us from far countries through the daily papers, never can be too great for us; the more admirable their dispositions, their talents, the more they rise above their surroundings, the more irresistible their ascendency over men is, the wider the circle of society extends in the minds of which their greatness is reflected, and the greater is the satisfaction with which we dwell on the description of them. This satisfaction ceases when this description becomes a reality for us, through personal contact, either through family ties, or the intercourse of society, or the same field of labour, and their real or supposed superiority makes itself felt to us; when we come to find that they succeed in what we have vainly attempted, that what we lack is cast into their lot. They gain confidence wherever they show themselves, or their manner is so attractive that they are liked everywhere, or their arguments prove acceptable to everybody, or they meet everywhere with people who are ready to carry out their wishes, to approve of their proposals and undertakings. Even if they do not possess all the qualities and advantages just mentioned in their highest perfection, they only need possess them in a somewhat higher degree than ourselves to give us the impression that everywhere they stand in our way, that they deprive us of the inclination of others, that they render us less popular, that they curtail the influence which we should exercise if they were not there. This experience is evidently not limited to those who are spurred by ambition to play a part in the world at large. Three persons, the lowliest position, the most secluded spot on earth, are sufficient conditions for this drama: one person wishing to please another, and a third animated by the same desire and more successful than the first, are all the elements required to bring it about. This drama is the same, day after day, for most people; the apparent difference consists in the simple fact that whilst the first remains the same, the second and third persons continually change. Meanwhile everyone who, through his peculiar individuality, causes him so painful a disappointment, remains for ever to him an object of anxiety and fear; for the individuality remaining the same through all changes of circumstances, what happened yesterday, can, as long as we live together, happen again under a new form.

The same sensation, by contact with people of

superior gifts, is produced on us again when our relation to another person presents that strange mixture of like and unlike, of similar dispositions and contrary, in consequence of which the two are to each other like the two ends of a magnet, so that what is sought by one the other shuns; and again, what is pleasing to one is disagreeable to the other. Natures of this description, when joined together by inexorable fate, do not generally contribute to heighten the enjoyment of life; in most cases they know so little how to enter into each other's peculiarities, that the most cheerful frame of mind in one of them can be disturbed by the mere appearance of the other. Nothing could prove more evidently that it is the whole individuality on the other side which is repelling, than the fact that what the one cannot forgive to the other, is that he exists at all, or at least that he is what he is. No doubt both will be obliged to admit that it would be absurd to make it a reproach to each other that fate has blended their lives together, or that nature gave to one what she refused to the other, or composed the one of qualities which seem so repulsive to his companion. Albeit the absurdity of reproaching each other with the existing circumstances is clear to everybody else, nevertheless men do not allow themselves, so long as they will not learn to forgive, to be led, by acknowledging their own contradictions, to self-cognition; they do not cease to deceive themselves; they have recourse to new errors to justify themselves with regard to the old ones. "Of course," they say, "no one is answerable for what nature and fate have made him;" but are nature and fate to be made responsible for what he does with these gifts? Whose fault is it that he foils our pleasure and our happiness in every way? that his existence becomes an evil for us? that he only needs appear to prevent others from being just to us? "No," they add, "the wrong lies in the use he makes of the gifts with which nature has endowed him." These accusers will assure everybody and persuade themselves, that, unsympathetic as may be the peculiarities with which nature has characterised this unfortunate person to their own individuality, they would bear them with perfect equanimity if he were not so quarrelsome, so overbearing, and conceited in all his doings, small or great, and if he did not show it in all his movements, and in every shade of expression that passes over his face. In the same way they will assure us that they would never feel humiliated by real superiority, but that what they cannot forgive to this particular person of whom they complain, is the deceitfulness, the mean tricks, the subtleties with which he dazzles the world, and tries to surround himself with a nimbus of intellectual superiority, and assume in society a position to which his mediocrity does not in the least entitle him. In one word, what they cannot forgive him, is not at all anything that he has done to offend them personally, but his offences against God Himself. Who is so weak in his understanding, if he does not himself pass such judgments on his neighbours, as not to see the hypocrisy that betrays itself in such accusations, condemnations, and calumnies? But such is the hypocrisy with which everyone will end who will not learn to forgive.

The way in which we judge of others is a sure

standard of what we are ourselves, the most infallible criterion by which we test whether we love good or evil. The assurance with which a person speaks of the guilt of his fellow-man, only proves the guilt of his own heart; by his complaint of the wrong he has met with at the hands of others, he only proves that he sets aside the law of justice. Not to forgive our fellow-man means that we are tormented by the idea that he stands in the way of our obtaining the goods which fate bestows.

The more greedily the heart of man strives after such goods, the more he must fret when he thinks that others are able, intentionally or unintentionally, to wrench from him what he possesses of these goods, or to withhold that which he wishes to earn. How is it that Jesus, and those who are like-minded, do not know this tormenting idea? The reason is this. They view these goods differently; their free soul considers the desire for goods, which depends on the power of fate, as a stranger to them, as degrading, and they keep aloof from it. But that anyone, or anything, could hinder them from obtaining the goods which they strive after, or disturb them in their aspirations to the perfect fulfilment of the law of liberty, or in the enjoyment of the happiness ensured by this imperishable good—that is not conceivable. On the path on which they advance none can do them any harm; they have nothing to forgive. Not to forgive one's neighbour means that we are possessed by the delusion that God has placed us as a judge over our fellow-men. Such a delusion is incompatible with obedience to the law of justice. Whoever recognises this law and loves it, is above all things convinced that, according to the will of God, according to the law that He has established in the self-determining will of man, every one of us is his own judge. "The son of man judges no one." Therefore every man, who is sincere with himself, can see by his accusations against his fellow-creature, by his whole judgment of him, that he is not what he ought to be. Let us strive to become what we ought to be by combating the illusion that our fellow-man is a trespasser against us. It is in our judging and condemning that evil first becomes flesh and blood in us; then it is, that this enemy first assumes a visible form, and stands before us; then it is, that we must begin the holy fight against the effects of evil, which, united with the love of goodness, with the cognition of truth, raises us to communion with the Eternal, and establishes in us the eternal life of freedom and justice.

In order to begin this fight so as to ensure success, we must give our task definite limits, for it is necessary that we should be able to embrace it in one glance, and that we should be conscious at all times whether we come nearer our goal, or whether we recede from it. In its effects, evil assumes a shape in time and space. In order to free ourselves from these effects, it is necessary to make a division of our work. Let us make a beginning, be it even with one person only, in purifying our judgment of our fellow beings, and keeping it free from all censure and condemnation. Let this be one of those with whom we are in daily intercourse, the one of whom we are conscious that it is not anyone of his special actions which jar upon us, but his whole individuality, and that he would be

the most likely object of our censure and condemnation.
To expect this feeling of repulsion to yield at these
first efforts on our part, would be hoping too
much, but this lingering ill-feeling ought not to make
us anxious, or to excite doubts in our minds as to the
ultimate success of our enterprise. Feelings are the
leaves and blossoms, the life of which depends on the
root, and the root of spiritual life is the deed of the
will that determines itself. The deed of which I now
speak is the conscious judgment we pass on this
person, whether outspoken or no. To judge him
otherwise than we have done hitherto, that is the condition which we have to fulfil. Let us start from this
rule: Do unto others as you wish to be done unto. How
often have we, when the world misunderstood or
suspected us, looked round for a friend who would
only think it worth his while to understand us! Let
us then render this man the service that we have
wished for ourselves from others! Let us cease to be
his accuser and his judge, let us become his advocate.
Are we still too much prejudiced against him to see
good impulses where we used to see evil only,
and where these good impulses certainly are, although
we did not see them; yea, however great his guilt
may be, let us be the advocate for that which is in
him, as it is in every one else, God's own perfection. The eternal laws, in which there is nothing
to censure, are the same in us as in him whom we
wish to learn to forgive. If we seek nothing in him
but the manifestation of those eternal laws of human
nature, we shall recognise ourselves in him, and him
in us, and a bond of union is henceforth growing

between him and us. The same alternations of pain and joy which constitute our existence, also constitute his. We shall then feel that his sorrow causes him no less suffering than our sorrow causes us; and if we only learn to suffer with him, the moment will not be far off when we shall also rejoice with him. The same voice of conscience which we hear in us also speaks in him; as it censures us, it censures him; *our* censure is therefore not needed. The only thing needed is that which helps him and us equally; and this help consists in striving more and more to free our own lives from the evil which we thought we saw in him. If concerning this man, we really suffer no other thought than this in our consciousness; if we faithfully persevere in shaping his image in our mind, so as always to remind us of what God demands of us; if in the presence of this man we demand nothing from life but faithfulness to ourselves, if the greed of transitory enjoyment is silenced in us, we shall no longer think it possible that his presence could ever disturb our happiness, and if it does, we shall scarcely perceive it.

The transformation here hinted at in these few words is certainly a work of life, which those in whom censuring and condemning has become a habit will not accomplish without efforts that require the concentration of their whole strength upon one point, not without a very unpleasant self-imposed restraint, not without hopes rashly conceived, and followed by bitter disappointments. But he who has learned in this way to forgive one person, henceforth forgives one and all; he has learned by his own experience that to learn to forgive is the way to free one's own self from evil; he knows by his own experience that Jesus is right when he says: "Forgive and it will be forgiven you." Amen.

XIII.—B.

FATHER, FORGIVE US OUR TRESPASSES, AS WE FORGIVE THEM THAT TRESPASS AGAINST US.

WHENEVER we avail ourselves of the teaching of others to acquire the knowledge of truth, we must beware of two lurking errors: either we think that we have understood it, or we think that we have not. If we think we do not understand it, we easily assume that it cannot be understood, at least by us, and we then think we act wisely in putting it aside altogether. But when we think that we understand it, we rarely consider that this assumption on our part is by no means a guarantee that we have really understood it, and that all whom we honour as masters in the art of cognition agree in this; that what people generally understand least of all, is just that which they consider is most simple in itself, and therefore most easy to understand. Of all the utterances of Jesus, the one which may most easily expose us to this latter error appears to me to be the words : "Father, forgive us our trespasses;" the latter part of the sentence, "as we forgive them that trespass against us," the relation of the offender to the offended, is presented to us in a similar way, although inversely, as in the parable of

the wicked servant who, having met with mercy,
treated his fellow servant without mercy. The teaching is the same whether we are told how to act, or
how not to act. It is the relation of the debtor to
the creditor in civil society; and without hesitation
we transfer to God's way of dealing with us the way
in which the acquittal of debts is carried on, when a
distinction between mine and thine must be made.
We know how an acquittal of debts is brought about
in commercial transactions; he who has become the
debtor of another man ceases to be a debtor the
moment his creditor destroys his bond or returns it to
him. But how is that? Has the debtor done or been
able to do anything that must bring about the decision
of the creditor to that effect? In some cases, even
the most fervent entreaties for release remain without
effect, whilst in other cases, a man finds himself set
free from his obligations, even without knowing how
that came about. The creditor is the only active
party in the acquittal of debts; for the debtor, the
change that has taken place is a turn of fate, an
accidental event. And in what does this change
really consist? Merely in this, that before the tribunals of the country, the one man is no longer considered as a debtor to the other, and that is all.
Important as this altered view of the relation may be
for me, on account of its consequences, the fact in
itself that I am unable to return the service rendered
to me by a similar service remains altogether unchanged, notwithstanding the annihilation of the bond.

Many people will be the more inclined to regard the
current view of this relation of debtor and creditor,

valid before civil tribunals, as a standard for our relation to God, since in our day one has grown accustomed to express one's moral and religious convictions by certain imposing pass-words accepted as a sort of mysterious vessels in which truth is supposed to be securely held. The word love belongs to that set of words which are in special favour. Many people are convinced that anyone still in doubt about the forgiveness of his sins, ought to be helped on, in his cognition of truth, when he is told: God is that love that denies its favours neither to the just nor to the unjust; God is the creditor who cancels all bonds.

Certainly God is love; but the comfort and the power of soothing our anxieties, for the sake of which alone these words are so dear to many, at once prove to be a vain illusion when we remember that the bond of our offences against truth is not a paper and cannot be destroyed like paper. True, Jesus has pronounced the faith in love to be the faith in the kingdom of God; but no one lives in the faith that Jesus meant by that word, who does not consider also that Jesus said at the same time: "Verily, verily, I say unto thee, except a man be born again, he cannot see the kingdom of God." Everyone who seeks comfort in the words that God is love, is a liar to himself, if he will not remember that the children of God who experience that comfort are free beings, determining themselves to what is good; that the divine Father makes the fundamental law of His will known to us clearly by the words: help thyself, *i.e.* seek, and thou shalt find; that no perfection is granted to him who does not, by his self-determining will, help himself. He who is too indolent to make up his mind to this change of spirit which Jesus characterises as a new birth, and who thinks to find a comfort for his indolence in the love of God, will, sooner or later, discover to his dismay that the love of God, in which he has believed, is as much help to him as painted bread to a hungry man. God is love; but often as we may say so to ourselves, our notions of God remain what they were of old; we only *feel* God to be, as we did before, an unjust, jealous, violent being, as long as we turn our consciousness, which is the power of vision in our soul, from divine love; and we remain the old man who worships as idols the false creations of his folly. God is also harmony and beauty; but *did* Solomon *see* it, so long as he imagined that his purple and gold could be anything better than the dress in which the lilies of the fields are arrayed? So, also, the belief in love is no better than a deceptive sound, so long as the old Adam in us, who will only receive and make no return, is not dead; so long as we have not entered on a love of freedom by a new birth. In our last meditation we found that Jesus gave us a sure test of that, by making the happy result of our prayer for deliverance from evil depend on our way of judging evil in others. Let us therefore use these words to-day as a self-examination, and consider accurately how the way of dealing, in the old man, will distinguish itself by our judgment of others, from that of the man who is born again to a life of spiritual freedom.

The old man, whether he call himself orthodox, or whether he follow the fashion of scepticism, whether he belong to the National Church, to the Baptists or to a free congregation, betrays his indolence in his judgment of his fellow-men by forgiving no one but himself. The indolent cannot act differently, for to judge others is easy, but to know one's self requires real exertion. As certain as it is that the indolent man cannot act differently, as little will he admit that his judgment of what is good or evil in the world, in every case, contains either an accusation against somebody else, or an attempt at self-justification. The indolent and slavish man will allege that he also is very often dissatisfied with himself. But we did not say that he reproaches himself with nothing, but that he is always ready to forgive himself what he has done amiss, that he always finds reasons to excuse the wrongs he has done. And we must add, that when he reproaches himself with something, it never springs from a free aspiration to the cognition of truth. If we observe ourselves and others impartially, we shall find that when men are dissatisfied with themselves, the cause is generally an external one. If a man fails in an enterprise, if he draws a humiliation upon himself, he takes that opportunity to blame himself. The blame therefore bears upon some want of skill, of knowledge or talent, which was unavoidable considering his peculiarity or his special development, or which he could not help in the least in this special case. The impurity of his will, the selfishness of his heart, is not what causes his displeasure; for what has this to do with the good or ill-success of our undertakings, with the judgment of the people about us? It is therefore not of his own accord that he decides to judge of his own moral state, to examine how he is minded and what were the motives of his actions; he occupies himself with the conditions of his inward life only when he is compelled to do so by the blame of others, and with the intention of defending himself in order to prove that he does not deserve the blame, that he is in the right.

The self-justification which, for the indolent man, is the only result of his supposed self-examination, does not consist in acquitting himself of all wrong. He may even be accustomed to bear all special accusations against him without any protest. With some, this is the result of the pietistic inclination to self-degradation; with others, it is a way of yielding which is supposed to belong to good-breeding. But this readiness to admit one's error on single points is quite compatible with the self-indulgence peculiar to indolence and slavishness; for everyone is persuaded that single acts do not determine the general worth of a man. A man may grant that he is guilty of much foolishness and even wickedness in his actions, if he is only sure that goodness is the predominant element in him. He does not dispute the fact that his life leaves much to be desired; the ultimate estimation, the total judgment of him must, after all, be in his favour, if he is convinced that these short-comings only concern accessory things, and that he is not found wanting in the essential. Thus the way by which the indolent arrives at self-satisfaction is found easily; he simply declares that in which he is found wanting to be the accessory, and that which he possesses to be the essential. In that, he acts like schoolboys who, in producing their examination-reports, declare that those subjects in which they have failed are of secondary importance. He is therefore ready to admit that his life never presents in its purity and completeness his own standard of goodness; that he often positively breaks the law of duty; but that causes him no anxiety; that does not lower him in his own eyes, for he considers that the fault lies in the general weakness of human nature. According to him, the essential for a man consists in knowing what is right and in the wish to do good. So, even the laziest appears justified in his own eyes; for if to carry out, to realise, to fulfil, is not the essential, the work of cognising and willing becomes a mere play with opinions, views, and wishes; and in order to play with all these things, to hold one's self convinced that one knows what is right, in order to comfort one's self with the idea that one wishes to do what is right, it is evident that no exertion whatever is required.

In this way the indolent establishes peace with himself as often as the blame of others obliges him to cast a glance into his inner life. Now, if we observe his attitude when he judges of his neighbours, the first thing which will force itself upon our notice will be that no special invitation is required for him to express his criticism, that it is an imperative want in him which compels him, that it is necessary to his satisfaction to give an exact estimation of the moral worth of all those with whom he holds intercourse, whilst he never applies this standard and measure of good and evil to himself, without being called upon to do so by some outward necessity. On the contrary, when others are concerned, he never can *refrain* from inquiring whether they are good or bad. His starting-point and the results he arrives at are always the same; the starting-point is, what duties they have, according to his opinion, to fulfil *towards him*, and the only answer which he can find to that question is, that they fulfil these duties very imperfectly. And although he may not think that all are so selfish as to try to injure his interests, still he finds that no one does full justice to him. Some deny him the love which he has a right to expect; others do not grant him the confidence which he thinks he deserves; most misjudge his best and noblest intentions; and no one gives him that support in his attempts to do good which he demands. And how does he account for this imperfect fulfilment of the duties of the world towards him? If he is not to doubt everybody's goodwill, which he does not wish to do, he can find no other reason for the wrong done to him, than that no one is sufficient in the essential, that no one quite knows what goodness is, that no one has acquired a clear notion of what ought to be done. Even those who at first seemed to agree with him, he gradually finds, as he knows them better, come very short of the mark, in what is essential. By what name he calls that which is wanting in them, whether it is the orthodox faith, or whether, on the contrary, what he has to reproach them with, is that they are still under the influence of old prejudices, depends on the standpoint of the criticiser.

The result remains ever the same for the indolent man, whatever his standpoint may be; and it is this: the others are all wrong, he alone is in the right. And that people will not see it, that is what he cannot forgive them. The thought that he is right, and that nobody will see it and admit it, forms the basis of all his feelings, thinking, and dealing, the centre of attraction of all foolishness, and evil inclinations round which they all gather, and on which rises that kind of power which the Creator has allowed evil to have in general.

How human society must shape itself under the influence of this indolence and thoughtlessness is clear. It assumes the aspect which the history of the world presents to us almost throughout, *i.e.* the aspect of the war of all against all. Peace no one has, except with himself. Naturally everyone carries on that war with the means he has at his disposal; one with his erudition, another with his ignorance; this man with his wit, that man with his eloquence; a third with his mute stubbornness; nations carry on the war with their enemies. Greece and Rome said: We are in possession of civilisation and culture: we are in the right; those who inhabit the rest of the world are barbarians: our victory and our dominion are the victory and dominion of right. In the same way the nations who, at the time of the Reformation, honoured the Pope as the representative of God on earth, said: "We have the right faith," and in the name of God they rushed upon the Protestants. Since glory is no longer sought in orthodoxy, but in civilization, behold, the same thing happens this side and that side of the sea in the name of civilization. Nations and parties formed within them must regulate their reciprocal treatment by their judgment of each other; and their judgment of each other is nothing else than the judgment which our individual indolence passes upon our neighbour, with this difference only, that it is multiplied as indefinitely by the sight and the consciousness of the many individuals that compose parties and nationalities, as an object which, being reflected many times in the several sides of a polished stone, becomes a multitude of objects.

And, again, the judgment which censures and condemns, only expresses in other words what the indolent man thinks of himself; it is only another turn of phrase to say: I am right. That peace it is indeed which the indolent man establishes with himself which gives every pretext for quarrels and disputes, for enmities and wars, and lends the mask of right and truth to selfishness and all low passions. This peace it is, the destruction of which all teachers of nations have considered as the first condition of the return of men to the knowledge of Self. So spoke the prophets of the Old Testament: "Woe to them who say, Peace, where there is no peace." And so speaks Jesus: "I do not come to bring peace but the sword." So long as this peace is not destroyed, the faith in the love of God and in the forgiveness of sins is itself death and sin; and since the wages of sin is always death, instead of helping man, instead of delivering him from evil, it must entangle him more and more in illusions and errors of all kinds.

The old Adam forgives no one but himself. He, on the contrary, who is born again to the life of freedom and cognition presents the contrary image: he forgives every one except himself. In order to retain our present meditation within the domain of experience known to us, let us again start from this: it is easy to censure others, but the knowledge of self cannot be acquired without trouble and exertion. We can readily believe that those who have persevered long and faithfully on the path of freedom at last succeed in pursuing the work of self-deliverance joyfully, and with pure satisfaction, and ever begin again with the keen feeling that this alone gives them perfect satisfaction. There may be some among us who, at times, at least, have felt the same satisfaction in that which they call the work of self-cognition. But even if it was self-cognition which we called so, these moments ought not to make us forget how often we fell again unintentionally into the censuring and condemning of others, nor how much exertion it requires generally to keep us free from this sin. The work of cognition is still a requisite with us; we can only be sure that we do not indulge and forgive ourselves anything if we are incessantly on the watch. The indolent man does not see why he should make himself a constant object of watching. He is convinced that he is in the right, and that those who differ from him in their views are in the wrong. The imaginary peace in which the indolent man lives with himself is indeed incompatible with the watching over one's self, this watching hinting at a kind of war with one's self. The necessity of it is comprehensible to those only who have become conscious that in themselves there are enemies from whom they have to fear surprises; and the more we convince ourselves that these inward enemies are the only ones that we have to fear, the more closely we shall watch ourselves.

From the discords with others to which we have exclusively devoted so much of our attention, we will now turn our thoughts to the conflict in our own spiritual life. Also, here, we shall have for some time still the prejudice of the weakness of human nature on our lips; but gradually it will lose its demoralizing influence over us, for, after having convinced ourselves that goodness is not conceivable without untiring efforts, without doing our part unremittingly, we shall become anxious to gain as much advantage as possible over this weakness of our nature. Our first care will be to establish a perfect harmony between that which we conceive as right, and the arrangements of our daily life, and the practice of all our business-concerns.

The new life of liberty shows itself first in the awakening from the sleep in which the charmed tale of the unattainablenesss of our ideal has kept us lapped. Human beings are free; therefore they can err: they can seek their good in the fancies of their own imagination, in the lust of passions, in certain institutions and conditions of public life which people of an unbiased mind at once recognise to be impossible, because they are in contradiction with the laws of nature. But if we fix on that which is truly good, and grasp it with our thinking and feeling, as certain as it is that our inner life is an indivisible whole, quite as certain is it also that this goodness must be within the reach of our will, that it must be realisable by the deeds of our inner life,* *i.e.* our feelings, hopes, inclinations, habits, and ways of thinking, and in the whole turn which our spiritual activity takes. To allow no contradictions between one's convictions and actions, to allow no such dualism in one's self, that is the first duty of a man who recognises the essence of freedom; the first, but by no means the only one. The other, to my mind, no less important task, consists in maintaining one's freedom relatively to one's views and convictions. To distrust himself appears the more important to such a man, when he feels tempted to say: "I am right; not you." To him these words are never the expression of real cognition; they are the unintentional testimony that ignorance bears to itself; they are a token of prejudice and spiritual narrowness; properly speaking, they are the confession of unbelief and of a mind which forgets God; for what God is that who belongs only to one man?

In thinking or saying: "I am right," and in so tying one's self to one idea, man becomes the slave of his thoughts. And single thoughts, single views and convictions, are the creatures of his spirit as well as deeds and actions. Anyone who has raised himself to the consciousness of the spirit, can find no satisfaction in being the slave of his own creatures. If I am to

---

* The reader who has followed the author in his reasoning through this series of discourses on prayer, will perhaps have familiarised himself sufficiently with his mode of thought and expression to see that the facts or deeds of which he speaks here are not those we perceive with our senses, but their unseen determining causes, without which the external facts never would be, namely, our thoughts and feelings; for these it is that give our actions their true character, and they are therefore the only facts truly important in our lives.

attain to the peace of freedom, I must never give up the struggle with my own thoughts. As long as a wise man has not been heard to say: "I have erred," I doubt his wisdom. I do not know if, in the course of the whole New Testament, there is anything that would fill me with more reverence for Jesus than the fact that He who had torn asunder all shackles of superstition, he who had opened to our race the path to freedom, did not think too little of even a woman belonging to the idolatrous race of the Canaanites to accept instruction from her. St. Matt. xv. 28. In order to follow his example, we ought never to forgive ourselves for allowing a predilection for our own convictions to be a bar in the way of inquiry.

If a man succeeds in never going out of the way of the struggle which he has to sustain in his inner life, if he sets his highest glory in never yielding to the craft and tyranny of the enemies that lie in wait for him there, that will show itself unmistakably in his attitude to his fellow-men. So long as a man perseveres in the indolence which will only receive, which values life in proportion to the succession of pleasant impressions that it brings, so long is the feeling of his responsibility a burden to him, which he wishes to lighten in proportion as he wishes to load his neighbour with it. The greater is the guilt of his neighbour, the lighter his own appears to him. He therefore becomes the accuser of all with whom he lives.

On the contrary, the more efficient, the more valiant a man becomes in the struggle with himself, the more jealous he becomes of his responsibility. He cannot at all consent to share it with anyone. He is convinced that no one can rob him of even the least part of this privilege, which he values more highly than any other good. No one can do him any harm there, where he finds his very life. He has not anything to forgive to anybody; whilst he is constantly on his guard against the prejudices which formerly used to darken, in him also, the consciousness of his responsibility, he excuses and defends before himself and before others those who are generally the object of the most virulent and unjust calumnies on the part of the indolent. Those whose individuality appears to be most unsympathetic and repulsive to him, as well as those whose superiority most frequently eclipses his doings, are just those who may reckon upon him as their steadfast advocate. That is the way in which he ultimately comes to enjoy the superiority of others as a manifestation of God's perfection, even when it deprives him of the credit due to his merits which he would otherwise obtain from those surrounding him; that is the way in which he learns to see that those individualities which appear repulsive to him, are just those which form the necessary completion of his own being; that are most favourable to his advancement, and, when he judges them impartially, preserve him most securely from one-sidedness and narrowness. That is the way which leads to the assurance and freedom in which man, according to his likeness to his eternal Father, never feels an offence as a wrong done to him; but, on the contrary, acknowledges in all the evil which he meets a call for help, a call to return good for it. He who does not tire in the good fight with the enemies in his own breast, and loves the eternal goods which no one can pluck from his grasp, above all things knows of no ill that he suffers from any one, knows of no one whom he has to forgive for anything; and by this consciousness he has established an everlasting peace in himself with God and the whole world.

In all ages there have been people who have won the victory in this good fight, and conquered for themselves the eternal inward peace. But when will such people meet together and found that community of God's kingdom which Jesus wanted to establish? A community the members of which have at least freed themselves so far from the love of appearances, that not the offender appears guilty to them, but the one who feels offended; a community which, without deceiving themselves, without misuse or abuse of words, can profess the belief in the love of God; a community who, proving by deeds that man can deliver himself from evil, can say in truth: "I believe in the forgiveness of sins."

The word that praises the glory of love resounds and dies away; the memory of those who have devoted their lives to the power and godliness of love are at last swept away by time: the bonds of a community alone resist these changes of birth and death, and remove the limits of time. When there will be again a community, the members of which have something more important to do than to feel hurt and offended, whose associates do not only speak of the power of love, but will not suffer the sun to go down upon their wrath against their brother; when the faith in love will have again embodied itself in a community of free men, among whom all forgive every one except themselves—then, my friends, the old words will be understood again which say that man's faith is a divine power that conquers the world. Amen!

XIV.—A.

"LEAD US NOT INTO TEMPTATION."

THE last three portions of the Lord's prayer answer the question how the essence of truth manifests itself in the self-determining will of man. The work of self-cognition, the task of fulfilling the holy laws of equality* and justice, begins by our ceasing to accuse and to censure our neighbours. We are reminded of it by the words: "Father, forgive us our trespasses, as we forgive them that trespass against us." This petition: "Lead us not into temptation," points to another order of aspirations on which depends the success of this work. The words that warn us against censuring and condemning, refer us to those errors into which we are often led by certain unpleasant feelings caused by the peculiarities or the ways of dealing in certain individuals. This petition, which is to protect us against temptations, brings before our minds the dangers to which we are exposed when dealing with men and things that cause us unpleasant impressions.

* See the special sense given to these words, equality and justice, in the tenth discourse, " Thy kingdom come." .

I do not mean to say that the word temptation in itself ought to limit our inquiry to that kind of danger alone, or that it ought to remind us solely of the inclination to, and habit of, being deceived by evil. Even in the collection of writings contained in the Old and the New Testament, the characteristic language of which we have foremost to consider in our study of the Lord's prayer, various meanings are combined in the word temptation.* Whilst our prayer calls upon us to apply ourselves with all diligence to avoid temptation, in other passages the temptation, on the contrary, appears just to be one of the ways intended to lead us to the cognition of truth and to confirm us in all that is good. In this sense we are told that God tempted Abraham. The apparent contradiction between such passages and the words of our prayer disappears if we consider that conditions as well as actions, thoughts, and feelings which point to a common origin, or appear to be alike when viewed from outside, and which are, for that reason, called by the same name, take a very different aspect when viewed from a different standpoint, in reference to different people. If, in treating of temptation, we set aside the standpoint of a person as determined by his general character and the momentary bent of his thoughts, we shall find that the words *temptation* and *trial* are only different expres-

---

* This is so true, that this word is rendered variously in the translations of various languages. Where the Germans have the one word *versuchen*, the English have to try, and to examine, to prove out; the French have also *examiner* and *éprouver* (see Psalm xxvi. 2). In the same way the English version of the Old Testament has it that "God *tempted* Abraham." The French has it, "Dieu éprouvant Abraham."

sions for the free will of men; that *trial* and *temptation* alike simply indicate the two ways which life always presents to the choice of this self-determining will in men. Whether men are conscious of it or not, various paths are open before them at all times; in every moment they are tried, and the attempt is made that is to show which of the various possible ways they will be disposed to choose. Thus, temptation brings before our minds the innermost life of man, the primitive unchanged organisation of our nature, the task of our life, ever repeating itself anew. But as soon as we regard the difference of position which individuals occupy relative to this general task of life, according to their past and present; as soon as we consider the ultimate turn which circumstances, whatever they may be, must take according to the spirit and tendency of thought in every individual, it will be seen that, as men seek God or reject Him, the same circumstances will become for one a trial and temptation which manifest his evil spirit by the new illusions to which he gives himself up and the wrong he does. When conscientiousness and perseverance at last bear their fruits in the holy work of self-culture, when a man at last has reached the point at which he does joyfully what duty demands of him, then, though evil be still existing in him,—he sees more of it than before, —he sees it there also, where the wise of the world bestow their praises;—but it has lost its power over him; it is in him as it is in the Eternal, rejected and condemned; henceforth it will even be serviceable to him; he will, by means of this contrast, recognise the essence of goodness and its broad universality more and more perfectly, and henceforth every temptation is a step onward. He, on the contrary, who is not certain yet that he does not consent to what appears to him to be wrong, or he who fears the revelations of self-cognition and shuns them, or he again who is not able to do what is good, without reluctance and a painful effort—if he does do it at all—for all these temptations rarely or never bring the victory; they only too frequently bring a defeat. What the temptations of life are to such men, that is the subject on which we dwell in our thoughts when we pray: "Lead us not into temptation."

Everything may become a temptation endangering the work of our self-culture; now it is some evil that we fear, now some advantage that excites our greed. We have often, in our previous meditations, touched upon the temptations that are concealed under our griefs and sorrows of all kinds. The dangers of feelings which make the actions of other men appear offensive and painful to us, and render their whole individuality repulsive, have been the subject of the immediately preceding discourses. We will therefore dwell more exclusively, to-day, on the temptations which threaten us when people and things promise us enjoyment and fill us with pleasant feelings.

The first question to which we shall limit our remarks is this: What can we do in order not to succumb to this temptation? when its hour has come, and when the struggle against it has begun, how can we conquer the evil by good? But before answering this question, we must examine what is meant by succumbing to temptation. Generally, the fault is considered to lie in the outward action, in that which we can see and hear in the doings of men; the offence is supposed to consist in the words that greed or passion have caused a man to utter, in the stretching out of his hand to grasp some object belonging to some one else, in his stepping on forbidden ground. But these outward actions are determined by a mixture of what is accidental with what is brought about by necessity, which has nothing to do with our guilt; for the wrong has been committed in thought and feeling, before the act that made it visible could take place. These outward actions will often remain undone because of some obstacle which arises, or some fear that keeps us back; but what thus remains undone only concerns the consequences which the action following our wrong might have, but not the wrong itself. The judges who pronounce their verdict according to the dictates of civil laws or public opinion, no doubt always seek what they call guilt and wrong exclusively in these outward acts; but for us, who, in our search after truth, take our stand on moral and religious grounds, and here recognise no other authority than conscience, the guilt does not consist in that which happens outwardly, and follows upon isolated decisions, it consists in the thoughts in which these our decisions originate. Human life is like a watch, with the internal organisation and competent treatment of which everyone ought to be acquainted and familiar. But most people content themselves through life with observing those movements which take place on the face of it, and putting the hands backwards or forwards, with what they call good intentions. As is the case whenever we strive after moral and religious cognition, we have in our present meditation, concerning temptation, only to deal with the inner mechanism of this watch, if we may be allowed to carry on the comparison. When we say that a man withstands a temptation, or that he succumbs to it, we mean that at a certain time of his life he has taken care that the mainspring and the working organisation of his soul is in proper order, or that he has failed to do so. Now, the only thing that determines the movement of the soul's organisation, is what notions we have of good or evil. Our actions depend on the verdict of our judgment, and these verdicts depend on what we think and feel in respect to good and evil. The question, what we have to do in order not to succumb to a temptation, is synonymous with the question what we have to do to form a correct conception of good and evil. A faithful adherence to our principles allows us but one answer to this question, and it is this: Man's conception of good and evil is correct as long as it is based on the consciousness of his moral freedom.

If a man must confess to himself, after having enjoyed a pleasure, that it has prevented the fulfilment of a duty; if after this enjoyment he feels a certain blank and discomfort, discontent with his position and his surroundings, reluctance and incapacity for his work; or if in some other way he feels the bitter after-taste which so frequently follows the cup of joy, and he thinks he may conclude from it that the pleasure he has enjoyed was not free from evil, he rarely fails to excuse himself by saying that what is agreeable exercises a powerful attraction on human nature, and that this attraction extends to evil, when evil is concealed under what is agreeable. When a man takes refuge in such excuses, he supposes evil to be something external, that can conceal itself, and being adorned in this way with the charms of what is agreeable, exercises a power to which human beings can oppose no resistance. Is this notion of evil compatible with the consciousness of our freedom? Can I be made responsible for that which is done by me? ought I to be considered as the originator of it, if a power over me has been given to it to which my power of resistance is unequal? when evil has been allowed to creep stealthily into my heart without my being able to recognise it? when it is allowed to assume a form which completely hides everything that would serve as a warning to me, and show that prudence is required—a form under which evil presents itself as a gift of God specially destined to me? The habit of speaking of the power of evil and its deceptions is so general, even among people who love goodness, that one must admit that freedom cannot be denied to all who use these expressions. And certainly these words are by no means in contradiction with the consciousness of freedom, if they are meant to express that the working of evil affects us too deeply to be set at nought altogether by the use of *outward* means, by laws and institutions which require compulsion to be kept up; that the aberration of the thoughts which come as the sequel of evil cannot be remedied by instruction alone, by the enlightenment of the understanding, much as these means may contribute to rectify our notions of nature and her laws.

If, by the power and deceptions of evil, that is meant which takes place in consequence of it, and the means which are to be used to prevent the manifestations of evil, then the significance of freedom is specially brought out, and this interpretation makes the power of the will that determines itself the pivot round which the whole world of our feelings and thoughts revolves; this interpretation of these words means that all that proceeds from the will, from faith and conviction, both error and the cognition of truth, evil as well as good, is infinitely superior to all the measures of prudence and material power which proceed from the calculation of advantages and disadvantages, and in the application of which the motive springs of fear and hope are taken into consideration. If, on the contrary, the words "power" and "deceptions" of evil refer not to the effects, but to the origin of evil—if they are not used to express what is the effect of the misuse of freedom on the working of all our other forces and faculties, and how human existence develops and shapes itself under the influence of evil—if these words are meant to attribute to evil a power over my will, and to explain my guilt by saying that evil subjugates my will by taking the mask of what is agreeable, and, with it, its irresistible attraction—then this is a conception of evil which is incompatible with the consciousness of liberty, and betrays an erroneous view of the fundamental laws of the human mind. In order to be able to speak of a power which evil exerts over me, I must presuppose that the evil which I perceive in me comes *from without;* whilst, on the contrary, evil is so completely *one* with the will, that it is born of it, and never has the power to overstep the threshold of its birth-place. The old words by which God characterises freedom in its essence, when He says, " I have placed good and evil before thee ; now choose,' are often as little understood now as they were in the times of Jesus ; and the various commands and defences of civil laws, the rules and manners of society, are taken as the only guide to judge of what is good or evil. But these ancient words only mean that man is to decide, according to the necessity of his nature, instituted by God, which, among the many ways that he sees open before him, is the right one. Not to *will* to decide what is right, not to *will* to care for it, not to *will* to pay, that homage due to justice under the law of freedom ; that, and that alone, *is the evil*. For me, there exists no evil outside my will. All in the lives of others that I call evil, is for my will an empty word, to which this will of mine first gives a purport, an existence, either by making it the expression of its own faithlessness and want of conscientiousness, in consequence of which it finds pleasure in the sight of it, or, on the contrary, by making use of it to recall to itself that which it *will* not, in order to make it the expression of its faithfulness and truthfulness. It must have been entirely forgotten that every one of us is as much protected, as safe against what is called evil, as the eternal God ; that everyone sins to-day precisely as did the first man, who, being exclusively surrounded by images and forms of goodness, of perfection and holiness, nevertheless scorned the thought of truth and justice, and that no one can transfer the least part of his responsibility to anyone else. The nature of freedom and the origin of evil must have been entirely forgotten, if we speak of a power and of a deceit practised by evil, by means of what is agreeable and the force of attraction peculiar to it.

As to the so-called deceptions of evil, which are supposed to disguise themselves, and thus obtain admittance into the soul, this notion arose in the childhood of our race, when all inward notions assumed a form perceptible to the senses; and later on it was retained by those who, being too sincere to deny the existence of evil in themselves, and too indolent to cast it away, did not disdain even the most shadowy excuses. But anyone who, for the sake of this, his gravest interest, allows no such admixture in his conception of human life, as that which would present evil as so subtle and crafty and superior to man, will agree with me, when I say that nature has taken more care to throw light upon, and to set aside, all doubts concerning the distinction between evil and good, than upon anything else. Even in the darkest times of superstition, whilst coercion was invested with a character of sanctity, and self-contempt stamped as a virtue, we find that the inner light, which renders it impossible to mistake wrong for right, never was extinguished. And even if we entertain so low an opinion of the development of the understanding in a man as to think that, being incapable of any finer distinction, he contents himself with this definition: to be good is to have God before the mind and in the heart—are these simple words not sufficient to protect him against all dangers? Does he not know enough of the difference between good and evil when he says to himself: Evil begins when the remembrance of God begins to make me feel uncomfortable; my life has become bad as soon as I cannot bear the thought of what is eternal, and the presence of what is holy. Can I ever be in doubt concerning any moment of my life, whether it is one of those when I have had God before my mind's eye and in my heart, or one of those when I have turned away from Him and forgotten Him? No, my friends, the distinction between good and evil comes from God, and He speaks equally distinctly to everyone. And we have the plain proof of it; it is only when we have rejected what is right, and made appearance and falsehood our masters, that, although we have chosen evil, we profess to be the pitiable victims of its wiles and its deceptions.

In order to give this shallow excuse an appearance of foundation, it is said that evil carries out its deceptions with the help of what is agreeable, and what gains admittance into the heart of men is this flattering, insinuating form. In this argument, also, the natural order of things is inverted, and the end presented as the beginning; for although by what is agreeable we do not mean here the sensation caused by smell or taste, which can evidently not help us to distinguish justice from injustice, and can therefore not cause us to mistake one for the other, but rather those enjoyments and pleasures of the heart which are very closely connected with the moral character of men, even so justice does not appear in the train of joys of one kind and injustice in the train of joys of another kind; on the contrary, as health gives to eyes and skin a different colour, a different brightness from that of illness, so the same meal of which justice* makes an occasion for the enjoyment of a man of pure heart, becomes for evil an occasion for the outflow of impure appetites. It is not because gold has a tempting brightness that it makes you hard and pitiless in the course of time; it is not because the ornament on your apparel is beautiful that in the end it makes you vain, or because it is great enjoyment to be the object of the admiration of many that this enjoyment makes you ambitious after a time, and gradually transforms your ambition into hypocrisy; not because the feeling of friendship is sweet will it bring you by and by to satisfy every desire of passion, and turn your heart away from God; on the contrary, it is because you would not listen to the voice of God in your soul that you now like to see gold in your possession rather than in that of some one else; because you have not God before your eyes and in your heart, simplicity and order ceased to be your ornament, and you then looked for a false one, the outer brightness of which is to conceal the paucity of your inner life. It is because you scorned the advice of your conscience that it became a necessity to see your own reflection in the praise of others, so as to have a compensation for displeasure with yourself; and because you have turned away from truth, you found pleasure in a friendship and love which require the screen of secrecy. In one word, it is not possible for the agreeable to lead you to evil, for the agreeable is not one of those things that are before you, around you, and out-

---

* The reader is referred again to the previous note on justice in the discourse on the words, "Thy kingdom come."

side yourself; the feeling of it is in you; it is you who clothe things in the apparel of the agreeable or disagreeable. It is a matter of course that, in the man who denies God and himself, evil alone can produce an agreeable feeling.

Evil cannot use the power of attraction of what is agreeable, and thus deceive you; on the contrary, it is when the will is evil in a man that it seeks to draw its like to itself and calls it agreeable. Altogether, evil does not deceive us; for any one who chooses to have his eyes open and to see, evil is stamped as evil by the hand of the Eternal. In short, evil is nothing that can approach man from the outside, as deeds, for instance, which are done from certain reasons. The love for God is itself the ground of all goodness. And what would you therefore think of anyone who would ask for grounds and reasons to love God? As man does good for the sake of goodness, so also he does evil because he will do it without requiring causes to determine him to do it. Every one acts to-day as did the mother of our race who plucked the apple, not in the hope of being like God, nor with any other intention, but because she had not God before her eyes and in her heart, and therefore the fruit pleased her. The only help available in the hour of temptation is to know that it is always man himself who produces the temptation out of his own breast; that the temptation never can come from outside, that there is no other tempter but the tempted himself.

It is scarcely necessary to add that this knowledge cannot be imparted to us by a sermon which we hear, or a treatise which we read; the utmost that the words of another person can do, is to help us to see that this cognition on our part is necessary. And this conviction can be acquired by the act itself, that is, through life. The ancient people of pre-Christian times called the possession of it the virtue of discretion; and our forefathers said of him who possessed that virtue, that he was in the discipline of the Lord. And indeed no one becomes an efficient co-operator in the creation of the Kingdom of God who has not learned to govern himself. The cognition of truth is an art and a science which can only be learned by valiant practice. He, indeed, who does not allow any day to pass without giving himself the proof that he is under the government of no external power, but that he is his own master, and who allows no day to pass without taking occasion of what is agreeable to gain the conviction that he can do without it, and let some one else have it; he who tries to equal others in willingness and perseverance in the practice of such kind of work as is most troublesome and disagreeable to him, will progress safely in the cognition of this truth, that as long as he breathes and his muscles last, it is self-deceit and nothing else to say, "I cannot!" The more we learn to recognise in this joyful work of self-cognition how often our greed and our unwillingness conceal themselves under the cover of necessity and the pretext of impossibility, the more decreases for us the danger of a fall in the hour of temptation. Amen.

XIV.—B.

"LEAD US NOT INTO TEMPTATION."

It is no new observation that the hopes of most people become more vivid and their expressions of joy louder as their state and position become more miserable and desperate. The sick man for whom there is no cure, and who would so gladly prolong his life on earth, considers the slightest improvement in his condition as a certain token of his complete recovery. As long as public enterprises and the affairs of individuals are flourishing, even the best news causes but little excitement; but with increasing danger arises the want of consolation; and the less likely the success of an enterprise, the more noisily welcomed is all news which at all admits of being interpreted as a happy turn of affairs. We meet with the same experience on the path of moral and religious life. A man who does not choose to legislate for his own soul and to judge it by divine and eternal principles, gives his first consideration to his business and his pleasures. Then, if he has any time and any strength left after having attended to these occupations and recreations, he may bestow them upon the work of cognition and deliverance from evil. And when a deep chasm has gradually formed between what a man is and what he ought to be, he never fails to represent the least emotion resembling a yearning after truth as a proof of his immovable faith in, and attachment to it; and that, he thinks, gives him a right to be in every way satisfied with himself. He judges like the thief who, being interrupted in his theft, for a moment hesitates whether he shall let his booty go or secure it by the death of the disturber, and then thinks highly of himself for having resisted the temptation and kept his hand from bloodshed. Most people will think this form of self-deceit incomprehensible; this is only because the kind of theft forbidden by civil laws, the theft which the doer must seek to keep secret, does not belong to the set of common faults which they may, and do, commit themselves, like everybody else, in broad daylight and without any fear. But setting aside this difference, we shall find that the large majority of people who think the good opinion which the thief entertains of himself so strange, are in precisely the same error as he, when they praise man's resistance to temptation as a virtue. A temptation to evil resisted is designated as a victory. This wrestling of man with himself formed the subject of our last discourse, and certainly we could not help considering this happy issue in a certain sense as a victory. But there are victories of different kinds; victories which entitle us to expect peace with certainty, and therefore fill those who were fortunate enough to obtain them with unmixed feelings of joy; there are other victories which not only bring no decided results, but are of so doubtful a character that the victors, if they have only sense enough to see their position, must say to themselves: "Another such victory, and we are lost." How many of those who look with high satisfaction upon the firmness which they have shown in temptation, would make eth same confession if they had a clear notion of the state of their inward life! Indeed, I do not believe that any temptation in which we have remained masters can be considered as one of those victories which give us real joy and show real progress. For, however great the strength may be of which we have given proof, we must not overlook the fact that this great effort in the hour of temptation was necessary only because we felt that we were inclined to the evil that presented itself, that we were listening to its devices, and had already begun to defend it before our conscience. The kind of faithfulness which protects us in such cases, and prevents us from giving way, always presupposes a previous betrayal of good faith. To be tempted only means that we have failed to preserve the purity of our heart. It is a state of transition in which the people and things with which we come into contact become a temptation. The experience that we have been steadfast so far, is no guarantee that we shall not succumb to the temptation in the end; that we shall not conceive a liking for some new form of evil, and that we shall not begin to persecute as the enemies of truth those who wish to free us from this new error. The prayer which is meant to protect us against evil, is therefore not granted until we are able to avoid the dangers of evil, to prevent the recurrence of a temptation which is nothing but the reflex of our guilt. Such is the conception of the prayer of our Lord that God may not lead us into temptation, which is to form the starting point of our meditation of to-day.

1. To prevent the return of temptations must be the ultimate object of our efforts. But many will think

it impossible to guard against the return of temptation. They will remind us that even wise people can hope to set aside threatening dangers in the future, and prevent their consequences, only when the circumstances under which they arise are always the same, and when what they have to fear has altogether a regular course, and presents itself under an appearance already known to them. In order to render this coming danger impossible, I must know the conditions without which it cannot happen, and have them under my control. You now ask whether that is possible in the case of temptations. We may know, you say, that under certain circumstances of life, and with certain persons, we lose our equanimity, that we find it hard to regard them with unprejudiced eyes and to judge them impartially. Perhaps it might be in our power to keep aloof from circumstances that so endanger our inner life. But what would be the advantage thus gained? This question may fairly be asked. For will the objects which have left their memories in my heart, or the people with whom I have become familiar by intercourse, cease to occupy my thoughts when I shun the sight of them? And even if we succeed in wiping away the features thus engraved upon our mind, where is the guarantee that there are not already within our horizon other persons and other things that will, ere long, re-awaken our slumbering passions and disturb once more the balance of our inner lives before we think of it? Were we not also taken by surprise on former occasions by the temptation, in mastering which we but just succeeded with extreme efforts? We did not, like the villain of a novel or play, go out in search of an occasion of evil for evil's sake, from sheer love of wickedness; we were not aware of anything but what naturally comes in the course of human life, and we were only comparing with others the difference of impressions caused by what is agreeable or disagreeable, when out of these agreeable impressions grew for us a power of attraction which assumed the appearance of something irresistible, a power which throws fetters around us when the work of liberty calls for us, a power which gives us over to evil, as if we could not refuse to serve it, with our feelings, thoughts, words and actions. This is the peculiar way in which all temptations arise: they attack men like a thief in the night; we do not see them when they approach us, so that we may bar the way to them; we first become aware of them when they have gained admittance into our hearts. If we consider temptations carefully—these people continue—we shall find that they are rarely connected with what comes gradually towards us from without; generally they are nothing but ideas which occur to us without our seeking, images which an invisible hand holds out before the mirror of our consciousness. We do not know when, whence and in what garb the tempting thoughts will arise in our souls; there is no connecting link between our present and that which we have to fear from the future! And can we think it possible to prevent the temptation?

And, indeed, that would be impossible, if there was no connecting link between our past and that which the future brings; but there is a connection, and we know it, even if we do not perceive it by our senses.

Nobody can see the connection between the metal point on the roof and the thunder-cloud above; nevertheless, anyone who is not quite unacquainted with the phenomena in nature knows that between that cloud and the lightning-conductor there is a close connection. And so with the ideas of which we say that they occur suddenly to us: we cannot see their origin, but still, anyone who is acquainted with the laws of the world of thought knows that thoughts which appear to cross our minds suddenly are by no means altogether accidental. He knows, on the contrary, that the element in our thoughts, which converts them into temptations, is in the closest relationship with our whole inward way of dealing, and our moral mode of thought and mode of life. In order to see clearly this relation, we must remember that even among the most cultivated people, only a very small number become conscious, at any given time, of the inexhaustible store of ideas, feelings, and aspirations, which form our inner world, even if it were that only of the most uncultivated. Human life in this respect resembles a river lit up by moonlight. Of the innumerable waves which form the river, only those few are visible which are lit up by the light of the moon. The only change which takes place is that the water which the darkness just now rendered invisible, now becomes visible: the kind of motion which we perceive in the lit up waves has remained the same; however gentle, calm, and slow, or however wild and raging, the motion remains alike, whether the light shine upon it or not.

And so it is with the thoughts that come uncalled

for. They are not an addition from without, and do not cause an influx and a swelling in the stream of our inner life. No! they have belonged to it for years, and decades of years, and are always in motion; they are in constant and reciprocal action with all the other thoughts and feelings in our souls. The only change which takes place in respect to them, is that we become conscious of them; for in that which we see of them, under the form in which the light of our consciousness shows them, nothing has been altered in the least by the fact that they have come out of the darkness of our hidden self. Although these thoughts come to us unbidden, and speak to us a language at once disturbing and flattering, prepossessing and confusing, as is peculiar to the whole progeny of error, do not let us imagine that it is the first time they have presumed to speak, or that they have had no utterance before. Ere we knew anything of them, or at times when we had forgotten them altogether, they always had a disquieting action upon our soul, and influenced the character of its life. In other words, the ever-narrow circle of those thoughts of ours, on which falls the light of our consciousness, is in the closest union with the unlimited space of our life of thought hidden in the darkness of unconsciousness. That of all thoughts and feelings which now dwell within us, just these and no other ones come before the eye of our consciousness, may be called accidental, but it is not so with the character which these thoughts assume. That the remembrance of a friend which suddenly rises in my soul is not under the influence of the aspiration to the knowledge of self, but is accompanied by feelings of pride; that the sight of the happiness of others on which I gaze, instead of filling me with joy, inflames my evil passions; that the pleasure I find in considering the fate of my enemy does not spring from a spirit of peace and forgiveness, but, on the contrary, from a vindictive hope in which I seek my satisfaction—that all these thoughts which suddenly start up in my mind are as many temptations to evil for me, that is in as close a relation with my past life as the fruit with the seed. Indeed, all our temptations are but the fruit of our former guilt. Illness, failure of crops, or other misfortunes, are not the punishment which strike evil by the decree of eternal order; but out of sin grow error, misunderstandings, confusion, discord, and all that causes the dismal light in which the world appears to the wicked, so that we must consider temptations as a part of the spiritual evils which our misuse of liberty and our selfishness draw down upon us.

The close connection between our several temptations and the bent which we give to our inner life, shows distinctly that it is within the power of man to prevent the return of these temptations. For if we convince ourselves that it is our own error and our own doing which transforms the circumstances of life into temptations, we shall see men and things again as they really are, as soon as we forsake the wrong path, and use the means which help us in our striving after the cognition of truth. The longer and the more exclusively a man has fostered the evil dispositions of his heart, the more luxuriantly the weed grows, and the more it abounds in fruit. Withdraw the care and nourishment you have hitherto bestowed upon it, and you make it impossible to it to produce new fruit; in other words, you prevent the return of temptation. Certainly, the change of which we now speak is not the doing of a moment; it is a gradual growth, as is the case with everything else in nature: and what we require to hinder the *working* of evil, we must borrow from the example of *nature*. The change which is to render impossible the return of our temptations, is a slow process, but a certain one; and the object which we pursue is one that can be completely attained. The moving forces of our mind, of which is built the vessel that is to carry us on the river of life, are organised like the parts of the ship which conveys us from one place to another. A whole ship, however large it may be, is governed from one point. The man at the helm determines the direction of the course which the ship is to follow. Is she to turn round, to enter on a course opposed to that which she pursued before, it certainly requires efforts and time, but the helm will do its duty; there is no doubt about it. It will accomplish its object so completely that when the vessel weighs anchor, everything about it has changed sides; what was on the right before, is now on the left, and *vice versa*. It is the same with human life. What on the ship is the place where the helm is at work, in human life is conscious labour. Faint as may be the outlines of this conscious labour, compared with the collective feelings, conceptions, thoughts and appetites, which are ours even when we know nothing of their presence, it is nevertheless this conscious labour alone through which human life as a whole is determined; and as the helm completely, though slowly, succeeds in turning round the ship which was hurrying to its destruction, so conscious efforts also succeed so completely in turning all the thoughts, feelings, wishes, and inclinations which were directed towards evil, that henceforth they pursue goodness with equal determination, and keep to the path, so that everything which formerly was a threatening danger is now behind the man, and getting always farther from him.

Secondly.—After having dwelt on this point so long, in order to prove that the power has been given to man to prevent the return of temptation, we have little time left to speak of the best ways and means to carry out what is in our power to do, and to purify our lives from pernicious temptations; and this question is probably the one to which most people will attach the greatest importance. And no doubt there is no progress conceivable without a careful consideration of it. But, consistently with the view we take of moral life, we think that a discourse can contribute but very little towards a satisfactory answer to this question. In those communities which are based on human authority, it is natural to give to those who are driven to the confessional by the consciousness of guilt, certain rules of conduct such as a physician gives to a patient. In our community, on the contrary, in which everyone is expected to honour his reason and conscience as the highest authorities, no one can presume to prescribe to others what path they are to choose in order to reach the goal of self-culture and self-deliverance from evil. We are conscious that this aspiration is our common bond of union, and we strive to confirm each other in it by common meditations in our meetings; but as to the most appropriate way, according to the several dispositions and peculiarities of each one, according to his general experience and his present position, that must be the result of his own scrutiny and his own determination. That individuals who live in the same age, under similar circumstances, agree together in the choice of this or the other means of self-education, is simple and natural enough; and if, to conclude, I am to name the means which to me appear the most effective against the temptations peculiar to the character of our time and our social standpoint, I can name no other than work. Work is the soil which contains the best food for the germs of goodness, and none whatever for the instincts of evil. Whoever is anxious to procure a safe and speedy result to his efforts in the attempt to prevent the return of pernicious temptations, let him learn to work.

It is evident that not all occupations called work can answer this purpose. There is even a kind of work which, far from being a barrier to the growth of evil which bears the fruits of temptation, may well be called the nursery-garden of temptation. I mean that kind of work which has been assigned to women, in consequence of the division of work according to sex, and which keeps the hand in motion whilst the faculties of the soul are left unemployed and the mind without food. Nothing favours dreaming and idle fancies so much as a position in which we, being outwardly occupied and therefore free from the reproach of idleness, foster the disinclination to serious efforts, and unconsciously become more and more lenient towards ourselves. The danger becomes greater when those whose allotted duty it is to perform day by day this mechanical motion of the hand, scarcely requiring the supervision of the eye, have received the appearance of culture, which, without training the heart, without awakening in them any real sympathy for, or any interest in, the beauty of pure human aspirations, has excited in them imagination, disquieted thought and feeling, and created a pernicious craving for amusement. It is in the hours of busy idleness that the soul, satisfied by the performance of some prescribed external duty, imagining itself free from evil, learns to enjoy the feeling of security in the comfortable dwelling, built up of the remembrances and hopes of past and future pleasures, and becomes entangled in the illusion that happiness is the object of life. Neglecting all the gifts with which God has blessed human life, it then develops the deplorable talent of detecting imperfections and shortcomings everywhere, and dwelling on all occasions in the consciousness that the world knows very little how to understand and share its sublime feelings.*

* This touch of satire seems to have been directed partly against the incessant knitting and similar occupations of German women at the time when these discourses were delivered. It is acceptable from one who has not waited for the time when women should clamorously claim their rights to higher education, to excite and foster an activity which claims the co-operation of all the talents, small or great, of those around him in both sexes. Scarcely any day passes in this fortunate community without some gathering taking place in the interest of some kind of mental work performed in common. The interesting collection entitled " Die Stimmen der Freiheit" owes its existence to this collective labour. Meanwhile great, though

When I designate work as a means of preventing the return of temptation, I mean that kind of work which calls forth the activity of the whole man, and founds its demands upon the most deeply-rooted wants of his nature, and opens to him a sphere of activity which proves to him that the fulfilment of his duty and his true inclination are in perfect harmony. It is obvious that the conditions just mentioned are not fulfilled by that kind of work which is undertaken for the satisfaction of our daily wants, or for the sake of securing to ourselves an existence free from care. Just as little as they are fulfilled by those kinds of occupations which we choose as our profession from mere inclination. In the exercise of a vocation chosen so entirely to suit our taste, we are

---

unconnected, efforts have been made in various localities of Germany to satisfy the demands for the higher education of women. In Hamburg lectures for women were held as early as the year 1848. The kindergarten, although representing but one side of the movement, has for many years been a pivot of activity with which high aspirations were connected among German women; it was often disturbed by the short-sighted interference of German governments, but the perseverance of the women has at last overridden all prejudices. Dresden is now the centre of a far-extending activity, which does not limit itself to the kindergarten, but embraces wider studies for women of high aspirations. The first kindergarten in England was established, under crushing difficulties, by a lady from Hamburg more than twenty-five years ago. There is now in Berlin a regular system of lectures for women, delivered by the professors of the university, which has been in existence for eight years at least.

The author's remarks are applicable to more than one kind of "idle occupation" and to every kind of superficial education, although he would be the last to advocate any change in one's position for the sake of any work which would tend to foster pride or diminish our esteem for lowly work done with all one's might, and concentrated attention with any real feeling of duty.

conscious that it is not a work of moral self-government, that we only obey dthe ictates of nature, that it is owing to the instincts of affinity and inclination that we choose one special side of human life instead of embracing its full range and penetrating to its depths. We are conscious that in choosing this occupation we do not assimilate it to our being, that we do not use our freedom to reproduce these given conditions of life as a creation of our own. If the activity of a man is to possess the power of freeing life from the temptations of evil, it must be, in the true sense of the word, a voluntary work; it must not therefore have been forced upon us by the requirements of physical existence, or the imperativeness of certain inclinations; its object must be the weal of human society, the realisation of eternal thoughts of truth and justice. Further, all that by which nature has distinguished one man from another, all that which belongs to our personal existence, must be no more to us than the materials for our work; and the instinct which excites us to consecrate ourselves to this work must be derived from the life of reason common to all, from the feeling and consciousness of the communion between the human and divine. A man who consecrates all his powers to the calling which binds all human beings together, without desecrating it by any admixture of selfish motives; who does not make it a mirror of his vanity, nor undermine his faith in it by cares and doubts concerning the uncertainty of outward results, but devotes himself to it with pure love; who does not content himself with looking from a safe distance on the holy struggle against violence and injustice, or with silently wishing well to those who fight for truth, and at best encourages them by exhortations when no one else is near enough to hear him: but who, on the contrary, takes his share in the struggle, and unremittingly strives to find out what can lead to its successful issue; who counts every day as lost on which he has not done anything for the cause of liberty and right— that is a man who may well be considered as one who learns how to work. And he who is able so to work, is able to be at the helm and to guide the vessel of life in such a way that the pernicious temptations to evil at last disappear, and the goal is happily reached. That is the kind of work which so transformed the Apostle John, that the sight of evil which once had tempted him to call upon Heaven to send fire on the heads of the guilty, reminded him only, later on, that the love of the Eternal "wills the death of no sinner, but rather that he may live." The sight of evil was now nothing to him but a new call to show this love more and more decisively by word and deed. And the effect which work on behalf of the general interests of humanity had on the members of the first Christian communities, will be the same in our time in the case of anyone who strives faithfully and with self-denial after moral and religious intercommunion.

And many an one among ourselves has experienced that as often as he could bring himself to persevere in the efforts made in our community, and was quite absorbed in the work of the Kingdom of God, evil lost its power over him. Men and things which formerly never met his eye without exciting his selfish instincts, are henceforth looked upon by him with an impartial eye and calm feelings. May the healing power indwelling in the work of moral and religious intercommunion show its virtue in us more and more! When the love of truth has been supplanted in our hearts by the passionate desire for transitory advantages; when we find it hard to do what is good, and evil appears promising to us; in one word, when we have not prevented the occurrence of temptation, we certainly can do no better than to withstand the temptation, to reject the evil and to choose what is good, even if it must be with reluctance and a divided feeling. But is it the true nature of the child to be obliged to constrain itself in order to follow the advice of his Father in heaven? Well for the man, therefore, who remains indefatigable in his search and his efforts until he has found the way which leads to no temptation. Well for him who in his unremitting efforts in the work of self-education regains this spiritual health, in the enjoyment of which we consider evil with repugnance wherever and under whatever form it may present itself. Well for him who through his indefatigable labour is ever raising himself to that freedom of mind in which we may be in intercourse with evil without danger, in which we can, as the Scriptures have it, tread on serpents and scorpions without being hurt. Amen.

XV.

"DELIVER US FROM EVIL, OR FROM WICKEDNESS."*

THE object aimed at in the last three petitions of the Lord's prayer is to secure for ourselves protection against the dangers to which we are exposed on our way to the cognition of the supreme good and the realisation of truth. The prayers for forgiveness of our sins, and for strength to resist temptation, bring vividly before us the dangers that lie in our intercourse with our fellow-creatures. The concluding petition which forms the subject of to-day's meditation is intended to lead us back to ourselves, and to the dangers lying in our past, dangers consequent on the course which we have followed in the special kind of culture which we have chosen.

Ever since the Reformation has put within the reach of every German the Bible in his mother-tongue, it has been a subject of discussion what is the right ex-

---

* The two expressions, wickedness and evil—*Böses und Übel*—must be given here to render this discourse comprehensible to the reader. Although English readers have not shared in the indecision of the Germans as to whether they should say, "Deliver us from evil, or from wickedness," the distinction between these two expressions must be kept in view, and the inquiry to which the author leads us ought not to be avoided, for there is a difference between the two ideas. *Wickedness* is the root in the abstract, *evil* is its fruit, its concrete result. I therefore translate this discourse entirely as it is in the original. There is no doubt that with a more philosophical view of religion the scrutiny of the mind, which becomes necessary, brings with it a more scrutinising analysis of language. If we rejoice in the progress of thought, we ought no less to rejoice in the corresponding progress of language, for the latter will greatly facilitate the spread of the first in society at large.

pression for the concluding petition of the Lord's prayer, in the German language. Some say, "Deliver us from wickedness;" others, "Deliver us from evil." If these words refer to the dangers that accrue for us from the course of moral and religious development, as we have carried it on until now, we cannot side with or against either party in their view of this matter. We consider neither of these two words as expressing that which causes our past to become a temptation for us in our self-determination. We will take as the subject of our meditation the fruit which is borne by wickedness. Can we call the fruit of wickedness an evil? We are accustomed to designate as good and evil those gifts which fate dispenses, that which birth and circumstances lavish upon one and withhold from another, that which nature appoints as enjoyment or privation to anyone. Wherever men have begun to think, they have found it necessary to draw a line between that which happens to them through nature, and that for which nature cannot be made responsible. With this intention, virtue or freedom has been designated as the highest good, and guilt as the greatest evil, to distinguish them from all other goods and evils. It is through the insufficient fulfilment of a just demand that the dangerous prejudice has arisen which consists in considering the mind as the highest development of nature, the blossom in the life of sense. Our starting-point has always been the conviction that those who consider the spirit in man, as a higher degree of the life of sense, wrong both spirit and nature. It is not a matter of degree, a more or a less, that distinguishes the self-determining spirit and will from the life of sense and soul in man;* the fruit of wickedness must be the sign, the proof by which we recognise that the good or evil will is of an absolutely different kind from the life of nature; we can therefore not call this fruit an evil. The act of the will that determines itself is the only thing that can be called good or evil; whatever is connected with it, be it ever so closely, is not the act of self-determination, whether we call it the fruit which it bears, the trace which it leaves, or the shadow which it projects; all that is but a testimony of this self-determination, the reflection of it, which the mirror of nature receives and gives back in the eye of the mind. Human language still lacks simple expressions for this evident, though invisible, creation, which owes its existence to the reciprocal action of mind and nature permeating one another. We are reduced to the expedient of circumlocutions; and, as long as this is the case, such words appear to be the best as bring out, in the most striking way, the contrast of the elements which they bind together, and thus show that these words are used to hint at an object for which the language of our

* It is evident from this sentence that the author does not use the word *soul* in the sense given to it, at a time when the analysis of mind and matter was in its infancy. Even now dictionaries tell us that *soul* means that in men which thinks and *feels*. We cannot accept this definition: the soul, if it *feels*, belongs to the life of the senses; it is that which feels and may form certain intelligent combinations, so far, for instance, as we see it to be the case in animals, affections and emotions which they have in common with men. By spirit, on the contrary, we mean the higher side in human beings as distinguishing them from animals—in short, that which constitutes our humanity. Whenever the author uses the word "spirit," the meaning is the same as that attached to it in the authorised version of the Bible.

nation has not yet created an appropriate name. This object will best be approximately designated if we call that from which we entreat God to deliver us, at the end of our prayer, as the disease of the spirit. Of course, we do not mean, by this expression, that disease of the soul and body to which the name of mental disease has been applied by those who were entirely unacquainted with the consciousness of spirit and freedom. And it is quite as much a matter of course that, by disease of the spirit, we do not mean any hurt or loss, or any weakness consequent thereon, through which the spirit and will might be prevented from fulfilling their task. Much as the several acts done by the spirit and its will may differ from one another, the spirit which has given them birth is, in its essence, always the same. The self-determining spirit and will (whether we think of the spirit of God, or of that of man, when we use these expressions) is not one of these forces for which effort or fatigue, increase or decrease, exists. So far as the distinction between good or evil is concerned, and the exercise of freedom and its deeds, we can only say either that a man does or does not make this distinction, or performs the duties dependent on it. The question whether man can or can not do this or that, is without sense in this case. We are, therefore, not speaking of a disease to which the spirit might be subjected—there is no such thing : we speak of the harm which the spirit can do by the misuse of its liberty in the sphere of its own creation. The activity of the will is closely bound up with moral and religious conceptions and feelings; and, as it embodies itself in this activity, these conceptions and feelings are uninterruptedly renewed and transformed. This edifice of thought is an invisible body with which the spirit and its will mantles itself, and enters into intercourse with its fellow-spirits. Everything in this edifice of thought is order and harmony, as long as man governs himself according to the law of justice ; but as soon as he misuses his liberty, his moral and religious life of thought becomes distorted by disorder, confusion, and contradictions, and can no longer lead him to the contemplated goal. *That* is what *we* call the disease of the spirit. What are its symptoms and its effects ? In order to answer this question, we will consider a passage of the evangelical tradition.

St. Luke relates that on one occasion, Jesus, after having addressed His followers in presence of many of the people and scribes, was asked by one of them by what authority He did all these things ? and that Jesus answered : " I will ask you a question : What do you think of the baptism of John ? was it from Heaven, or of men ?" Thereupon they began considering that, if they said from Heaven, Jesus would ask them why they did not believe on Him ? and if they said of men, they would expose themselves to be stoned by the people, who held John to have been a prophet. They therefore said that they did not know whose was the baptism of John. Let us now set aside in this narration the details which are only intended to characterise the learned divines of the time, their official position, and other circumstances. What is then left is a perfect illustration of the disease produced in the life of thought when men, misusing their spiritual freedom, unexpectedly find that they are at variance with themselves. In the eyes of the scribes, it seems dangerous to express their opinion concerning John the Baptist; therefore they deceive the people, and say: "We do not know whence this baptism was." But they had long ago agreed together, that this man had broken the law of God, and that the fate which had fallen upon Him was a just chastisement of Heaven; and they were convinced now, as they had been before, that their opinion of the work of John, and its issue, was the only correct one. We know how they had come to this opinion. They derived that which they considered the knowledge of truth, from their national sacred writings, in which it was held that the manifestation of Divine will had been deposited for them. It was not from having convinced themselves, by independent inquiry, that their own reason and conscience confirmed this opinion, that they held it; for such an investigation itself, made on their own authority, would have appeared to them a disobedience to God. What they called truth, was called so, because it was written in those books. Now, if from this remark we go back to the answer by means of which they tried to conceal their real opinion from the people, we shall see in that conduct of theirs that irony of fate to which everyone exposes himself, be it ever so much against his will, who receives truth as an external gift. What happens is this. The very thing such a person says, in order to conceal his thoughts from others, is the very picture of what is really going on in his mind. He thinks he keeps people in the dark as to his true opinion, but it really is as he says, and, instead of deceiving others, he deceives no one but himself, thinking all the while that his conscience is quite clear about the matter. The ignorance which remains unseen by the man whom it holds captive, yea, which he often considers as his knowledge, that is the disease which unavoidably follows in the wake of guilt.

The attitude of a man towards truth is an absolutely true manifestation of the spirit that lives in him, whether he recognises it in its integrity or whether he misapprehends it. Such a manifestation of the spirit is its necessary and living embodiment in all forms of human consciousness or unconsciousness; and every thought, every feeling and every deed, which the self-determining will of man produces in its incessant activity, is necessarily a part of this embodiment of the spirit in him. But we must be careful to make a distinction between this attitude towards truth, in which our spirit manifests its eternal essence from the want which, in the course of time, we experience to account for it to ourselves and to others; to make it an object of reflection and even of conversation. This want which man experiences to bring before the eye of his consciousness in groups, or pictures of ideas, what he has practised even as a child, makes itself felt, in some people early, in others late, according to the more or less precocious maturity of their understandings. It arises from the observation that the same objects produce very different impressions upon us at different times. Man then attempts to distinguish that which is transient in things from what they are in themselves; and he considers everyone who sees in things what is their transient form only, as blinded by the delusions of transitory phenomena. Whether he will succeed in his attempt, whether he will be able to penetrate into the inner working and meaning of nature, to reach the root and essence of things, to behold the truth, to recognise what things are in God and what God is in them; or whether, on the contrary, it will be his fate to obtain no answer to all his questions, and whether this is his personal fate only, or whether it is a condition of human nature in general that the true essence of things is concealed from every human being alike, and everyone is condemned by an irrevocable necessity to be subject to the delusions of mere phenomena, these are questions which man naturally has not answered, at the time when the difference between essence and phenomenon, between what is eternal and what is transient, begins to form the subject of his thinking. He does not know yet what is possible to man, but nature knows it. Nor does he know what he himself will be able to do just now, within the limits which it is possible for the forces of men to fill, but although he does not know it himself, it is already decided and has even now been decided by himself. For just at the beginning of this thinking over the world and himself (even if there are no generally received opinions, confirmed by a long tradition, or when, if there are any such confirmed opinions, he has not yet accepted them)—that which this man conceives, the character of the ideas or pictures which he presents to his soul's vision, stands in the closest relation with that which his self-determining spirit wills and does. If the will of man is turned towards God's holy will in free obedience, and is already familiar with it, and the will of man is in concord with the law of justice, with the eternal order of things, this concord will create its natural expression, by producing the conviction that the cognition of truth is placed within the reach of man. If, on the contrary, man turns his will away from what is godly, if he turns away his heart from that which is permanent, from this life of the spirit which never is at variance with itself; if he seeks in the changing phenomena of outward things a satisfaction which they cannot give, so as to flee from the tormenting feeling of his inner discord and his estrangement from God; if he takes refuge in the foolish self-justification which makes his nature answerable for that which he has committed *against* the will of his nature—the involuntary expression of his error is this: all his thinking and his inquiries concerning the origin and limits of human knowledge lead him to the conclusion that man is denied the power of penetrating into the essence of things, that the divine being cannot be recognised by man; that man's spirit is too weak to solve the problem of life, that it is condemned to entertain narrow, superficial and contradictory views of the world and of life. The certainty that the pure source of cognition wells up in the mind of man is nothing else than the consciousness of a pure heart translated into the language of the understanding. The inverse fact is this: the feeling of guilt, translated into the language of the understanding, is the doctrine that it is denied to man to see God face to face; that the pure light of truth would unavoidably dazzle and destroy his sight; that a dim mixture of light and darkness alone is available for the power of vision in the mortals whose fate is eternal ignorance.

There will be no one among us who can deny that this last degrading doctrine, so misrepresenting man's nature, has long exerted a powerful influence over him, and that even now there are moments when he is tempted to acquiesce in it. We cannot be surprised at it, after our preceding remarks, so long as free obedience is not the ruling character of our self-determination. A servile* heart has no other confession of its own faults, than that the life of man is an unbroken chain of contradictions. Ignorance and the consciousness of it is a disease inseparable from the misuse of our liberty. And nevertheless the notion that blindness to eternal truth and perfection is born with man is so diametrically opposed to the deepest and most pressing want of our nature, that everyone is prevented by the voice of his conscience from giving himself up unconditionally to this superstition. But until now, only very few have conscientiously taken advantage of the warning of their conscience to return to obedience to the law of liberty. Instead of taking this warning and beginning with determination to fight against the deceits of guilt, most people have done the contrary; that is, they have tried to soothe their conscience and taken refuge in the evil art of shifting between error and truth. In this way two opinions have gained credit which have governed the world, now in succession, now simultaneously, and have perhaps, more than any other superstition, con-

* A servile heart here means serving evil still, though with reluctance.

tributed to estrange men from the study of their moral and religious self-education.

The Pharisees, who clung to the idea of a supernatural revelation confirmed by signs and miracles, held the most ancient of these two opinions. To believe in a revelation which comes to man from an external source is a superstition which considers truth as one of those things that man can be taught by others, and which he is incapable of drawing out of himself. But there is no substitute, no proxy available in the work of the spirit. That which one gives to another is but words and nothing else, and man never wants words for the cognition of truth; what is required and is too often wanting is the sense for it, the spirit of it. Everything that God or man has to tell us will only lead us to the cognition of truth in proportion as we strive after it. We no sooner cease to seek it, than that which was light becomes opaque and turns to darkness. Moreover, everything which man cannot derive from himself belongs to what is accidental, and therefore the truth which he finds out of himself he only finds again, for he had it in himself before and had only lost sight of it. But there is no need for us to dwell any longer on the superstition of the Pharisees, since there can hardly be any attraction for us in the attempt to replace the word of God, which our conscience alone is able to perceive, by a revelation which addresses itself to our senses.

The danger for us is much greater in another form of that same superstition; I speak of the new opinion according to which truth in itself—absolute truth—is to be considered as distinct from relative truth, *i.e.* from the conception of some one side of it; truth in itself which is presented as the prerogative of the infinite and distinct from a one-sided view of it, the only one of which the creature is supposed to be capable, according to its limited horizon. And it is not alone the truth that is one and the same for all—that alone which deserves the name of truth, which, according to this new opinion, is supposed to be an eternal mystery for human nature; but also that which is left of it after this truth which is one and indivisible by its nature has been anatomised, disjointed, and distributed among men according to times and parties, and is then still too great for individual men to be able to enter into direct communication with it. This way of viewing the cognition of truth stigmatises the individual man with the characteristics of the most excessive narrowness and weakness; he is supposed never to be able to raise himself by his own strength even to relative truth, to the contemplation of any of those many truths into which divine thought is subdivided and portioned out for the finite reason of man, if this enigmatic being, which has been made of the spirit of the time, did not undertake to step in, as the intervening link between finite and infinite reason. That is, if we are to express it in a more intelligible manner, he who will recognise relative truth, who will know which of the many truths is just the truth of the day, is referred to the spirit of the time, the reigning one, or the one which is about to be so; he is referred to the "accomplished facts" in which this truth finds its expression; he is referred to the result through which it proves its power. Most of the leaders of public opinion of the day agree in these and similar opinions, in that distinction between absolute and relative truth, which forms their common ground and their starting-point; all agree here, from those who make their unbelief their boast, and exert themselves to prove to the world that the belief in God and in conscience is the root of all prejudices, down to those orthodox men who are anxious not to remain behind the time, and the philosophers who have turned pious. The worldling and the enthusiastic dreamer, the historian and the poet, dramas, novels, and devotional books, everyone and everything without exception preaches this doctrine. Notwithstanding the positive fact established by this doctrine, that there is no possibility of cognition, and no knowledge for man beyond the limits of the life of sense, and that doubt alone is in the right, the adherents of this doctrine are ready for the sake of their imagination to tell us the contrary the next moment, by asserting that the distinction between absolute and relative truth and the complete separation of God and men are an absolute certainty. When our descendants write the history of our time, this doctrine will be the chief explanation of the entanglements and the wonderful confusion of this generation. The indifference for truth, the feverish excitement accompanying surprising events, and whirling past like a hurricane without leaving anything behind but devastation; the complete loss of all firmness and self-respect, the servile spirit and all other infirmities which disfigure public life* in the present

* This was written during the reaction that followed the revolutions of 1848.

time, have, so far as faults of character can be attributed to opinions, their common origin in the delusion that there is no direct communion between the spirit of man and that of the Almighty; that man's nature excludes the cognition of the eternal will of God; that for mortals, what is folly in one age will be wisdom in the next; that within the limits of one nation that may be error, which beyond these limits becomes truth. The most striking proof of the thoughtlessness of our age which will meet the gaze of our descendants when they dwell on the sorry sides of our age, is not only the countless number of people who have renounced the privilege of thinking for themselves, but more especially the number of so many learned and pious men who accept this distinction between an absolute and a relative truth, and nevertheless honestly think that they have a right to call themselves Christians, and who continue to honour Jesus either as the son of God or as a wise man; whilst, if this distinction were a correct one, there could be nothing more erroneous, more foolish and pernicious, than the doctrine which this Jesus of Nazareth has preached and the activity He has exercised. For He never spoke a word, never did a single act, that did not rest on this conviction that there is an everlasting communion between man and God based on the equality of a common essence; on the conviction that the holy will of God, which is the fundamental law of the universe, becomes manifest to anyone who has not special motives for closing his heart to these manifestations; on the conviction that ignorance concerning the will of the Eternal does not arise from the nature of man; but that this ignorance is the disease produced by the misuse of our liberty.

Can we, my dear brothers and sisters, consider ourselves, as far as this disease is concerned, as being among the healthy ones? The signs by which this kind of disease or health can be recognised are easy to indicate. Can we say that life, notwithstanding its privations and pains, never is a burden which oppresses us, or causes us to consider death as a friend who tarries too long? Do we never feel as if we knew not what we lived for? Do we in truth rejoice in life? When I speak of joy, I do not mean that keen disposition, that excitement with which youth or passion seizes the desired gifts of life. I mean: is life in itself an object of gratitude? Does it give us a lasting, pure, inmost feeling of joy? Do we conceive it as pure and natural that people have been found ready to bear ruin or shame for their faith, without being fantastic dreamers, or being spurred on by ambition? Have we any convictions which have made comprehensible to us the words of the poet that among the goods of life, life itself is not the highest? Have we any convictions for the sake of which we should do more than for wife or child, more than for a friend or a beloved one? The answer to these questions will be a very different one according to our respective points of view. It will depend on whether we follow the reigning professions of faith of the time concerning the essence and limits of human cognition, and consequently drag down truth into the domain of scholastic opinions which change according to times and nations; or whether we are convinced, on the contrary, that in the cognition of truth there is, notwithstanding the changing expression it assumes, something unchangeable which remains eternally equal to itself. The cognition of truth is the work of the spirit and will; it is the source, the being, and the aim of all things. He who not only rises in isolated moments to this conviction, but embraces it with the whole strength of his soul, receives it in his heart with all his power; he whose whole feeling, thinking, and striving is permeated with it, never can experience a moment in which existence becomes a burden—he knows of a price for which he is ever ready to give up every one of the single gifts of life. Amen.

THE END.

www.ingramcontent.com/pod-product-compliance
Lightning Source LLC
Chambersburg PA
CBHW032047220426
43664CB00008B/902